Parallel
Programming

INTERNATIONAL COMPUTER SCIENCE SERIES

Consulting editors   **A D McGettrick**   University of Strathclyde
                        J van Leeuwen   University of Utrecht

OTHER TITLES IN THE SERIES:

Parallel
Programming

R.H. Perrott
The Queen's University of Belfast

ADDISON-WESLEY
PUBLISHING
COMPANY

Wokingham, England · Reading, Massachusetts · Menlo Park, California
New York · Don Mills, Ontario · Amsterdam · Bonn · Sydney
Singapore · Tokyo · Madrid · Bogota · Santiago · San Juan

The programs presented in this book have been included for their instructional value. They have been tested with care but are not guaranteed for any particular purpose. The publisher does not offer any warranties or representations, nor does it accept any liabilities with respect to the programs.

Cover graphic by kind permission of Laurence M. Gartel
Typeset by Quorum Technical Services Ltd, Cheltenham, UK
Printed in Great Britain by The Bath Press
First printed 1987

British Library Cataloguing in Publication Data

Perrott, R. H.
 Parallel Programming. — (International
 computer science series).
 1. Parallel Programming (Computer science)
 I. Title II. Series
 004'.35 QA76.6

 ISBN 0–201–14231–7

Library of Congress Cataloging in Publication Data

Perrott, Ronald.
 Parallel programming.

 (International computer science series)
 Bibliography: p.
 Includes index.
 1. Parallel programming (Computer science) I. Title.
II. Series.
QA76.6.P463 1987   005.2'1   87–1182
ISBN 0–201–14231–7

To Simon

.

Preface

This textbook is concerned with the topic of parallel programming and is aimed primarily at undergraduate students. The subject matter covers the following areas:

- multiprocessor/distributed programming;
- programming array and vector processors;
- data flow programming.

Historically each of these three aspects of parallel programming has been developed independently and this is the approach followed in this book. After an examination of the main requirements for each category of parallel programming, representative languages are used to illustrate the current thinking or state of the art in that particular language group. Each language group suggests a particular hardware configuration which matches its language primitives best. However, this book advocates the concept of abstract programming which hides the underlying architecture from a user by presenting program and data structures which are independent of particular architectures.

In Part One the major hardware and software developments which have taken place are considered. Since a knowledge of some machine features helps in the explanation of some of the programming concepts, a broad hardware overview, at a very elementary level, is given in Chapter 1. In it the rapid progress that has taken place over the last 50 years is emphasized. This contrasts markedly with the slower developments which have taken place for programming languages, an aspect which is considered in Chapter 2.

Part Two of the book is concerned with asynchronous programming languages. These languages can be used for programming multiprocessor or distributed systems and have been the object of most attention from researchers. This arose because of the many systems applications which required, or could benefit from, the introduction of parallelism in the solution of problems. The task of devising suitable notations and implementing languages based on these notations has been ongoing for the last 20 years. The particular problems associated with this area are now well understood and several notations and languages have been successfully implemented. In addition, much theoretical work has been carried out in this area resulting in several well documented case studies which provide a pedagogical platform for the introduction to the topic given in Chapter 3. The two major mechanisms which have been used in high level languages to provide communication between independent actions within a program are considered in Chapters 4 and 5. These are then illustrated by an examination of the concurrent features of several languages, namely, Modula-2 (Chapter 6), Pascal Plus (Chapter 7), Ada (Chapter 8) and Occam (Chapter 9).

In Part Three programming languages suitable for use on supercomputers such as array and vector processors are considered. These languages support synchronous parallel solutions to problems. Synchronous parallelism has not received as much attention from the academic community as the asynchronous variety. Languages for array and vector machines have usually been provided by computer manufacturers and as a result they have been influenced by the architecture of particular machines. The result has been that a user must possess a detailed knowledge of a machine in order to exploit effectively its power. In addition, no well established programming principles have been laid down; rather, a series of *ad hoc* programming techniques associated with a particular language implementation or a particular machine have been used.

The main users of supercomputers were originally engineers and scientists. However, the situation is changing as these machines become more widely available. The best techniques to be used when programming such machines are neither widely agreed nor understood. To illustrate current approaches the languages available on two well known vector processors, namely, Cray-1 (Chapter 10) and CDC Cyber 205 (Chapter 11), are discussed. Following this a discussion of languages which specifically reflect the architecture of the underlying machine is presented. This reflects the situation for one of the earliest array processors, the Illiac IV (Chapter 12) and a more recent array processor, the ICL Distributed Array Processor (Chapter 13). Work is currently in progress to produce a more abstract basis for programming supercomputers and initial results of these investigations are considered. The language being developed in this work is based on Pascal rather than FORTRAN and is presented in Chapter 14.

In the remaining part of the book the most youthful area of parallel programming is addressed, namely, data flow programming. The data flow model requires a completely different approach to programming from that required in the other cases. The languages developed earlier can be described as control flow languages since it is the statements which govern the order of program execution. In data flow programming it is the availability of data which drives the program's execution. Under such a requirement several instructions may be executed in parallel if the data required is available. The requirement for a language which facilitates such programming is the ability to represent the solution to a problem in such a way that data dependencies are either avoided or easily identified. Machines are currently being constructed which embody this principle but it is too early to say whether this approach will contribute significantly to large scale computation in the future. One of the earliest data flow languages, VAL, is considered in Chapter 15.

Finally, I would like to thank all those people who directly or indirectly helped in the production of this text. In particular, A. Aliabadi, M. Clint, L. Harper, the series editors and the reviewers.

R.H. Perrott
November 1986

Contents

PART ONE

HISTORY AND DEVELOPMENT

The main objective of this part of the book is to review in general terms the developments which have taken place in the evolution of computer hardware and high level programming languages. In the case of computer hardware the objective is not to give an in-depth treatment but rather to establish the concepts and terminology which are mentioned in later chapters.

The first chapter traces the evolution of computers, taking as the starting point the pioneering work of Charles Babbage in the last century. The rapid and substantial improvements in component technology which led to the identification of three generations of computers are then considered. These computers were all based on the von Neumann model of computer architecture and had therefore a sequential approach to processing. This is followed by an examination of some models of parallel computers such as vector, array, multiprocessor, distributed and data flow systems. These computers represent a departure from the von Neumann model.

1

The review has been selective as only architectures which are relevant to the languages considered in later chapters are mentioned. As a result many significant architectural developments of recent years have not been considered. This review has been included because in some situations a knowledge of the architecture of a machine is desirable when constructing a program. For example, the current state of the art for programming an array processor requires that the programmer chooses data structures which are related to the number of processors in the array. However, for sequential, multiprocessor, distributed and data flow systems this is not the case as abstract programming techniques can be applied.

The second chapter considers the evolution of high level languages by tracing their historical development, taking as the starting point sequential programming languages which represent the first generation of programming languages. The distinction between each language generation is not easily identified. The second generation is taken as those sequential languages which offer data abstraction features. The third generation is taken as the parallel programming languages and within this generation three distinct themes can be identified, namely asynchronous, synchronous and data flow.

The asynchronous languages have been designed and implemented mainly by academics until the recent interest of the US Department of Defense who commissioned the language Ada.[†] For these languages independent operations can be applied to different parts of a program simultaneously. Synchronous languages are those languages in which the parallel processing is applied to the data in synchronized operations. These languages are used to program array and vector processors. Their development has largely been associated with supercomputer manufacturers and the progress of FORTRAN. A new FORTRAN, FORTRAN 8X with array processing features is currently being considered. Data flow programming languages are much more recent and have been developed mainly at universities. In these languages the availability of the data drives the program's execution, in parallel when possible.

Chapter 2, therefore, traces and identifies the major developments and principles of each language category and quotes examples of each language.

Finally the words concurrent and parallel are used interchangeably in this text, conforming with common usage. However, there is a difference as concurrent expresses the possibility of simultaneous computation while parallelism refers to the ability of a machine to perform simultaneous computation.

---

† Ada is a registered trademark of the US Government.

Chapter 1 Hardware Technology Developments

1.1 Sequential architectures

In 1821 Charles Babbage proposed what he called a Difference Engine (Randell, 1975). The Difference Engine was to consist of a set of linked adding mechanisms and its purpose was to generate automatically successive values of a polynomial by using the method of finite differences.

The prototype, which he actually built, was capable of calculating to two orders of difference, in other words, it could handle a second degree polynomial. Babbage then went on to design, but not build, a more powerful Difference Engine capable of dealing with a sixth degree polynomial. In addition, he designed an Analytical Engine which was proposed as a general purpose digital computer. The Analytical Engine consisted of a store, arithmetic unit or mill, punched card input and output. There was also a card controlled sequencing mechanism that provided iteration and conditional branching. This pioneering work of Babbage is widely regarded as the basis for the architecture of modern computers. The component technology that Babbage was working with was based on gears and wheels. Babbage estimated that his machine was capable of an addition or subtraction in one second and that a multiplication or division would take one minute.

Over a hundred and fifty years later proposals were being made by organizations such as the US National Aeronautics and Space Administration to build a computing engine which would help with the design of aircraft and spacecraft (Stevens, 1979). The aerodynamic flow problems which affect such craft are governed by a set of equations known as the Navier-Stokes equations. These equations have been known since the early 1900s but sufficient computing resources have not been available to solve them in their full generality. The techniques used for solving these equations are usually based on the method of finite differences. The designers of these systems were, like Babbage, proposing systems which were orders of magnitude more powerful than those systems which were currently in use.

The component technology available to these system designers was based on Large Scale Integration (LSI) and it was estimated that the number of arithmetic instructions executed per second would be in excess of 1 billion ($1 \times 10^{+9}$) using this component technology.

Charles Babbage worked on his designs until the time of his death in 1871. His ideas were too advanced for the technology which was available and so many of his designs were not implemented. The realization of his computing engine had to wait until the middle of the next century.

In fact, parallel developments in the UK and the US led to the implementation of what are called the first stored program computers, namely the Electronic Delay Storage Automatic Calculator (EDSAC) at the University of Cambridge, England (Wilkes and Renwick, 1949) and the Electronic Discrete Variable Arithmetic Computer (EDVAC) at the University of Pennsylvania (Rosen, 1969). The term, stored program, is used because the data and instructions of the problem resided in the computer's store. These machines and their commercial equivalents are usually referred to as first generation computers (Hockney and Jesshope, 1983; Hwang and Briggs, 1985).

These machines are classified in this way because of the component technology used in their construction, in this case thermionic valves. One of the major characteristics of a valve is what is known as the gate delay time, that is, the time taken for a signal to travel from the input of one logic gate to the input of the next logic gate. A typical delay time for such components was 1 microsecond (1×10^{-6} second). This technology was in use during the period 1945–1958.

The disadvantages of valves were that they required large amounts of power and generated large amounts of heat. This, in turn, meant that they were large, cumbersome and prone to frequent breakdowns. However, a successful example of a machine from this generation was the IBM 704.

The second generation of computers was based on the transistor. Transistors had decided advantages over valves in that they were much smaller, more reliable and produced very little heat. Their compactness meant that the number of active components in the computer could increase by an order of magnitude over their predecessors. The gate delay time for these components was typically 0.3 microseconds. An example of a computer which was built using this component technology was the IBM 7090.

These computers, like those of the first generation, were based on what is called the von Neumann model: that is, they consisted of an input and output device, a single memory for storing data and instructions, a single control unit for interpreting the instructions, and a single arithmetic and logical unit for processing the data. Such a configuration was based on the structure proposed by Babbage over a hundred years earlier and is illustrated in Figure 1.1.

The era of the second generation computer lasted from approximately 1959 to 1965 when a new component technology enabled a third generation to be designed and built. This component technology was based on solid state integrated circuits.

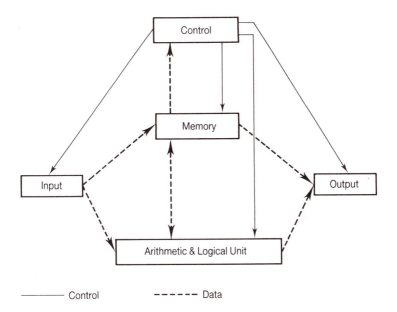

Figure 1.1   von Neumann model.

The chief characteristic of these circuits was the silicon chip where several components were combined on a silicon wafer. Initially only a few gates were placed on a chip giving a gate delay time of about 10 nanoseconds (1 nanosecond $= 1 \times 10^{-9}$ second). This was gradually improved until around 1975 when the delay time was reduced to approximately 1 nanosecond. Examples of computers belonging to this generation were the IBM 360 series, Burroughs 6500 and the UNIVAC 1108.

Hence the component technology as represented by the gate delay time has shown an improvement of the order of a thousand. From 1 microsecond of the first generation component technology to 1 nanosecond for the component technology of the third generation. The time in years for this 1000-fold improvement was approximately 30 years.

Another way of examining the impact of this technological change is by examining the performance of a machine from each of these generations. In this way how the components of the machine have been joined together is also being measured. All of the machines are assumed to have an architecture similar to that proposed by von Neumann.

A typical measure of the performance of a computer is the time taken to execute one arithmetic operation or the number of arithmetic operations executed per second. For the EDSAC in 1951 a figure of 100 arithmetic operations per second was quoted. By 1959 the IBM 7090 was capable of approximately 10^{+5} arithmetic operations. An average figure for a third generation machine such as the IBM 360/195 showed that it was capable of

10^{+7} arithmetic operations per second. This is more usually represented as 10 Mflops where 1 Mflops is a million floating point operations per second.

Hence over a period of three decades the component technology as measured by the delay time has improved 1000-fold, while the computer performance as measured by the number of operations executed per second has improved by a factor of 10^{+5}. This improvement as measured by the number of floating point operations executed per second is illustrated in Figure 1.2.

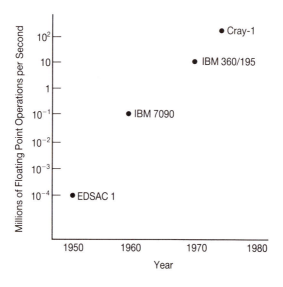

Figure 1.2   Computer development.

This extra improvement, over that provided by a comparison of the gate delay times, is attributable to the improvement in the design of the computer's architecture.

1.2   Parallel architectures: pipelined processors

The concept of having different components of a computer operating in parallel had been proposed in the last century. For example, Babbage had proposed a parallel addition algorithm. More recently the concept of parallelism had been introduced to machines such as the CDC 6600 which had separate execution units for floating point and integer address calculation, each of which could operate in parallel. However, in the next two sections we consider the introduction of parallelism to machines which departed from the traditional von Neumann model, machines such as array processors and vector processors, which are commonly referred to as supercomputers.

As each new generation of computer was implemented it enabled the user of these machines to solve much larger and more demanding problems. In particular the scientific and engineering communities were continually demanding an increase in the number of operations executed per second. In many cases, such as in aerodynamic flow problems, scientists knew how to solve these problems, but they lacked the computing power to achieve a solution within a reasonable time.

As a consequence computer designers began to re-examine the concept of the von Neumann architecture and eventually came up with designs which were radically different. These designs were based on the introduction of parallelism and enabled a substantial increase in the number of operations executed per second to be achieved.

How these machines enable the number of operations per second to be increased can be understood by considering the various stages that are involved in performing an arithmetic operation.

An operation such as addition can be divided into 4 distinct stages after the operands are converted into their binary equivalent; for example

$A = P \times 2^Q$ and $B = R \times 2^S$

which is then manipulated as follows:

Stage 1. Compare the exponents to obtain the value $(Q - S)$.

Stage 2. The value $(Q - S)$ determines the number of places to shift P with respect to R to line up the binary points.

Stage 3. Add the mantissas P and R.

Stage 4. Normalize by shifting the result until the leading non-zero digit is next to the binary point.

If this is executed on a serial machine then one stage is executed after the other in the order given above. The time taken for each stage may be different but to simplify the analysis we assume that the time to execute each stage is the same, say T seconds. Thus a result is produced in $4 \times T$ seconds.

A more general situation is where there are D stages and N pairs of operands to which the floating point operation is to be applied. In this case one pair of operands is added before another pair is considered. Thus the time for N operand pairs is

$N \times D \times T$

or the number of floating point operations performed per second is

$1 / (N \times D \times T)$.

This process is shown in Figure 1.3(a).

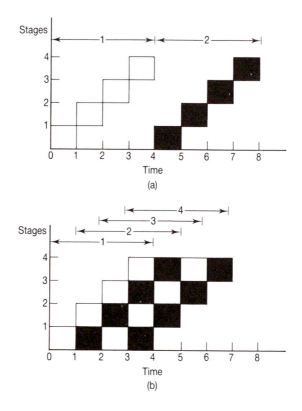

Figure 1.3   Stages of execution: (a) sequential execution; (b) pipelined execution.

An examination of this figure shows that after the first pair of operands pass through the first stage, that stage lies idle until the second pair of operands is considered. This means that it is possible to consider the second pair of operands (compare their exponents) after the exponents of the first pair of operands have been considered. The same principle can be applied to all N operand pairs that have to be processed. This can be represented as in Figure 1.3(b).

This technique is usually referred to as pipelining. It is not a concept which is unique to computers or in fact which was discovered by computer scientists. Henry Ford used this conveyor belt approach to construct his model T car back in the 1920s.

As a result of having identified four stages in the addition operation it is possible to have four operand pairs being processed in parallel. Each operand pair is at a different stage of completion of the addition operation.

Thus, the time to process N operand pairs using pipelining is

$$D \times T + (N - 1) \times T$$

The first term represents the time to add the first two operands after which a result is produced every T seconds. This formula ignores the time taken to compute the addresses for the operands and other overheads such as transfer between memory and the pipeline unit.

The number of floating point operations performed per second is thus

$$1 / ((D + N - 1) \times T)$$

which represents an improvement over a serial machine of

$$N \times D / (D + N - 1).$$

This same principle of pipelining can be applied to other arithmetic operations and a separate unit can be introduced to handle each operation. This is the basis on which machines such as the Cray-1 (Russell, 1978) and the CDC Cyber 205 (Lincoln, 1982) have been built. Such machines are usually referred to as vector processors since it is a vector of operands which is presented to the pipe (the collective name for the stages) for processing. In certain cases it is possible for more than one pipe to operate in parallel, for example, the addition and the multiplication pipes. As a result the number of operations executed per second is further increased. For example, the peak performance rate of the Cray-1 has been measured at 160 Mflops.

1.3   Parallel architectures: array processors

Another means of introducing parallelism into the design of a computer is the approach taken in the construction of an array processor. In this case a processor equivalent to that used in a serial computer is duplicated a number of times, say P times, and each processor is given its own local memory. Each of these P processors can perform an arithmetic operation on two floating point numbers in its local memory in the same time and in a manner similar to that of a serial computer. Thus the number of operations that can be performed per second has, in theory, been increased by a factor of P.

In addition to a number of processors an array processor has a single control unit whose function is to direct the activity of the array of P processors. It does this by broadcasting instructions to the processors after which the processors perform the instruction broadcast. The action of the processors is in lockstep or synchronized mode, in that they all perform the same instruction only using different data; the data in their local memory.

There is some flexibility in such systems in that any combination of the processors can be enabled (or disabled) meaning that they execute (or do not execute) the broadcast instruction. This type of computer configuration is shown in Figure 1.4.

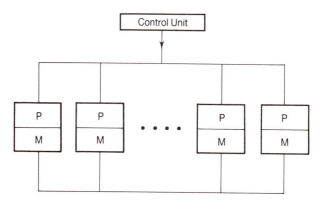

P - processor   M - memory

Figure 1.4   Array processor model.

Hence P pairs of operands can be added in the time required to add one pair of operands on a serial computer; that is, using the earlier notation

$D \times T$

and the number of floating point operations performed per second is

$P / (D \times T)$

where D is the number of stages and T the time to execute one stage. However, if the number of pairs of operands to be added is greater than P then the operands must be considered P at a time.

In the case where N is greater than P the time to process N operand pairs is

$[N / P] \times D \times T$

where $[N / P]$ represents the ceiling function, the smallest integer that is either greater than or equal to N / P.

Several machines have been designed and built on the basis of this principle. For example, the Illiac IV (Barnes *et al.*, 1968) which had 64 processors capable of a full range of arithmetic operations. More recent is the design and implementation of the ICL Distributed Array Processor

(Parkinson, 1983) consisting of 4096 processors (a grid 64 by 64) and the Massively Parallel Processor (Batcher, 1979) with 16 384 processors (a grid 128 by 128). The arithmetic capabilities of the individual processors of these last two machines have been restricted to simple operations.

There are disadvantages associated with this type of architecture in that each processor has its own local memory, and the task of one processor obtaining an operand from another processor's local memory can be an expensive operation.

The cost of such an operation depends on how the processors are connected together, the interconnection network. If, for example, each processor is connected to its adjacent neighbours then moving operands between adjacent local memories is relatively inexpensive compared to other moves. Other moves have to be performed in terms of the single moves provided by the hardware.

1.4   Multiprocessor/distributed architectures

As the speed of the component technology increased the price of these components decreased. This enabled computer designers to build more efficient and reliable computers and also for experimental parallel architectures to be designed and implemented. Such was the case with multiprocessor architectures where several processors, each with its own instruction set and capable of independent action, were combined. Thus the restriction of lock-step operation enforced upon an array processor configuration was removed.

On such a system different parts of an application program could be assigned to different processors for execution with the result that the time for execution of the complete program would be substantially reduced. If there were P processors in the multiprocessor configuration then in an ideal situation a P speed-up over the single processor configuration might be expected. However, this assumes that the program can be divided up among the P processors uniformly and that communication between the processors is not a substantial overhead. In fact, the control of the processors and their interconnection is now much more complex.

We shall confine our attention to two configurations only: first where the P processors share a common memory which is regarded as the basis of a multiprocessor configuration. The structure of such a system is shown in Figure 1.5.

An example of a configuration reflecting this philosophy was designed and built at Carnegie Mellon University and was known as Cm* (Swann et al., 1977). The processors were based on the DEC LSI-11 and all processors shared access to a single virtual memory address space. A system with 50 processors was implemented. Efficient use of the system depended on ensuring that most of the code and data references made by a processor were held locally to that processor.

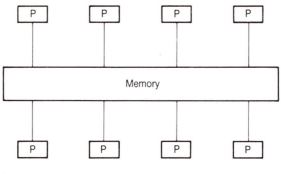

P - processor

Figure 1.5 Shared memory model.

Several experiments were performed on the system and it was found that such a multiprocessor system can provide a linear speed-up factor. That is, P processors, at best, can perform the same task as a single processor in $1/P$th of the time. However, there are many factors which can affect the performance such as:

- **synchronization**, some of the processors may be idle waiting on other processors to catch up,

- **algorithm**, an algorithm designed for a serial machine may not be the most efficient on a multiprocessor machine,

- **contention**, if several processors require the same resource they may have to use it one after the other.

The second configuration that we shall consider briefly is what is described as a distributed computer system. In this case the processors have their own local memory and there is little or no shared memory. Such a system is illustrated in Figure 1.6.

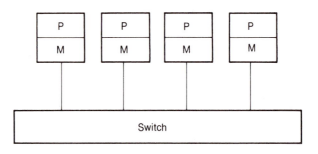

P - processor   M - memory

Figure 1.6 Local memory model.

In this configuration the processors can be described as loosely coupled as opposed to the tightly coupled system of a multiprocessor configuration. Now when two processors wish to communicate, perhaps to exchange results, they send messages to each other. One of the advantages of this type of architecture is that as the cost of hardware decreases such systems will become more feasible and can be expanded.

An example of such a system is the Heterogeneous Element Processor (HEP) which was manufactured by the Denelcor Corporation (Smith, 1981). A HEP consisted of a number of processors, one to 16, that were connected to as many as 128 memory modules. Each processor had its own memory with which it could communicate directly, in addition, it could communicate through a switch or interconnection network to other memories. A 4-processor HEP was estimated to be capable of executing 160 million instructions per second.

This concept has been developed further giving rise to computer networks. In a network there is no necessity for the processors to be physically located in the same area, they could be quite far apart. An example of a geographically spread network is the ARPA network which has been used by a number of universities and government agencies in America. Users of this network are able to share data bases and programs constructed and in use in different parts of the United States.

1.5 Data flow architectures

The architectures which were considered in the previous sections do in fact have something in common when we come to consider how they should be programmed. The order in which the programmer has composed the program statements determines the sequence of instructions that govern the operation of the computer. Data flow computers are based on a different concept, namely, the availability of the data determines which instruction is to be executed. If the data is available for several instructions at the same time these instructions can be executed in parallel. In this way parallel processing can be introduced to the program and to the machine architecture.

These data flow machines, like array and vector processors, are also a radical departure from the von Neumann model. In these machines an instruction is ready for execution when its operands arrive; the position of a statement within the program does not determine when it is executed. Hence if the architecture provides multiple processing elements and if instructions and data are matched, multiple instructions can be executed in parallel.

For example, consider the assignment

$$A = (B + C) \times (D - E)$$

On a von Neumann type machine this would produce an instruction
sequence similar to

        add   B, C
        store T1
        sub   D, E
        store T2
        mult   T1, T2
        store A

taking a total of six instructions to perform the assignment. On a data flow
machine the addition and subtraction can take place in parallel and then
the multiplication performed. This can be represented as shown in Figure
1.7 where instructions on the same line can be executed in parallel and an
instruction is executed whenever its inputs or operands have arrived.

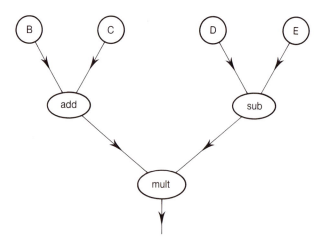

Figure 1.7 Data flow execution.

A simpler example illustrating how operands can be broadcast is

$$(2 + 5) \times (3 \times 5) + (4 + 5) \times 5$$

which can be represented as in Figure 1.8.

This expression can be evaluated in three steps on a parallel machine
as opposed to six steps on a serial machine. Broadcasting multiple copies of
data values gets around the problem of calculations interfering with each
other by accessing values in shared memory.

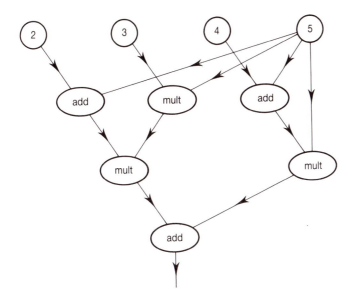

Figure 1.8   Data flow representation.

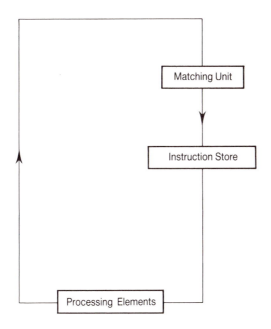

Figure 1.9   Data flow architecture.

If this principle can be applied to a complete program then the program can be executed in parallel as determined by the availability of the data. In such a system there is no concept of control flow, as the name suggests it is data flow control.

An outline of a data flow architecture is shown in Figure 1.9. The basic machine consists of a pipelined ring structure to which are attached a group of processing elements, matching unit and instruction store. The data flows around the ring and enters the matching unit. This unit arranges the data into sets of matched operands which are then released to obtain their required instruction from the instruction store. After this the processing elements are activated. Any new data produced as a result is passed into the ring and the process continues.

Several prototype machines have been constructed based on this philosophy at MIT, Irvine, California and Manchester, England. The results of using these machines have not been fully analysed, however a number of experiments which have been performed give very encouraging results. For example, Gostelow and Thomas (1980) have shown that a data flow machine can perform matrix multiplication of two $N \times N$ matrices in a time proportional to N rather than N^3 which is required by a serial computer.

1.6 Summary

The foundations of modern-day computers are attributed to the work of Babbage in the last century. His ideas were realized in the von Neumann model of computer architecture some 40 years ago. Since that time improvements in component technology have led to the classification of computers into three different generations. With each generation there has been an improvement in performance and reliability of the machine.

However, the scientific and engineering communities still required an increase in computer performance. In order to achieve better performance architectures, machines which departed from the von Neumann model were introduced. These machines are usually referred to as supercomputers and can be subdivided into array and vector processors. A vector processor overlaps the operations on a vector of operands by means of a pipelining technique. An array processor duplicates the number of processors and applies them simultaneously to a vector of operands. Both configurations produce substantial improvements in computational rates.

Other configurations such as multiprocessor and distributed systems have been implemented. In these systems processors act independently either sharing a common memory or with their own local memory. In either case performance can be improved over a single processor system.

The improvement is not so dramatic as with the supercomputer case due to processor contention problems.

In recent years data flow computer models have been designed and implemented. In this model the availability of the data drives the computation. The experience with these machines is not sufficient to quantify fully their computational performance.

Chapter 2 Software Technology Developments

2.1 Sequential programming languages

The analysis of the development of sequential machine architectures based on the von Neumann model reveals that there were three distinct innovations in component technology. These progressive refinements of the hardware enabled the construction of computers which were more reliable, faster and cheaper.

The programming technology advances to enable a user to capitalize on these hardware developments did not proceed at such a rapid pace. The development of new programming techniques was hindered by the prevailing state of language design and compiler construction and the resistance to change by programmers.

The mismatch of hardware and programming technologies led to cumbersome project implementations usually delivered late and operating inefficiently.

Another reason for the delay in the introduction of programming innovations was the large investment that had been made in essential software and program libraries. Not unnaturally programmers and managers were reluctant to discard and rewrite these systems.

However, as the cost of software production continued to escalate and the movement of programmers increased the need for better methods of programming etc. became more acute.

Before the introduction of FORTRAN most programmers worked with machine language or assembly language. It was felt that this was necessary to achieve a high utilization of the processor. Several attempts at introducing a higher level notation had been unsuccessful thus encouraging the belief that efficient programming could not be achieved using a high level translator or compiler.

However, the cost of programming (programmers) began to increase and in many cases exceeded the cost of the hardware. In addition, as the scale of programming projects grew the debugging problems became more severe. As a result the potential benefits of high level language programming became easier to promote among the user community.

It was into such an environment that John Backus of IBM proposed the introduction of FORTRAN (Backus, 1981). One of the major considerations in the design of FORTRAN was the necessity to produce a translator which would produce efficient object code on a particular machine – object code which would be comparable to that produced by a programmer and would ensure a high degree of utilization of the expensive hardware. This, in turn, meant that language features were chosen to facilitate the construction of the translator. Many of these features have subsequently been enshrined in several language standards.

Thus the construction of the translator or compiler was felt to be the major problem, rather than language design. The name of the language being an abbreviation of FORmula TRANslator reflects much of the thinking on language design at that time. FORTRAN, therefore, had the objectives of making programming on a particular machine, the IBM 704, very much faster, cheaper and more reliable.

FORTRAN proved the viability of using a high level language to solve many problems. However, the spread and acceptance of FORTRAN was not without resistance. Many programmers saw no reason to change as they felt that machine code was the best way to obtain efficient use of a computer. Also, it takes time and effort to learn a new language and a lot of courage to abandon working programs or to start a project in a new language, especially when there is no obvious guarantee of improvement or success.

The interest in developing a high level language was not confined to the USA. In Europe a committee had been engaged on such a task from 1957. The considerations of this group produced the algorithmic language known as Algol 60 (Naur, 1963).

Unlike FORTRAN, the design and development of this language proceeded in parallel. The syntax (grammar) and semantics (meaning) were described in a report which used a special notation to describe the syntax. This notation or metalanguage is now widely known as the Backus-Naur form. Algol 60 was moderately successful in Europe but made little impact in the United States. It was the first language with a complete syntactic specification and reasonable semantic specification. It has acted as a model for subsequent language designers.

A successor to Algol 60 known as Algol 68 was proposed. Algol 68 turned out to be a controversial language in that many people regarded it as too complex. As a result, Niklaus Wirth of the Eidgenossiche Technische Hochschule in Zurich embarked on the design and implementation of what is now known as Pascal (Wirth, 1971).

There were two principal aims in the development of Pascal:

1. to make available a language suitable for teaching programming as a systematic discipline based on certain fundamental concepts clearly and naturally reflected by the language (structured programming),

2. to develop implementations of the language which were both reliable and efficient on presently available computers.

The language benefited from the experience gained in the design and use of other high level languages,

1. by identifying what was missing, and what was necessary,
2. by using more modern techniques to produce a reliable and efficient compiler.

The first version of Pascal was drafted in 1968 with the first compiler available in 1970. Pascal gained widespread acceptance as a teaching language to illustrate the concepts of structured programming and soon it was being used in other application areas.

Pascal is a simple language the interaction of whose features is well understood. Both the data and control structures can be developed hierarchically. Pascal has few machine dependent features which has enabled the movement of programs between different machines to be relatively easily achieved.

Eventually the concept of abstract programming coupled with the reliable and efficient implementation of languages like Pascal allowed a much greater degree of control to be exercised over software projects. As a result the software produced was more reliable and was amenable to adaptation, thus allowing the solution to similar problems.

There were, of course, many other developments taking place at the same time. In particular, COBOL for business data processing, APL for array processing, LISP for symbolic computation, Snobol for string processing and PL/1 as a general purpose language designed to meet the needs of scientific, commercial and systems programmers.

However, if FORTRAN is regarded as a first generation computer language in that it provides control structures and an abstraction mechanism in the form of the subprogram, then Pascal could be regarded as a second generation language which, in addition, provides data abstraction features. Subsequent languages contained features which enabled the construction of large programs and parallel processing features. Such languages can be regarded as the third generation. It is these third generation languages that are the main subject matter of this book.

2.2 Asynchronous programming languages

The next major area of programming to receive attention from the research community was that of parallel programming, in particular, asynchronous parallel programming. In this situation it is possible to specify actions which can proceed independently; such actions are usually referred to as processes or more recently as tasks. Each individual process can be specified by using the features that are recognized as necessary for abstract programming. In addition, language features are required to regulate the situations where the processes are required or wish to interact.

The situations in which processes interact can be divided into two categories. The first situation occurs whenever processes wish to update a shared variable or a resource at the same time. For example, when several processes wish to use the same resource, only one process must succeed in gaining access to the resource at any time. Once a process has obtained the resource it must be able to use the resource without interference from the other competing processes.

The second situation occurs when processes are co-operating and must be correctly synchronized with respect to each other's activities; for example, when one process requires a result not yet produced by another process. The first process must be able to wait on the second process and the second process must take the responsibility to resume the first process when it arrives with the result. The processes are communicating or scheduling one another and are now aware of each other's existence and purpose.

Two main techniques have emerged to solve these problems: first, where the processes use a structure called a monitor to deposit information and to communicate their intentions; and second, where the processes wait for each other and then pass information directly.

Languages have been developed using both techniques. For example, a language Concurrent Pascal was developed by Brinch Hansen (1975) and based on the first technique. Concurrent Pascal provides a process which consists of a private data structure and a sequential program that can operate on the data. One process cannot operate on the private data of another process. A monitor defines a shared data structure and all the operations that can be performed on it. These operations are defined by the procedures of the monitor. In addition, a monitor defines an initialization operation that is executed when its data structure is created.

In general a process can access the shared data of a monitor by calling one of its procedures. If there is more than one call then only one of the calling processes is allowed to succeed in entering the monitor at any time; this guarantees that the data of the monitor is accessed exclusively. Only when a process exits the monitor is it safe for one of the calling processes which was delayed to enter the monitor.

It is also possible for a process to enter the monitor and discover that the information it requires has not yet arrived. In such a situation, it can join a queue associated with that condition and thereby release its exclusive access over the monitor. Another process is now able to enter the monitor. Eventually, another process may enter the monitor and enable a delayed process to continue. The queues within a monitor are usually identified by condition variables and a process can append itself to a single condition variable queue by executing a **wait** operation. Another process executing a **signal** operation on a condition variable queue will cause a process delayed on that queue (if there is one) to be resumed. These are the main additions to sequential Pascal to enable parallel programming to be specified. The whole question of monitors and conditions is considered in more detail in Chapters 3 and 4.

Niklaus Wirth (1977), the designer of Pascal, also designed and implemented an extended version of Pascal called Modula. Modula is described as a language for modular multiprogramming and was intended for programming dedicated computer systems, including process control systems on smaller machines. It includes a module which is a set of procedures, data types, and variables where the programmer has precise control over the identifiers that are imported and exported. The user can declare processes in order to specify those activities which can take place in parallel. These activities can be synchronized by means of signals (conditions). Such synchronizing actions can only take place within an interface module which is similar to the monitor. Wirth subsequently designed and implemented Modula-2. Although a successor to Modula its means of synchronizing concurrent processes is much simpler. Modula-2 is considered in Chapter 6.

A more recent language based on the process and monitor concepts is Pascal Plus (Welsh and Bustard, 1979). Pascal Plus also has an abstraction mechanism similar to the module of Modula-2 but called an envelope. The envelope is an aid to program modularization and data abstraction and defines:

1. a data structure;
2. the operations that can be applied to the data structure defined as procedures and functions;
3. a control structure which brackets or envelops the execution of any block which creates an instance of the data structure – this control can be used to guarantee initialization and finalization of the data.

The parallel programming features of Pascal Plus are based on monitors and conditions and this language is used as the language to illustrate these features in Chapter 7.

In 1974 the US Department of Defense realized that it was spending a lot of money on software. This situation had arisen because, among other things, different installations were using different languages on similar projects leading to unnecessary and expensive duplication. Even in the cases where the same language was being used local variants had been introduced thus preventing or reducing the possibility of portability. This, in turn, increased the maintenance costs and the cost of training the personnel involved.

A series of requirements for a language to meet the demands of the Department of Defense in the embedded systems application area was drawn up in 1975 and widely circulated to the academic and industrial communities. The requirements were refined in the light of the comments received. The computing community was then invited to submit designs for a language to meet these requirements. Of the 17 submissions four were chosen and funded for further study. These proposals concluded that no existing language met the requirements but that Pascal was a suitable base on which to design the new language. Eventually a new language was approved and was called Ada (Reference Manual, 1983).

It was hoped that the language would be used widely in the next century and it should therefore push the state of the art in language design and implementation of the 1980s. One area where this was particularly true was in the area of parallel programming.

The origins of Ada's parallel processing method can be traced to languages like Communicating Sequential Processes (Hoare, 1978) and Distributed Processes (Brinch Hansen, 1980) which were proposed as notations for the design of parallel systems. Like the earlier languages a process or task in Ada terminology is used to indicate those parts of a system which can be executed in parallel. However there is no data structure like a monitor for the tasks to deposit data for later collection or in which to wait for data to arrive. Instead the tasks first synchronize their activities and then communicate directly without the help of an intermediate data structure. Hence one process may have to wait for another process to arrive. When it does the processes can exchange messages directly; such an encounter is referred to as a **rendezvous**. Ada is considered in Chapter 8.

The final language considered under the heading of asynchronous languages is called Occam (Inmos, 1984).[†] Occam is also a language which can be used to program parallel systems independent of the underlying hardware. The number of language features has been kept deliberately small to avoid obscuring the treatment of parallelism. Occam lacks many of the features which are to be found in a general purpose parallel programming language like Ada.

Occam enables a programmer to write a parallel program in which the processes communicate by sending messages along channels. This gives rise to a clear and simple structure as the individual processes operate largely independently. This, in turn, means that a program can exploit the performance of many computer components as each process may be executed by an individual processor. To further promote this idea Occam has an associated piece of hardware known as the transputer. Both Occam and the transputer are considered in Chapter 9.

2.3 Synchronous parallel programming languages

A section of the programming community, consisting of those interested in large scale scientific computations, has consistently demanded an increase

---

[†] Occam is the registered trademark of Inmos Ltd.

in the number of instructions executed per unit time. Their demands exceeded what could be provided by the most advanced sequential computer architectures. To satisfy these continually increasing requirements new computer architectures, which departed radically from the von Neumann model, were designed and constructed. Examples of these architectures are array processors like the Illiac IV, and the ICL Distributed Array Processor in which an arithmetic unit was duplicated many times, and vector processors such as the CDC Cyber 205 and Cray-1 in which the functional units were pipelined.

The effect of this revolution in computer architecture has been that the number of instructions executed per second is greatly increased and that numerical experiments which previously had been uneconomical or too time consuming became feasible.

On such processors a sequence of instructions can be applied concurrently to disjoint sets of data – the array processor philosophy. Or instructions can be overlapped on disjoint sets of data – the pipelining philosophy. We refer to this as the synchronous parallel programming environment. Consequently these machines do not have the mutual exclusion or synchronization problems of an asynchronous parallel programming environment. Array and vector processors are best suited for grid or mesh type problems in which the processing of data in regular patterns is the dominant feature. The problems of communication are now concerned with the movement of data between the various disjoint sets.

Many physical phenomena can be simulated effectively by parallel processors of these types. One example is weather forecasting in which a grid is used to encompass the earth and information is collected at each grid point. The data at each point of the grid can then be processed in parallel, using a technique based on finite differences. Another application area which requires large amounts of processing power is computational fluid dynamics. The equations specifying aircraft design can also be solved using a grid of points and processing in parallel the grid points. It can be argued that parallel machines of this kind require the best hardware and programming technologies available since many of their application programs produce information which have a direct influence on our daily lives.

An examination of grid-type problems reveals that dynamically varying data structures are not essential. Rather, what is required are arrays with primitive, enumerated, subrange or record components similar to those available in Pascal. A mechanism is required for specifying the parallel nature of such data and the means of applying parallel operations to such data. Thus many of the program and data abstractions which have been found to be beneficial in the construction of sequential programs can be utilized in this type of parallel programming environment.

It would appear that history is repeating itself as the developments in synchronous parallel programming technology have not kept pace with the architectural advances. The result is that many programmers and researchers are expected to use very sophisticated hardware with primitive and inadequate software tools. The current situation is similar to that which faced programmers of the early sequential machines.

The historical analogy with the development of sequential programming languages becomes even more apparent when the languages which are currently available for array and vector processors are considered.

These programming languages can be separated into two groups:

1. where the language provides either a syntax which directly reflects the architecture of the machine or demands that the programmer must explicitly encode hardware instructions in separate subroutine calls. This effectively turns these languages into higher level assembly languages. However, the implementation problems which are a major challenge are considerably simplified;
2. where the programmer uses a sequential programming language for the application and it is the responsibility of a compiler to determine which parts of the application can be executed in parallel. The major motivation for such an approach, in theory, is to utilize existing sequential programs and consequently save the development costs. However, to gain any substantial benefit the user must restructure the code or design it to suit the compiler.

The existing languages in these groups have ignored many of the recent developments in sequential program and data structuring which are relevant in this new environment. In addition, the knowledge accumulated in language design and compiler construction has not been utilized.

A third approach (Perrott, 1979) has recently been proposed which provides a programmer with data and program structures which reflect the type of parallelism under consideration. The syntax is independent of the hardware or the compiler and makes the language suitable for implementation on both array and vector processor configurations. This, in turn, should enable some measure of program portability to be achieved.

Subsequent chapters consider in more detail languages which have been designed and implemented for the synchronous parallel programming environment. Languages have been selected from each group to illustrate the programming techniques which must be used when programming array or vector processors. Unfortunately there is not the same agreement as to what is required in a language for this environment as there is for the asynchronous languages.

2.4 Data flow languages

More recently a new approach to both architecture and programming has gained momentum under the heading of data flow. In a data flow program it is the availability of the data which determines when an instruction is executed. This is in contrast to the above languages in which the order of execution is determined by the program text and referred to as control flow.

Hence in a data flow program if the data is available for several instructions these instructions may be executed in parallel. This means that there must be no data dependencies between these instructions. To ensure that this is true, new rules are required for data flow languages, for example, there must be no side effects or multiple assignments to variables.

Conventional languages are not well suited for data flow programming and this has led to the introduction of several new languages: for example, the language VAL developed at MIT (Ackerman and Dennis, 1979) and ID developed at the University of California, Irvine (Arvind *et al.*, 1978). In these languages the programmer is not provided with explicit sequencing features, such as the process or monitor, rather the programmer is given certain guidelines in which to construct the program. The parts of a program which can be executed in parallel are then determined by constructing a data dependency graph.

Prototype machines are now emerging with their associated languages and this approach may prove to be highly significant in providing greater computer performance. This topic is considered in more detail in Chapter 15.

2.5 Summary

High level programming languages have evolved much more slowly than the machine architectures on which they are implemented. In the sequential environment languages developed from being machine specific as the cost of programmers began to exceed the cost of the underlying hardware. Eventually the concept of abstract programming was established with program and data structures independent of the hardware being successfully implemented.

In recent years attention has focused on the problems of parallel programming which can be separated into two areas, namely:

- asynchronous parallel programming where relatively independent parts of a program compete and co-operate with each other to improve the efficiency of the program's execution;
- synchronous parallel programming where the regularity of the data enables the same operations to be applied in parallel by constraining all processes to act in unison.

A new approach which is now receiving attention is based on the idea that if the data for several instructions is available and there are no data dependencies then these instructions can be executed in parallel. This is referred to as data flow programming.

PART TWO

ASYNCHRONOUS PARALLEL PROGRAMMING

During the seventies it was the design and implementation of operating systems which led the research into techniques to regulate the concurrent activities which can occur in such systems. At the same time the development of cheaper hardware components enabled the construction of truly parallel configurations such as multiprocessor and distributed systems. The result was that many more applications became appropriate for the introduction of parallelism. This, in turn, meant that concurrent programming languages were required by programmers other than systems programmers.

The problems that are related to concurrent actions can be understood by considering the execution of a batch of programs in a sequential and a concurrent environment.

In a sequential programming environment each time a program is submitted for execution with the same data the series of states which the machine passes through is identical and the results obtained are the same.

27

Each instruction is executed without interference by the other instructions of the program.

In a multiprogramming system the processing unit is switched from one program to another, causing their instructions to be interleaved at (unpredictable) points in their execution. While in a multiprocessor system more than one program can be active at the same time with each program proceeding autonomously with its execution. In such systems the programs will interact and affect each other's progress.

The term **process** is used to describe a sequence of program instructions that can be performed in parallel with other program instructions. A program can therefore be represented as a number of processes which can be executing concurrently. The point at which a processor is withdrawn from one process and given to another is dependent on the progress of the processes and the algorithm used to assign the available processor(s). The simple and well defined processor allocation strategy of a sequential system is replaced in order to achieve greater processor utilization. The net effect is that processes are capable of interacting in a time-dependent manner. As a result of this time-dependent interaction the series of states which the system passes through is not necessarily identical when the same batch of programs is presented with the same data for execution.

Thus in a concurrent programming environment a programmer requires not only program and data structures similar to those required in a sequential programming environment but also tools to control the interaction of the processes – processes which are proceeding at fixed but unknown rates.

The situations in which the processes interact can be divided into two categories. The first situation occurs whenever processes wish to update a shared variable or a resource at the same time (or in an interleaved fashion). For example, when more than one process wishes to use a resource each process must be able to reserve and use the resource without interference from the other processes; this is described as **mutual exclusion**. The second situation occurs when processes are co-operating on some task, they must be correctly interleaved in time. For example, when one process requires a result not yet produced by another process, the processes must communicate or schedule one another and be aware of each other's existence and purpose; this is described as **process synchronization**.

In the sequel some of the techniques which have either been proposed or used to solve these mutual exclusion and process synchronization problems are considered.

The pedagogical approach as first illustrated by Dijkstra (1968) is used to examine the problem of mutual exclusion and to determine the properties required of any solution. This is followed by an examination of the evolution of techniques which have been proposed for the solution of these problems. The last of these techniques is based on a monitor construct plus condition variables. In this solution the processes deposit shared information in a data structure and synchronize each other by means of queues using special operators. This is then followed by an examination of the same problems using a different approach where processes pass information directly when they wish to communicate. There is no shared data structure and such a technique is referred to as a message passing technique.

The following chapters consider languages which have been designed and implemented using either monitors plus condition variables or message passing primitives as their means of regulating the activities of parallel processes. In particular, the languages Modula-2 (Wirth, 1983) and Pascal Plus (Welsh and Bustard, 1979) are considered as languages which use shared variables for synchronization while Ada (1983) and Occam (Inmos, 1984) are considered as languages which pass messages directly when communicating.

A typical problem in concurrent programming, known as the bounded buffer or producer/consumer problem, is programmed in several of these languages to enable a comparison of these two main techniques to be made.

Chapter 3 **Mutual Exclusion**

3.1 Introduction

To illustrate the problem of mutual exclusion, consider a concurrent system in which it is required to keep a count of the number of completed output commands issued by all the processes. A shared variable COUNT can be used to represent this number, and inside each process the instruction COUNT := COUNT + 1 should be placed after each output instruction. The inserted instructions will translate into several machine code instructions and if two processes execute these instructions simultaneously (or in an interleaved fashion) then the number of lines output by the processes may be counted incorrectly.

The instruction

COUNT := COUNT + 1 ;

may translate to the following sequence of pseudo-machine instructions:

```
LD      COUNT
AD      1
STO     COUNT
```

in the workspace of each process. Thus if two processes are allowed to execute this sequence simultaneously the following interleaving of instructions may occur:

```
LD      COUNT     (* process 1 *)
LD      COUNT     (* process 2 *)
AD      1         (* process 2 *)
STO     COUNT     (* process 2 *)
AD      1         (* process 1 *)
STO     COUNT     (* process 1 *)
```

The effect of these two simultaneous increases is to increase the value of COUNT by only one. This will occur on rare but unpredictable occasions which are unlikely to be detected by program testing. To avoid such a situation occurring requires the introduction of a **critical section**, that is, a section of code which can only be executed by one process at a time and which, once started, will be able to finish without interruption.

31

Such sections of code should be as short as possible to avoid, as far as is possible, other processes being delayed while they are being executed.

3.2   A software solution

An interesting question arises as to whether it is possible to protect a critical section by software, using only the assumption that individual accesses to storage locations are indivisible, that is, if several processes attempt to store or access a single value in a particular location the hardware decides arbitrarily which one succeeds first. Under this assumption a positive answer was first given for the two process case by the Dutch mathematician Dekker and for the general case of N processes by Dijkstra (1965, 1968).

Several attempts to achieve the mutual exclusion of two cyclic processes, each with a critical section, are now considered. Each solution is introduced to solve a defect in a preceding solution; the unsatisfactory solutions help to illustrate the pitfalls to be avoided and the criteria to be fulfilled when solving a mutual exclusion (or process synchronization) problem.

Solution 1

As a first attempt at achieving mutual exclusion for two concurrent processes assume that the critical sections are protected by a variable

```
var   DOOR : (OPEN, CLOSED) ;   (* shared *)

      DOOR := OPEN ;
      (* initially no critical section is occupied *)

(* process 1 *)                 (* process 2 *)
repeat                          repeat
  (* continue testing *)          (* continue testing *)
until DOOR = OPEN ;             until DOOR = OPEN ;
DOOR := CLOSED ;                DOOR := CLOSED ;
  critical section                critical section
DOOR := OPEN ;                  DOOR := OPEN ;
```

Figure 3.1   Mutual exclusion. The critical sections are protected by a single variable DOOR.

DOOR which takes the values OPEN and CLOSED only. If the value of DOOR is CLOSED it means that one of the processes has entered its critical section; if it is OPEN then a process can enter its critical section. A possible solution, on this basis, for the two process case could be coded as shown in Figure 3.1. In order to aid the clarity of the solution only the main parts of the processes are given. A Pascal type syntax is used in the program fragments.

An examination of the code of either process gives the impression that mutual exclusion is guaranteed. Unfortunately the processes communicate via the shared variable DOOR and it is possible for both processes to find the door open at the same time. Hence, in good faith, both processes will enter their critical section at the same time. Thus communication by means of a single variable is not sufficient to guarantee mutual exclusion.

Solution 2

Now consider the use of a variable to order the processes as they try to enter their critical sections. For example, consider the introduction of an integer variable TURN which has the value 1 when process 1 is able to enter its critical section and the value 2 when process 2 is able to enter its critical section. On this basis the solution given in Figure 3.2 has been constructed.

```
var  TURN : 1..2 ;   (* shared *)

     TURN := 1 ;
     (* initially it is the turn of process 1 *)

(* process 1 *)                (* process 2 *)
repeat                         repeat
until TURN = 1 ;               until TURN = 2 ;
  critical section               critical section
TURN := 2 ;                    TURN := 1 ;
```

Figure 3.2 Mutual exclusion. The value of the integer TURN indicates which process can enter its critical section.

This solution does, in fact, guarantee mutual exclusion but only by placing an unacceptably severe constraint on the two processes, namely, that in the execution of their critical sections, the processes adhere to the order 1,2,1,2, ... etc. Hence, if process 1 stops or goes slower then so must process 2. This solution must therefore be rejected.

Solution 3

This alternation of the processes can be avoided by assigning to each of the processes its own variable which takes the values INSIDE and OUTSIDE only; INSIDE indicates that the process wants to enter or has entered its critical section; OUTSIDE indicates that the process is outside its critical section. Each process can examine its competitor's variable before entering its critical section as shown in Figure 3.3.

```
var   PROCESS1, PROCESS2 : (INSIDE, OUTSIDE) ;

PROCESS1 := OUTSIDE ;          PROCESS2 := OUTSIDE ;

(* process 1 *)                (* process 2 *)
PROCESS1 := INSIDE ;           PROCESS2 := INSIDE ;
repeat                         repeat
until PROCESS2 = OUTSIDE ;     until PROCESS1 = OUTSIDE ;
  critical section               critical section
PROCESS1 := OUTSIDE ;          PROCESS2 := OUTSIDE ;
```

Figure 3.3   Mutual exclusion. Each process has its own variable which indicates if it wishes to enter or is outside its critical section.

In this solution there is no shared variable and the halting of one process outside its critical section will not affect the progress of the other process. However a new difficulty has arisen. If both processes simultaneously make the assignments

PROCESS1 := INSIDE ;   PROCESS2 := INSIDE ;

then both processes will loop indefinitely each waiting for the other process to take action.

Solution 4

The infinite looping mentioned in the last solution arises because the processes always wait for each other to take action whenever a conflict occurs. If, instead, the process which detects that both processes are trying to enter their critical sections changed its value, perhaps the problem could be solved. A solution using this strategy is given in Figure 3.4.

Unfortunately, showing consideration towards the other process can also lead to blocking if both the processes are proceeding exactly in step. An everyday example of the occurrence of this type of situation is when

```
var PROCESS1, PROCESS2 : (INSIDE, OUTSIDE) ;

PROCESS1 := OUTSIDE ;              PROCESS2 := OUTSIDE ;

(* process 1 *)                   (* process 2 *)
repeat                            repeat
  PROCESS1 := INSIDE ;              PROCESS2 := INSIDE ;
  if PROCESS2 = INSIDE then         if PROCESS1 = INSIDE then
    PROCESS1 := OUTSIDE ;             PROCESS2 := OUTSIDE ;
  repeat                            repeat
  until PROCESS2 = OUTSIDE         until PROCESS1 = OUTSIDE
until PROCESS1 = INSIDE ;         until PROCESS2 = INSIDE ;
  critical section                  critical section
PROCESS1 := OUTSIDE ;             PROCESS2 := OUTSIDE ;
```

Figure 3.4   Mutual exclusion. Each process is willing to let the other process proceed whenever a conflict occurs.

two subscribers telephone each other and encounter the engaged tone. They will continue to fail to communicate if both replace their receivers and try again, after the same interval of time.

Solution 5

Dekker was the first to present a correct solution which avoided the earlier difficulties. His solution is essentially a combination of the two previous proposals, that is, each process has its own value to indicate if it wishes to enter its critical section and, whenever both processes try to do so simultaneously, an integer variable is used to resolve the conflict. This solution is given in Figure 3.5.

As in the previous solution, a process operates only on its own process variable. It can inspect the other process's variable to see if a conflict is occurring. It will only enter its critical section provided the other process is outside its critical section. The integer TURN is used to resolve conflicts by enabling the process which has its process number currently assigned to TURN to enter its critical section (after the other process has given up its attempt to enter). On exit from its critical section it changes the value of TURN and the other process can now enter its critical section. Hence blocking cannot occur. Whenever a conflict does occur it is resolved in a finite time.

Dijkstra (1965) considered the more general problem of providing mutual exclusion for N cyclic processes, each with a critical section. As in

```
var PROCESS1, PROCESS2 : (INSIDE, OUTSIDE) ;
   TURN : 1..2 ; (* shared *)

TURN := 1 ;
PROCESS1 := OUTSIDE ;              PROCESS2 := OUTSIDE ;

(* process 1 *)                   (* process 2 *)
PROCESS1 := INSIDE ;              PROCESS2 := INSIDE ;
if PROCESS2 = INSIDE then         if PROCESS1 = INSIDE then
begin                             begin
  if TURN = 2 then                  if TURN = 1 then
  begin                             begin
    PROCESS1 := OUTSIDE ;             PROCESS2 := OUTSIDE ;
    repeat until TURN = 1 ;           repeat until TURN = 2 ;
    PROCESS1 := INSIDE                PROCESS2 := INSIDE
  end ;                             end ;
  repeat                            repeat
  until PROCESS2 = OUTSIDE          until PROCESS1 = OUTSIDE
end ;                             end ;
  critical section                  critical section
TURN := 2 ;                       TURN := 1 ;
PROCESS1 := OUTSIDE ;             PROCESS2 := OUTSIDE ;
```

Figure 3.5 Mutual exclusion. Dekker's solution for two processes.

the two process case, each process has its own variable to indicate that it wishes to enter its critical section and an integer variable TURN is used to ensure that only one process does.

The provision of mutual exclusion using this method is cumbersome and impractical. However, the development of the solution does illustrate the conditions which are required by any technique which claims to guarantee mutual exclusion, namely:

- at any moment there can be at most one process inside a critical section;
- the stopping of one process outside its critical section does not affect the other processes;
- no assumptions can be made about the relative speeds of the processes;
- processes about to enter a critical section should not block each other indefinitely.

Hence a detailed examination of the software solution enables a fuller understanding of the mutual exclusion problem from a theoretical point of view. The following sections consider more practical methods which have either been proposed or used.

3.3 Disabling interrupts

Historically, the first solution to the mutual exclusion problem was achieved by hardware. The hardware, by means of an interrupt, was used to indicate when an entry to a critical section was being attempted by a process. In a system which has only one processor, the only possible cause of interleaving sequences of instructions from different processes is, therefore, an interrupt. Hence, if on each occasion that a process wishes to enter a critical section it causes an interrupt and further interrupts are inhibited until it exits from its critical section, then the mutual exclusion of competing processes can be guaranteed.

If there is more than one processor in the system then the handling of interrupts becomes much more complex. In practice the hardware must ensure that one processor is responsible for the servicing of interrupts otherwise mutual exclusion will not be guaranteed. Hence, if interrupts are always handled by the same processor, no interleaving of the critical sections can occur.

The advantage of such a technique is the simplicity and the efficiency of its implementation; the critical sections are catered for without complex coding.

However, the ability to inhibit (and allow) interrupts is spread throughout the system and must be programmed very carefully. Also the inhibiting of interrupts is not selective and as a result large and probably important parts of the system are prohibited from general use. This can cause other processes to be delayed, especially if the critical sections are long.

3.4 The exchange instruction solution

The earlier software solution assumed only the indivisibility of single store accesses. However, if two particular operations could be performed without interruption, such as exchanging the value of a location with (say) a local register of a process then mutual exclusion can be programmed much more easily. This is the principle used in the exchange instruction solution.

In this solution a global variable EXCLUSION is initially set to a unit value. A process before entering a critical section must acquire the unit value stored in EXCLUSION and set the value of EXCLUSION to zero in a single indivisible operation. At the end of the critical section, the process returns the unit value to EXCLUSION. Since there is only one unit value in the system at most, one process can acquire it at any time and enter its critical section. If a process is unable to enter its critical section it must loop continually, this is called the **busy form of waiting**. When the exclusion on a critical section is released one and only one of the looping processes is able to proceed. This method of solution is illustrated in Figure 3.6.

```
type RANGE = 0 .. 1 ;
var EXCLUSION : RANGE ;              (* shared *)

   EXCLUSION := 1 ;                  (* initialization *)

   procedure EXCHANGE(var LOC, EXC : RANGE) ;
      begin
         LOC := EXC ;                (* indivisible *)
         EXC := 0                    (* operation *)
      end ;
(* process x *)
LOCAL := 0 ;
while LOCAL = 0 do
   EXCHANGE(LOCAL, EXCLUSION) ;
critical section
EXCLUSION := 1 ;
```

Figure 3.6 Mutual exclusion using the exchange instruction method.

This technique may be acceptable if there is little demand for the resource and if the critical sections are short, that is, the amount of busy waiting is not a substantial overhead.

3.5 Binary semaphores

A characteristic of the previous technique is that if a process is trying to enter its critical section and it is unable to do so it will waste processing effort by continually looping in its attempt to gain access to its critical section.

It is preferable that a process which is unable to enter its critical section goes to sleep and is woken up whenever access to its critical section becomes possible. In this way its processor can be more usefully employed.

On the basis of this idea Dijkstra (1968) introduced the Boolean or binary semaphore. His proposal has a direct analogy with the signals available on a railroad system to avoid a collision between trains (processes) on the same track (critical section). A Boolean semaphore is an integer variable taking only the values 0 or 1. The only operations permitted on a semaphore (other than initialization) are:

1. a P operation[†] which causes the semaphore's value to be decreased by 1 (provided it is not already zero);
2. a V operation which causes the semaphore's value to be increased by 1 (provided it is not already 1).

Both operations are indivisible operations such that once a P or V operation is started by a process it is completed without interruption by other processes.

The critical sections of a program can now have a semaphore associated with them (initially 1) and a process wishing to enter a critical section performs a P operation on this semaphore. The process is allowed to do so only if the decremented semaphore value is zero. Otherwise the process goes to sleep and its processor can be redeployed. Thus a semaphore has the value zero if a process is in its critical section, otherwise the value one.

On exit from a critical section a process performs a V operation which causes the value of the semaphore to be increased by 1; if there are any sleeping processes one of them is awakened (arbitrarily chosen) and is allowed to proceed. Care should be taken by a user to ensure that an attempt is not made to raise the value of a semaphore which is already 1.

Hence a process remains blocked on a semaphore until another process indicates that it is now safe for it to continue. When a process is blocked its processor can be more profitably employed.

If several processes simultaneously perform P and V operations on the same semaphore these operations will be performed sequentially in arbitrary order. Similarly if several processes are waiting on a P operation and a V operation is performed then an arbitrary choice is made from the waiting processes as to which process proceeds.

Hence mutual exclusion between competing processes can be achieved by merely bracketing the critical sections by the primitives P and V on a chosen semaphore as shown in Figure 3.7.

```
var MUTEX : SEMAPHORE ;
    MUTEX := 1 ;   (* initialization *)

(* process x *)
P(MUTEX) ;
    critical section
V(MUTEX) ;
```

Figure 3.7 Mutual exclusion using a binary semaphore.

[†] P is now identified as the first letter of the Dutch word *prolagen* formed from the words *proberen* (meaning to try) and *verlagen* (meaning to decrease). V is identified as the first letter of the Dutch word *verhogen* (meaning to increase).

The primitive operations, P and V, can be implemented in hardware, but normally are implemented by software under the protection of disabling interrupts. A queueing technique is used to avoid the busy form of waiting with the insertion and removal of processes being performed under the protection of disabling interrupts. If the processes are awoken in the order in which they were delayed this will ensure fairness in that no process is delayed forever. For example, if MUTEX is a binary semaphore then the P and V operations have the following interpretation:

```
P(MUTEX) = if MUTEX = 1 then
                MUTEX := 0
            else
                wait on the queue associated with MUTEX ;

V(MUTEX) = if QUEUE ≠ EMPTY then
                remove a process from the queue
            else
                MUTEX := 1
```

Semaphores are logically complete but often lead to complex constructions which are difficult to comprehend and sensitive to minor changes. The disadvantages lie in the need for careful-programming. For example, if a P operation is written instead of a V operation then the processes are blocked indefinitely. Also a programmer may forget to include in the critical section all statements that refer to shared variables.

3.6   Simple critical regions

To help alleviate the coding problems associated with the correct use of semaphores it is possible to employ a high level language construct which will be translated by a compiler into one of the techniques described above. Such a language construct, as suggested by Hoare (1972), is the **simple critical region** which can be specified as

with RESOURCE **do** S ;

Such a construct permits the critical statements S to operate on the shared structure RESOURCE. Shared variables are explicitly placed in RESOURCE and each shared variable can be in at most one such structure. Mutual exclusion is guaranteed by ensuring that the execution of different critical regions with the same RESOURCE is not overlapped.

The notation removes the necessity of writing P and V operations around the set of critical statements S, and removes the burden of checking that the entry and exit to critical sections are properly complemented, and in the correct order. Furthermore, the compiler checks that shared variables are used only inside critical regions and the updating of shared variables is thus protected. The programming effort and the likelihood of error is therefore reduced.

The implementation of critical regions is relatively straightforward if there is a hardware or software semaphore available. The declaration of a shared variable causes a binary semaphore to be created and each critical section is preceded by a P operation, and followed by a V operation.

3.7 Monitors

One of the problems with the earlier techniques is that the statements performing the operations on shared variables are spread throughout the program. This means that the complete program must be studied to see all the ways in which the shared variables are used.

Another approach to the mutual exclusion problem is to gather together the shared variables and the operations which can be performed on this data into a single construct; such a construct is called a **monitor** or **secretary** (Brinch Hansen, 1973; Dijkstra, 1972; Hoare, 1974). The monitor therefore collects critical sections into a single structure and only one process can have access to this structure at any time. The critical sections are removed from the bodies of the processes and become procedures (or functions) of a monitor. Whenever a process wishes to enter its critical section it invokes the appropriate procedure of the monitor. Only one process can succeed in entering a monitor at any time and any subsequent calls of the monitor's procedures must wait until the monitor becomes free. Only when a process exits the monitor is it safe for one of the calling processes which was delayed to enter the monitor.

Such a language construct takes the form

```
monitor MONITORNAME ;
(* declaration of local data *)
  procedure PROCNAME (parameter list) ;
    begin (* procedure body *) end ;
  (* declaration of other local procedures *)
begin
  (* initialization of local data *)
end ;
```

and the user can declare as many different monitors as the program requires.

The monitor procedures should not access any non-local variables other than those local to the monitor in which they are declared and these non-local variables should be inaccessible from outside the monitor. If these restrictions are imposed it is possible to guarantee mutual exclusion.

On declaration the monitor initializes its local data and all subsequent calls use the values of the local variables obtained on completion of the previous call. To invoke a monitor procedure the monitor name and the required procedure with its parameters are specified as follows:

MONITORNAME.PROCNAME (actual parameters)

Using such a construct makes the programming of mutual exclusion situations much easier and less prone to difficult-to-detect errors.

There are other features available within a monitor, namely, condition variables which represent queues and their associated operations, wait and signal. Since these features are concerned with synchronizing the activities of co-operating processes they are considered in the next chapter.

3.8 Summary

In a concurrent environment there are certain situations when the processes require to update a shared variable or resource without interference from their competing colleagues. This is referred to as a mutual exclusion situation. Mutual exclusion can be guaranteed on the assumption that single store accesses are indivisible. However, the solution is cumbersome and impractical and serves mainly to illustrate the problems and requirements for mutual exclusion. Other solutions utilizing the hardware have emerged; these include compound instructions such as the exchange instruction where two operations can be performed without interruption, and the binary semaphore where special P and V operations are introduced. Eventually in order to make the programming of mutual exclusion situations easier a monitor structure evolved. Using this technique it is easier for a programmer to specify a solution and for a compiler to check that the shared variables are accessed only within a monitor.

EXERCISES

3.1 Two concurrent processes $P1$ and $P2$ each have their own local variable A and B respectively. The values of these variables are to be exchanged using the following sequence of indivisible machine level operations:

load A into register R1
load B into register R2
store value from register R1 into B
store value from register R2 into A

What is the effect of concurrent execution if $P1$ and $P2$ do not execute the exchange under conditions of mutual exclusion?

3.2 Devise two solutions for the mutual exclusion problem for $N(>2)$ processes each with its own critical section under the assumption:

(a) only single store accesses are indivisible; and

(b) an exchange instruction is available.

3.3 The IBM 360 computer provides an indivisible machine instruction called test and set (TS). If X and Y are two Boolean variables the execution of the instruction

> TS(X,Y)

copies the value of Y into X and sets Y to false. Show how this instruction can be used to provide mutual exclusion for two competing processes.

3.4 Show how to implement P and V operations on semaphores by using the exchange instruction.

3.5 Describe in detail what happens if the following incorrect code is written to ensure mutual exclusion.

> P(MUTEX) ;
> **critical section**
> P(MUTEX) ;

3.6 Consider a system in which one process is producing data items (one at a time) while another process is consuming them (one at a time). A buffer is available which can hold a single data item produced by the producer process. Show how binary semaphores can be used to guarantee mutual exclusion of the data being passed between the processes.

3.7 Show, using binary semaphores, how

(a) a critical region; and

(b) a monitor

can be implemented.

Chapter 4 **Process Synchronization**

The techniques of the last chapter can be used to organize processes whenever they are competing for the use of some shared resource or variable. Now we consider situations where processes wish to co-operate with each other and are therefore to some extent aware of each other's purpose. In such circumstances they are still competing to gain entry to a critical section, but once this has been achieved their actions within the critical section may make a condition true which previously had caused another process to be delayed. Hence some method is required to enable a process to indicate that a particular event has occurred (or to wait until a particular event has occurred). The emphasis is now on finding ways of ensuring that processes co-operate with each other to their mutual benefit, that is, process synchronization.

4.1 General semaphores

As well as the Boolean semaphore Dijkstra introduced the **general** or **counting semaphore** which can be used to ensure that processes are synchronized. The general semaphore is an integer variable taking only non-negative values, and the only operations apart from initialization which can be applied to it are the P and V operations. The P and V operations are indivisible such that no two processes can be executing such operations on the same semaphore at the same time.

A general semaphore is initialized with a value greater than 1, say X, and the P and V operations can be applied provided the semaphore's value is within the range 0 to X. If several processes simultaneously attempt P and V operations on the same semaphore these operations will be performed sequentially in arbitrary order. If the semaphore's value is zero a process attempting a P operation is suspended and waits for another process to perform a V operation. This V operation causes one of the waiting processes to proceed; the choice of which process is arbitrary. The definitions of P and V on a general semaphore N take the following form:

```
P(N) = if N > 0 then
           N := N − 1
       else
           suspend current process
```

V(N) = **if** is there a suspended process on this semaphore **then**
    wake up a process
else
    N := N + 1

The essential difference between the general and the binary semaphores is that it is possible for several processes to perform a P operation on the general semaphore and continue execution.

If conditions can be associated with the maximum and minimum values of a semaphore these conditions can be used to synchronize the activities of a number of parallel processes. If a process makes a condition true it signals that it has done so by executing a V operation on the associated semaphore, while a process is delayed on a particular condition by executing a P operation on the associated semaphore.

The effect of a general semaphore can be achieved by using two binary semaphores and an integer variable, as shown in Figure 4.1. In this figure the binary semaphore MUTEX is used to ensure that all operations on the variable K, which simulates a general semaphore, are performed in a mutually exclusive fashion. The other binary semaphore DELAY is used to delay processes once the value of K has reached zero.

```
var MUTEX, DELAY : SEMAPHORE ;   (* binary semaphores *)
    K : INTEGER ;   (* represents a general semaphore's value *)

MUTEX := 1 ;   DELAY := 0 ;
K := X ;   (* initialization *)

P(K) = P(MUTEX) ;
        K := K − 1 ;
        if K < 0 then
          begin
            V(MUTEX) ;
            P(DELAY) ;
          end
        else
          V(MUTEX) ;

V(K) = P(MUTEX) ;
        K := K + 1 ;
        if K <= 0 then
          V(DELAY) ;
        V(MUTEX) ;
```

Figure 4.1 A general semaphore expressed in terms of binary semaphores.

Figure 4.1 also illustrates the careful programming required when using semaphores and the difficulty of reading and understanding programs which use semaphores. As an example it is mainly of historical interest to demonstrate the use of semaphores and relies on the P and V operations being complementary.

To further illustrate the use of general semaphores, consider the situation where several processes (known as the producers) wish to communicate a series of items to other processes (known as the consumers) with all processes executing in parallel at unknown speeds. This can be achieved by means of a buffer of finite capacity into which the producers deposit items and from which the consumers remove items when ready. The processes must be synchronized in such a way that the producers will not deposit an item in the buffer when the buffer is full and the consumers will not attempt to remove an item from the buffer when the buffer is empty. This is known as the **bounded buffer** or **producer-consumer problem** and this problem is used in several of the following sections to illustrate the various synchronization techniques.

The necessary process synchronization can be achieved by using general semaphores to represent the possible waiting conditions, namely, a full or an empty buffer. If a general semaphore FULL is used to represent the number of full buffer elements then a consumer should be delayed when the value of FULL is zero. Thus, if a producer performs a V operation on FULL after it has placed an item in the buffer and a consumer performs a P operation before removing an item then the consumers will be delayed whenever the buffer is empty. In a similar fashion a second general semaphore EMPTY can be used to delay producers when necessary and a signal must be given by a consumer process when it is safe for a delayed producer to continue.

To avoid the overwriting or skipping of any of the items in the buffer the operations of depositing or removing an item must be performed in a mutually exclusive fashion. Consequently a binary semaphore MUTEX has been introduced to the solution, as shown in Figure 4.2. The other variables used are COUNT which records the number of items in the buffer at any time and POINTER which indicates where the next item in the buffer to be removed can be found.

In this solution a producer process first decreases the general semaphore EMPTY by means of a P operation. If this operation is successful it means there is an empty element in the buffer and it is safe for the producer to proceed and to deposit an item. The depositing of an item must be performed in a mutually exclusive fashion so that other producers and the consumers do not interfere. This can be effected by means of the binary semaphore MUTEX. The element of the buffer in which the next item is to be deposited can be calculated using the expression (POINTER + COUNT) **mod** N; this will ensure that the elements are used and re-used (cyclically) if the situation demands it. The producer must then increase the value of COUNT by 1, release exclusion on the buffer and

```
var  BUFFER : array [0..N − 1] of MESSAGE ;   (* shared *)
     POINTER : 0..N − 1 ;
     (* position of next item to be removed *)
     COUNT : 0..N ;  (* number of items in the buffer *)
     FULL, EMPTY : SEMAPHORE ;  (* general semaphores *)
     MUTEX : SEMAPHORE ;        (* binary semaphore *)

     COUNT := 0 ; POINTER := 0 ;  (* initialization *)
     EMPTY := N ; FULL := 0 ; MUTEX := 1 ;

     (* producer *)

     ITEM : MESSAGE ;
     (* produce item *)
     P(EMPTY) ;
       P(MUTEX) ;
         BUFFER[(POINTER + COUNT) mod N] := ITEM ;
         COUNT := COUNT + 1 ;
       V(MUTEX) ;
     V(FULL) ;

     (* consumer *)

     ITEM : MESSAGE ;
     P(FULL) ;
       P(MUTEX) ;
         ITEM := BUFFER[POINTER] ;
         COUNT := COUNT − 1 ;
         POINTER := (POINTER + 1) mod N ;
       V(MUTEX) ;
     V(EMPTY) ;
     (* consume item *)
```

Figure 4.2   Solution of the bounded buffer problem using general semaphores.

finally perform a V operation on the FULL semaphore to indicate that another item has been successfully deposited. A consumer process is similarly controlled in the actions it can take only now it is making sure that there is an item to be consumed and that it can perform such a task without interference.

In general, if a process wishes to wait until a certain condition holds, a semaphore must be associated with this waiting condition and any process which might make this condition true must take the responsibility for performing a V operation on it. Therefore the programmer must build into each process an awareness of the requirements of the other processes. Because of this awareness, even more care is necessary when coding synchronization problems using semaphores.

If several consumers are waiting they will eventually be scheduled in a neutral manner as the result of V operations after new items are produced. In many cases, however, a more complicated or partisan scheduling algorithm is required, for example, in cases where all of the consumers are not identical. This can be regarded as a disadvantage of using general semaphores for process synchronization.

4.2   Conditional critical regions

To avoid the programming difficulties associated with general semaphores, Hoare (1972) introduced the high level language construct, the **conditional critical region** which takes the form

with RESOURCE **when** B **do** S ;

where B is a Boolean expression and S a critical section operating on the shared structure RESOURCE. It specifies that the critical section S is to be executed only when the condition B holds. If the condition B is false the process is delayed and the mutual exclusion associated with the critical section is released.

Brinch Hansen (1972) proposed a more generalized construct:

with RESOURCE **do**
begin
  statement1 ;
  await B ;
  statement2
end ;

where the **await** statement is allowed anywhere within the critical section. In this construct a process can, for example, indicate in critical section statement1 a request for a resource and then wait until the resource becomes available before executing the critical section statement2.

The implementation of either form of conditional critical region is possible if the compiler associates a binary semaphore with the RESOURCE. A process must first perform a successful P operation to gain exclusive access to the critical section before testing its condition B. If its condition B is false the process releases exclusion and joins a queue of processes waiting for their condition B to become true. If, however, the condition B is true the critical section is executed without releasing exclusion. On completion of the critical section the queue of waiting processes must be examined in case any of the conditions has become true. One of the waiting processes whose condition is now satisfied is chosen and enters the critical section. If none of the waiting processes is able to continue a new request for the critical section can be considered.

It is possible, therefore, for a process whose condition B is not immediately satisfied to evaluate its condition B several times before

---

```
var RESOURCE : record
                 BUFFER : array [0..N − 1] of MESSAGE ;
                 POINTER : 0..N − 1 ;
                 (* position of next item to be consumed *)
                 COUNT : 0..N
                 (* number of items in the buffer *)
               end ;

  with RESOURCE do   (* initialization *)
  begin
    COUNT := 0 ; POINTER := 0 ;
  end ;

      (* producer *)

      (* produce item *)
      with RESOURCE
        when COUNT < N do
        begin
          BUFFER[(POINTER + COUNT) mod N] := ITEM ;
          COUNT := COUNT + 1
        end ;

      (* consumer *)

      with RESOURCE
        when COUNT > 0 do
        begin
          ITEM := BUFFER[POINTER] ;
          COUNT := COUNT − 1 ;
          POINTER := (POINTER + 1) mod N
        end ;
      (* consume item *)
```

Figure 4.3   Solution of the bounded buffer problem using conditional critical regions.

entering its critical section. Brinch Hansen (1973) has called this the **controlled amount of busy waiting** because the retesting is done only occasionally whenever some other process has completed a critical section with respect to the same resource.

The conditional critical region is a more natural construct to use than the general semaphore when a process wishes to wait until a certain condition is satisfied This is illustrated by the solution of the bounded buffer problem in Figure 4.3. In this solution the buffer and the variables which are required for its manipulation have been combined into a record structure.

The **when** condition is used to specify the possible waiting conditions under which it is safe for the producers and consumers to continue execution: namely, COUNT < N for a producer, since there would be space left in the buffer for a producer to deposit an item and COUNT > 0 which ensures there is an item for a consumer to remove. This solution is much easier to understand than that using semaphores since the conditional critical regions hide most of the synchronization details.

If this construct is used with arbitrarily complex conditions it is possible for processes to remain unaware of the synchronization problems. However, in the case of a heavy demand on a resource it is probably necessary to restrict the condition to a simple Boolean expression to limit the cost of re-evaluating the conditions after a process completes its execution of the critical region.

4.3 Condition variables

In Section 3.6 the monitor was introduced as a means of providing mutual exclusion. It was shown how the monitor can be used to bring together the critical sections which in other solutions are part of the processes. Only one process can be active at a time in a monitor. A new data type, called a condition, was also proposed to provide process synchronization within a monitor. It can be used on those occasions when a process wishes to delay itself or re-awaken a previously delayed process.

Condition variables can only be declared within a monitor and take the form:

POSITIVE : CONDITION ;

POSITIVE identifies a queue of waiting processes which can only be manipulated by the operations WAIT and SIGNAL, as follows:

POSITIVE.SIGNAL

and

POSITIVE.WAIT.

The WAIT operation deactivates a process and appends it to a queue associated with the specified condition variable POSITIVE. A WAIT operation automatically releases the exclusion which would otherwise prevent other processes entering the monitor. The SIGNAL operation causes the resumption of the first process on a queue associated with the condition variable, indicating to the signalled process that the reason for its delay no longer holds. If there are no processes waiting the SIGNAL operation has no effect. The process which performs a SIGNAL operation and causes a delayed process to be resumed is suspended until this process exits the monitor or performs a WAIT operation.

This form of process scheduling is necessary in case the condition for resuming a delayed process is subsequently changed by the signalling process or another process intervening. The exclusion is 'passed' from the signalling process to the newly woken process, and the signalling process regains the exclusion and continues execution only when the newly woken process exits the monitor or waits again.

Hence by specifically detailing the conditions under which the processes may be delayed and resumed the scheduling of the processes can be more explicitly handled than with conditional critical regions. This means that no repeated evaluations of conditions are required. Each

---

```
monitor SEMAPHORE ;
var MUTEX : INTEGER ;
    POSITIVE : CONDITION ;
    (* declaration of a queue POSITIVE *)

    procedure P ;
    begin
      if MUTEX = 0 then POSITIVE.WAIT ;
      MUTEX := MUTEX − 1
    end ;   (* P *)

    procedure V ;
    begin
      MUTEX := MUTEX + 1 ;
      POSITIVE.SIGNAL
    end ;   (* V *)

begin
  MUTEX := 1   (* initialization *)
end ;   (* SEMAPHORE *)
```

Figure 4.4   A binary semaphore expressed by means of a monitor.

condition variable queue is served on a first come first served basis whenever a signal operation is applied to that condition variable.

To illustrate the properties of the monitor the earlier technique of semaphores is implemented as shown in Figure 4.4.

This illustrates a monitor SEMAPHORE with two procedures P and V. When the monitor is declared the initialization code is executed, in this case MUTEX is given the value 1, after which the monitor waits for calls from the processes. At a later time if a process, after calling the P procedure, finds the value of MUTEX to be zero then it joins the queue associated with the condition variable POSITIVE and releases the exclusion of the monitor. If several other processes call the P procedure they will also join the queue, in the order of their call to the procedure. These processes will remain on this queue until some other process calls the V procedure, increases MUTEX by 1, and then signals the first process on the queue FOSITIVE. The newly awoken process will decrease MUTEX by 1 and exit the monitor. The signalling process can then continue. The procedures of the monitor are called by the processes as either SEMAPHORE.P or SEMAPHORE.V.

There are situations, however, when first come first served scheduling is inadequate, and to give closer control over the scheduling it is possible, when performing a WAIT operation, to specify a priority for the process, this takes the form

POSITIVE.PWAIT(NUMBER)

where NUMBER is a non-negative integer. The queue of delayed processes will then be sequenced in order of increasing NUMBER and a SIGNAL operation activates the highest priority process, that is, no explicit queue scanning is necessary.

To illustrate this feature, consider the construction of a monitor to control simulated time which can be represented as follows:

```
monitor CLOCK ;
type RANGE = 0..MAXINT ;
var TIME : RANGE ;
    TIMEQUEUE : CONDITION ;

    procedure HOLD(T:RANGE) ;
    var ALARM : RANGE ;
    begin
      if T > 0 then
      begin
        ALARM := TIME + T ;  (* wake up time *)
        TIMEQUEUE.WAIT(ALARM) ;
        (* processes appended according to priority,
           i.e. wake up time *)
```

```
      TIME := ALARM
      (* advances time to restart time of the
         newly awoken process *)
   end
end ;   (* HOLD *)

procedure NEXT ;
begin
   repeat
     TIMEQUEUE.SIGNAL
   until TIME < > TIMEQUEUE.PRIORITY or
         TIMEQUEUE.LENGTH = 0
   (* remove all processes which should be woken up at this
      time, checking to make sure there are sleeping processes *)
end ; (* NEXT *)

begin
   TIME := 0
end   (* CLOCK *)
```

The monitor provides a procedure HOLD which enables a process to delay itself for a period of T units of simulated time. Such a procedure is activated by a process calling CLOCK.HOLD(T). The calling process will be resumed when simulated time reaches the appropriate restart time, that is, current simulated time plus T. The current value of simulated time is recorded in the variable TIME which is advanced whenever all process activity at a particular time has been completed; the new value of TIME is determined by the earliest restart time of any process which has called the HOLD procedure.

The other procedure NEXT is used to remove processes from the time queue one at a time until all processes which should be resumed at that instant have been. To achieve this it requires the help of operations such as PRIORITY which determines the priority of the first process on a queue and LENGTH which determines the number of processes currently on a queue.

The above solution ignores the problems of termination and the possibility of exceeding the time limit. These problems are left as an exercise for the reader.

4.4 Summary

If processes are required to co-operate with each other to their mutual advantage they require program constructs which enable them to suspend themselves and to resume a previously suspended process. This synchronization can be effected using a general semaphore. However, this can lead to programs which are difficult to understand and sensitive to minor change.

To overcome these disadvantages higher level language constructs such as the conditional critical region and condition variables have been proposed. These constructs simplify the programming of such concurrent activities.

Hence, the monitor structure when used with condition variables:

1. combines the requirements of mutual exclusion and process synchronization;

2. provides a systematic method of isolating synchronization problems, that is, processes no longer need to share data explicitly, instead shared data is gathered together and accessed within the monitor;

3. provides a systematic method of solving a synchronization problem, by listing the conditions and then considering the problem sequentially;

4. enables complex process interactions to be specifically ordered within the monitor which makes them easier to understand.

EXERCISES

4.1   Consider the set of processes represented in Figure 4.5:

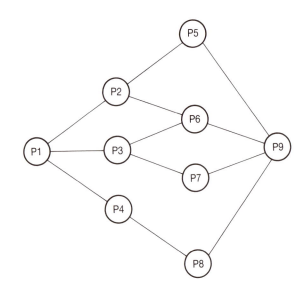

Figure 4.5

Using *P* and *V* operations show how the processes can be synchronized such that they adhere to the conditions imposed by the Figure.

4.2 In the bounded buffer example of Figure 4.2 suppose that V(MUTEX) is written incorrectly as P(MUTEX) in process PRODUCER. How does this affect the program? If the order of execution of V(MUTEX) and V(FULL) is reversed what effect does this have on the solution?

4.3 Devise a monitor which will control the allocation of *N* identical resources among *M* competing processes.

4.4 *The readers and writers problem*   A database may be used either for reading or writing. Any number of users may read from it simultaneously, but any user who is writing must have exclusive access to the database. Whenever a writer is ready to use the database, he should be allowed to do so as soon as possible.

Construct solutions to this problem using

(a) conditional critical regions; and

(b) monitors with condition variables.

4.5 *The spaghetti eaters*   Five philosophers spend their lives either eating or thinking. Each philosopher has his own place at a circular table in the centre of which is a large, and continually replenished, bowl of spaghetti from which he helps himself when seated at his own place. To eat the spaghetti requires two forks but only five forks are provided, one between each pair of plates. The only forks a philosopher can pick up are those on his immediate right and his immediate left.

Construct solutions to this problem using

(a) conditional critical regions; and

(b) monitors with condition variables.

Chapter 5 **Message Passing Primitives**

Message passing primitives, like the previous constructs, were introduced to solve the problems associated with low level synchronization primitives. As the name implies processes pass messages between each other when they wish to communicate; there is no shared data structure in which they deposit messages. With such a technique the processes must first synchronize their activities before they pass information. The origin of message passing synchronization techniques is attributed to the work of Conway (1963) on co-routines which provide a limited form of message passing primitives.

More recently two languages or notations, namely, Communicating Sequential Processes (Hoare, 1978) and Distributed Processes (Brinch Hansen, 1978) have been proposed which provide the programmer with synchronization primitives based on passing messages. These languages have, in turn, influenced the design of the languages Ada (Reference Manual, 1983) and Occam (Inmos, 1984) which are considered in later chapters.

5.1 Co-routines

In most programming languages when a procedure A calls another procedure B to perform a particular task, the procedure B is regarded as a slave procedure. Procedure B performs the requested task by executing its statements and then returning control to procedure A which can now proceed. However, there are many programming situations in which such a relationship between procedures is very restrictive and it is desirable to express the relationship in terms of procedures operating at the same level. In this situation control would be transferred backwards and forwards between the procedures without any one procedure being the master and the other the slave.

In such a system the transfer of control is effected in a symmetrical manner rather than in the hierarchical manner associated with languages like Pascal. To represent this symmetry in procedure calling Conway introduced the **co-routine**. This is a routine some of whose statements may be executed before returning control to the calling routine. At a later time if the routine is called again execution is resumed at the point where it relinquished control on the previous call. So a co-routine may only execute some of its statements when called by another co-routine. How many of the statements are executed is explicitly indicated by a new language primitive which indicates transfer of control. Such a procedure calling relationship can be easily extended to a system consisting of a number of co-routines with explicit transfer of control indicated in each co-routine. For example, co-routine A could transfer control to co-routine B which could transfer control to co-routine C which could transfer control to co-routine A, etc. depending on the application being programmed.

More specifically in a two co-routine system, control can be passed back and forth as each co-routine is executed thus introducing a symmetry into the calling procedure/called procedure structure. For example, a two player game such as chess can be more appropriately represented as a pair of co-routines rather than two player procedures under the control of a third procedure, which would be the case in a Pascal program. Each co-routine can store data local to itself rather than non-locally as in the procedural representation.

In a co-routine system a primitive such as

resume (PLAYER)

is required to transfer control between co-routines. In this example control is transferred to the named co-routine, PLAYER, which then resumes execution at the point where control was previously relinquished. Thus the **resume** primitive is the means of transferring control between co-routines. It is therefore possible for one co-routine to transfer control to any other co-routine in the system by simply naming it as a parameter. Each co-routine can be viewed as an implementation of a process with the execution of a **resume** primitive causing process synchronization. As a result process synchronization is completely specified by the **resume** primitives.

Another primitive **detach** is required to return control to the point at which the co-routine was originally activated. Thus the **detach** primitive can also be used to initialize the local data of a co-routine.

For example, the structure of a chess game could be expressed as two player co-routines declared as part of a main program as follows:

```
coroutine PLAYER1;                    coroutine PLAYER2;
begin                                 begin
   initialize local variables ;          initialize local variables ;
   detach ;                              detach ;
   (* return control *)
   while TRUE do                         while TRUE do
   begin                                 begin
     make a move ;                         make a move ;
     if game won then                      if game won then
       begin                                 begin
         print message ;                       print message ;
```

```
        detach                          detach
      end                             end
    else                            else
        resume (PLAYER2)                resume (PLAYER1)
  end                             end
end ;  (* player 1 *)           end ;  (* player 2 *)
```

When the co-routines are declared their local variables are initialized by executing the statements up to the first **detach** primitive. Control is then returned to the main program as a result of executing this **detach** primitive. The game is started by a call to one of the co-routines in the main program, for example, **call** PLAYER1. Execution then resumes after the **detach** primitive at the while loop in co-routine PLAYER1. After executing some statements which simulate a chess move PLAYER1 resumes PLAYER2 which will start to execute at its while loop. Control is then transferred between the players as they make their moves until eventually one of the players wins; no account has been taken of the possibility of a draw in the above program skeleton. Whichever player wins causes a **detach** primitive to be executed which returns control to the main program.

The parallel activity associated with this particular example is more appropriately described as quasi-parallelism since only one of the processes (co-routines) is active in real time at any moment. It is therefore an appropriate technique to use when concurrent processes share a single processor or in a multiprogramming system. Co-routines, in the form described above, are not adequate for truly parallel processing, for example, they do not provide a means for transferring data between processes. However, they do provide the basis from which the message passing techniques of the next sections have been developed. Co-routines have been included in many discrete event simulation languages such as SIMULA (Dahl and Nygaard, 1966) and BLISS (Wulf, 1971).

5.2   Communicating sequential processes

Programs written in languages like Pascal and FORTRAN are deterministic since the choice between several alternatives can always be determined by the variables of the program at any time. Dijkstra (1975) introduced alternative and repetitive constructs that allow non-deterministic behaviour in that, given several choices, one is chosen at random.

These new constructs are based on a concept known as a guarded command. A guarded command consists of a guard, which is a Boolean expression, followed by a command, which is a list of statements. The statements may only be executed if the guard is true. Alternative and repetitive constructs may be expressed using these guarded commands. In both constructs a list of statements belonging to a true guard will be arbitrarily selected for execution from among those guards which are true.

Using these guarded commands the alternative construct takes the following form:

```
[ GUARD1 → COMMAND1
[ ]GUARD2 → COMMAND2
[ ]GUARD3 → COMMAND3
[ ]– – –
]
```

where [ ] is used to separate guarded commands. GUARDn is a Boolean expression and COMMANDn is a list of statements of the language.

For example, the assignment of the larger of two variables X and Y to a third variable M is represented as

```
[ X >= Y → M := X
[ ] Y >= X → M := Y
]
```

Both guards are first evaluated, if only one is true the statement associated with it is executed. If both guards are true either of the commands will be executed; one is selected at random. If neither of the guards is true the process will abort. The case of two true guards will occur if X and Y have the same value, hence selecting either command will give the correct result.

The repetitive construct takes the following form:

```
*[ GUARD1 → COMMAND1
 [ ]GUARD2 → COMMAND2
 [ ]GUARD3 → COMMAND3
 [ ]– – –
 ]
```

This is similar in structure to the alternative construct with the addition of an asterisk, *, to indicate repetition. In this construct as many iterations as possible are performed, that is, until all the guards are false.

For example, calculating the greatest common divisor of two variables, X and Y, is represented as

```
*[ X > Y → X := X − Y
 [ ] Y > X → Y := Y − X
 ]
```

On each repetition both guards are evaluated and a true one selected; the statement associated with this true guard is then executed. This process is repeated until both guards evaluate to false, in which case the greatest common divisor of the two numbers will have been found.

With values of 36 and 24 for X and Y respectively two repetitions will be performed before both guards evaluate to false. On the first repetition the first guard is selected and on the second repetition the second guard is selected.

Another example of the use of this notation is

```
I := 1 ;
*[ I <= N ; A(I) < > 0 → A(I) := B(I)/A(I) ;
   I := I + 1 ]
```

which causes the first N elements of the array A to be reset except in the cases where A(I) is zero. The guard ensures that the value of I is less than or equal to N and that the value of A(I) is not zero.

These constructs do not by themselves introduce concurrency to a computation. However, if combined with processes which behave non-deterministically in that if there are several choices available at any time one is chosen at random then a new approach to the problems of concurrent programming is possible. It is felt that this non-deterministic approach more accurately reflects the input from unpredictably ordered external events, many of which occur at the same time in a concurrent environment.

Hoare (1978) incorporated the concept of guarded commands and processes into an experimental parallel language called Communicating Sequential Processes (CSP). He used input and output as the basic synchronization primitives for programming concurrent situations, that is, message passing by input and output commands.

In CSP process communication is achieved by means of these input and output commands and can occur between two processes whenever the following conditions hold:

1. an input command in process A specifies as its source the name of another process B,

2. an output command in process B specifies as its destination the process A,

3. the target variable of the input command matches the value denoted by the expression of the output command.

This is a substantial extension of the co-routine concept in that two processes must first indicate that they want to communicate with one another and then synchronize their activities before passing information.

For example, a process SENDER outputs or sends information to a process RECEIVER by executing an output command of the form

RECEIVER ! LINK(expressions)

where ! indicates output and LINK identifies the type of the message being passed. The parameters are the actual values to be transmitted.

The process RECEIVER inputs or receives information from the process SENDER by executing an input command of the form

SENDER ? LINK(variables)

where ? indicates input and LINK identifies the type of message being passed. The parameters receive the data being sent.

An input command fails if its source is terminated. An output command fails if its destination is terminated or if its expression is undefined.

Each process must name the process with which it wishes to communicate. Thus there is a symmetry in the synchronization relationship. Both the LINK and the expression and variable parameters must correspond if communication is to succeed. The synchronization of the two processes is known as a **rendezvous**; they come together, and pass information after which they proceed on their separate ways in parallel. No buffer is required to hold the information as it is passed directly between the processes. If there are no parameters it corresponds to the sending and receiving of a signal between two processes.

Whichever process encounters its input or output command first must wait for the other process to reach its corresponding output or input command in which the waiting process is named. Only then will both processes execute their communication statement, that is, the rendezvous takes place and the information is passed. The processes are first synchronized after which messages can be passed.

It is also possible for input parameters to be assigned directly to variables, in which case an input command takes the form:

SENDER ? (X,Y)

meaning: input a pair of values from the process SENDER and assign them to the variables X and Y. The output command

RECEIVER ! Y

means send to the process RECEIVER the value of the variable Y.

To enable non-deterministic waiting an input command such as PRODUCER ? C is allowed to appear as a guard in a guarded command. Such a guard is only true when process PRODUCER executes a corresponding output command, it is false if process PRODUCER has terminated but otherwise implies waiting to determine the result.

As an example of a CSP process consider the passing of characters one at a time from a process PRODUCER to a process CONSUMER. This can be formulated as

```
X ::  (* process name *)
  *[ C:CHARACTER ;
     PRODUCER ? C → CONSUMER ! C
   ]
```

where C has been declared as a local variable in process X. Process X consists of a repetitive construct with one guarded command. The guard inputs a value from the process PRODUCER and assigns it to the variable C. After this guard has been satisfied, the value of C can be output to process CONSUMER. Thus process X acts as a single character buffer between the producer and the consumer processes. When the producer process has finished the input PRODUCER ? C will fail, this causes termination of the repetitive command and of process X.

An alternative solution without a local variable is

```
X ::
  *[ PRODUCER ? DEPOSIT(C:CHAR) → CONSUMER ! REMOVE(C)
  ]
```

where the identifiers DEPOSIT and REMOVE with their parameter have been introduced to enable communicate.

To illustrate other features of CSP consider the implementation of a general semaphore SEMAPHORE shared among two processes identified as X(1) and X(2).

The semaphore must be described as a process which loops continually and is willing to communicate with processes wishing to perform a P or V operation. Since there are two processes the possible action of each must be specified by guarded commands, as follows:

```
SEMAPHORE ::
  VALUE : INTEGER ; VALUE := 0 ;

  *[   X(1) ? V( ) → VALUE := VALUE + 1
   [ ] X(2) ? V( ) → VALUE := VALUE + 1
   [ ] VALUE > 0 ; X(1) ? P( ) → VALUE := VALUE − 1
   [ ] VALUE > 0 ; X(2) ? P( ) → VALUE := VALUE − 1
   ]
```

On each iteration either a V( ) signal or a P( ) signal from one of the two processes X(1), X(2) is accepted. In either case no parameters are required since no data value is to be passed. A P signal cannot be accepted if the first part of the guard is false, that is, if VALUE is less than or equal to zero. This condition has been incorporated into the last two guarded commands.

The process X(1) or X(2) may increment the semaphore by means of an output command of the form SEMAPHORE ! V( ), and decrement the semaphore by the output command SEMAPHORE ! P( ). The semaphore must not be decremented if the value of the semaphore is not positive.

More specifically if process X(1) executes the statement SEMAPHORE ! V( ) it must wait until the process SEMAPHORE selects the guarded command

```
X(1) ? V( ) → VALUE := VALUE + 1
```

only then can a rendezvous take place and the value of VALUE increase by 1.

The process SEMAPHORE will terminate whenever all other processes have terminated.

As another example consider the programming of an alarm clock process which enables user processes to wait for different time intervals. The alarm clock receives a signal from a timer process after each time unit.

A possible CSP solution is shown below where the notation

```
*[(I : 1..N) USER(I) ? WAIT(INTERVAL) → statement
 ]
```

represents N processes each identified by a parameter I and output from any of them will be accepted.

```
ALARM ::
  TIME : INTEGER ; TIME := 0 ;   (* initialization *)
  DUE : (1..N) INTEGER ;   (* declares an array of N integers *)
  I : INTEGER ; I := 1 ;

    *[ I <= N → DUE(I) := −1 ; I := I + 1 ] ;
      (* −1 indicates that processes are not to be woken up *)
    *[ (I : 1..N) INTERVAL : INTEGER ;
        USER(I) ? WAIT(INTERVAL) → DUE(I) := TIME + INTERVAL

      [ ] (I : 1..N) DUE(I) = TIME → USER(I) ! WAKEUP( ) ; DUE(I) := −1

      [ ] CLOCK ? TICK( ) → TIME := TIME + 1
      ]
```

Each process I has a wakeup time which is stored in the array DUE(I), if it is not to be woken up this value is set to −1. Initially all values of DUE are set to −1. A process sets its wakeup time by performing an output command to the ALARM process of the form ALARM ! WAIT(T) when this is input by the ALARM process its due time is set. A process is woken up whenever the guard DUE(I) = TIME is true since this causes the output command USER(I) ! WAKEUP( ) to be executed. At each time interval the real time clock outputs a signal to the ALARM process that it is now time to increase the value of TIME.

The user processes have a structure such as

```
ALARM ! WAIT(T) ;
ALARM ? WAKEUP( );
```

so that they are ready to receive a wake up signal after they have set the alarm.

Thus in CSP interprocess communication is expressed by matching input and output commands in which each process names the other, and parameters describe the data to be transferred. The data is transferred directly between the processes after they have been synchronized; it is not deposited in a structure such as a monitor for collection at a later time.

5.3   Distributed processes

A second language or notation based on guarded commands and message passing primitives was proposed by Brinch Hansen (1978) and is known as Distributed Processes (DP). Communication between processes is achieved by one process calling a procedure defined in the process with which it wishes to communicate. The parameter list of this procedure is used as a channel for the transfer of data between the processes.

For example, if two processes SENDER and RECEIVER wish to communicate then process SENDER would execute a command of the form

call RECEIVER.LINK (values # variables)

where the process RECEIVER contains a procedure declaration of the form

proc LINK (value parameters # result parameters)
(* statements *)

and # is used to separate the different types of parameter. The value parameters carry information from the process SENDER to the process RECEIVER; the result parameters carry information back.

A process, such as SENDER, which calls a procedure of another process is delayed until the requested execution of the procedure is completed. Only when the called procedure is completed can both processes resume in parallel.

Another difference between the DP communication mechanism and the CSP mechanism is that the process defining a procedure does not require the identity of the processes which call it. Thus there is an asymmetric relationship between the called and the calling processes. It is argued that such a relationship is useful for programming a service process, particularly a library process, which may not or cannot know the identity of its users. If it is necessary to distinguish between callers this requirement must be catered for explicitly.

Non-determinism has been introduced into the language by means of guarded commands. A guarded command in DP has the following syntax:

GUARD : COMMAND

where GUARD is a Boolean expression and COMMAND is a list of statements. The Boolean expression must be true before the statement can be executed.

An alternative construct takes the form:

if GUARD1 : COMMAND1
| GUARD2 : COMMAND2

```
| ---
end
```

where | is used to separate guarded commands. This construct means that if some of the conditions GUARD are true one is selected arbitrarily and its command executed. If none of the guards is true the program stops. For example,

```
if X >= Y : M := X
 | Y >= X : M := Y
end
```

will assign the larger of the two variables X and Y to M.

The repetitive construct has the form

```
do GUARD1 : COMMAND1
 |  GUARD2 : COMMAND2
 |   ---
end
```

and means that while some of the guards are true select one of them arbitrarily and execute its corresponding command. This action is repeated until all the guards are false. For example

```
do X > Y : X := X – Y
 |  Y > X : Y := Y – X
end
```

will determine the greatest common divisor of X and Y by continually selecting a true guard for execution until all guards evaluate to false.

In addition special **when** and **cycle** statements, known as guarded regions, are used to express waiting, that is, a process can wait until a condition is true. The **when** statement takes the form

```
when GUARD1 : COMMAND1
 |      GUARD2 : COMMAND2
         ---
end
```

When this statement is encountered by a process it means wait until one of the guards is true and execute the corresponding command. The **cycle** statement takes the form

```
cycle GUARD1 : COMMAND1
 |      GUARD2 : COMMAND2
         ---
end
```

and corresponds to endless repetition of a **when** statement.

If several conditions are true within either a guarded command or guarded region then it is unpredictable which one of the corresponding statements will be selected. This uncertainty reflects the non-deterministic nature of real time applications.

To illustrate some of these features consider the earlier problem of passing characters one at a time between two processes. In DP this can be programmed using an intermediary process to hold the character as follows:

```
process X
  C : CHAR ; READY : BOOL ;   (* data declarations *)
  proc DEPOSIT(A:CHAR)
    when not READY : C := A ; READY := TRUE end
  proc REMOVE(#B:CHAR)
    when READY : B := C ; READY := FALSE end
  READY := FALSE   (* initialization *)
```

The initialization statement is executed first after which process X waits for requests from other processes to use its procedures, by invocations of the form **call** X.DEPOSIT or **call** X.REMOVE. An ordering has been imposed on the deposit and remove calls by means of the Boolean variable READY; this ordering was implicit in the CSP solution. For example, the DEPOSIT procedure can not be executed until the condition READY = FALSE is satisfied. Also in the DP solution the identity of any calling processes is not required as was the case in CSP.

As another example consider the implementation of a general semaphore which can be defined as a process with P and V procedures as follows:

```
process SEMAPHORE
  VALUE : INT   (* integer *)
  proc P
    when VALUE > 0 : VALUE := VALUE − 1 end
  proc V
    VALUE := VALUE + 1
  VALUE := 0   (* initialization *)
```

If a process calls the V procedure it is delayed while the V procedure is executed. If a process calls the P procedure it will not be executed until VALUE is greater than zero. If the process SEMAPHORE is to be used by two processes this fact is not apparent in its definition since the identity of a calling process is not required, as was the case in CSP when a similar example was coded.

The alarm clock example of the last section can be programmed in DP as

```
process ALARM
  TIME : INT
  proc WAIT(INTERVAL:INT)
    DUE : INT
    begin
      DUE := TIME + INTERVAL
      when TIME = DUE : skip (* empty statement *) end
    end
```

```
proc TICK
  TIME := TIME + 1
TIME : = 0   (* initialization *)
```

In this solution a separate copy of the local variable DUE is created for each process which calls the procedure WAIT thus avoiding the need for an explicit data structure.

This solution is easier to understand than the equivalent CSP solution, due mainly to the ability to express waiting directly in DP by means of the **when** construct. Further comparative examples of CSP and DP can be found in Welsh *et al.* (1980).

Thus DP, like CSP, uses a message passing technique as a means of process communication. In addition, both languages have introduced non-deterministic constructs to better reflect the unpredictable requests which can occur from external events in a concurrent system. It is these features which have influenced the design of the languages Ada and Occam which are considered in following chapters.

5.4 Summary

The origin of message passing primitives can be traced to the solution of the problem of representing a series of routines such that there is a symmetrical rather than a hierarchical relationship between them. This resulted in the introduction of a co-routine which is a block of code which resumes execution at the point where it previously relinquished control. Special language primitives are required to enable co-routines to co-ordinate their activities.

This technique was later expanded and combined with the concept of a guarded command to produce a different solution for the problems of mutual exclusion and message passing primitives. A guarded command consists of a Boolean expression guard and a number of statements; only if the guard is true can the statements be executed. If several guards are true one is selected at random for execution. The user can not rely on or use the processor scheduling algorithm which is operating in the system. Such a random selection accurately reflects the interruptions which can occur in a concurrent programming environment.

Several notations based on this principle, such as CSP and DP, have been developed and this is the principle for process communication which has been adopted by the designers of the more recent concurrent languages such as Ada and Occam.

EXERCISES

5.1 Design a program using co-routines which simulates a 4-player card game such as bridge.

5.2 Design a program using co-routines to read characters from an input file and print them. Every occurrence of a pair of asterisks in the input file is to be replaced by the single character upward arrow in the output. All other characters are to be copied as they occur.

5.3 Design a program using co-routines which copies characters from an input file to an output file. Every occurrence of a pair of asterisks is to be replaced by the single character, upward arrow. If a pair of upward arrows is produced they are to be replaced by a downward arrow in the output. All other characters are to be copied as they occur.

5.4 Devise a CSP and a DP process which will implement an integer semaphore which is to be shared among 100 processes.

5.5 Devise a CSP and a DP process which will control the allocation of a single resource among a number of competing processes.

5.6 Compare and contrast CSP and DP solutions to the bounded buffer problem as described in Section 4.1.

5.7 *Sieve of Eratosthenes*   In this method all the numbers are first put in the sieve. The smallest number is selected (a prime) and removed together with all multiples of this number. This process is repeated until the sieve is empty. Devise a CSP program which will print all primes less than the value N. Use an array of processes to form the sieve in which each process inputs a prime from its predecessor and prints it. The process then inputs an ascending stream of numbers from its predecessor and passes them on to its successor, suppressing any that are multiples of the original prime.

Chapter 6 Modula-2

6.1 Introduction

Pascal was created by the Swiss computer scientist Niklaus Wirth in the late sixties and the first implementation was available by 1971. After that time the use of Pascal, particularly for teaching, spread rapidly throughout the academic community. As a result of the experiences with Pascal, many of its advantages and disadvantages became apparent. One of its major disadvantages was when it was being used for the programming of large systems; it was unable to hide data objects. To solve this and other problems Wirth proposed Modula (Wirth, 1977). This was a special purpose language designed for programming large systems and also real time control systems.

Modula was based on Pascal but included an important structuring feature known as the module (see Section 6.2). In addition, it included general multiprocessing facilities, namely, processes, interface modules and signals. An interface module is essentially the same as the monitor structure while a signal has a similar function to that of a condition variable. As was shown in Chapters 3 and 4 these features can be used to control the interaction between parallel processes. Modula also allowed the specification of device modules to represent a computer's peripheral devices.

In 1977 Wirth began the design of both the hardware and the software of a computer system, subsequently called Lilith. This system was to be programmed in a single high level language such that detailed control over the hardware could be effected.

In order to satisfy the requirements of the Lilith system Wirth proposed Modula-2 (Wirth, 1983). Modula-2 combined some of the better features of both Pascal and Modula. It was a simpler language than Modula since it was designed primarily for implementation on a conventional single processor. As a result it required less sophisticated tools for controlling the interaction of processes. In Modula-2 the tools for handling concurrency have been simplified and are based on co-routines (Chapter 5) with transfer procedures rather than processes with interface modules (monitors).

Before considering some of the features of Modula-2 we first consider some of the changes which have been introduced to remove deficiencies in Pascal.

1. One frequent criticism of Pascal, particularly by scientists and engineers, is the fixed size of arrays. As a consequence a procedure defined with formal array parameters could not be used with different sized actual parameters at the time of activation. Modula-2 has removed this restriction by introducing the concept of an open array parameter which allows arrays of arbitrary bounds to be substituted. For example, the declaration

    procedure P(A: **array of** CHAR) ;

    allows calls with character arrays of arbitrary index bounds. The ISO Pascal Standard has introduced a similar concept referred to as a conformant array parameter in its Level 1 description.

2. There have been several improvements in syntactic conventions to enhance the readability of programs. For example, upper and lower case characters are considered as distinct while reserved words such as **if**, **for**, **while** and **end** replace Pascal's **begin – end** as statement delimiters. For example, in Modula-2

    if X > 0 **then** Y := Y − 1 ; X := X + 1 **end**
    else X := 0 ; Y := 0 **end**

    replaces

    if X > 0 **then begin** Y := Y − 1 ; X := X + 1 **end**
    else begin X := 0 ; Y := 0 **end**

    in Pascal.

3. Improvements have been made to certain of Pascal's statements. For example, the **case** statement can now have an **else** part for the situation in which the case value does not match any of the case labels. Also the number of language constructs has been reduced, for example, there is no **goto** statement.

4. Procedures are no longer regarded exclusively as program parts but can be regarded as objects that can be assigned to variables. This has given rise to a new type known as the procedure type. Variables declared with this type are called procedure variables since they take procedures as values. A procedure type declaration specifies the number and types of parameters and, if it is to be a function procedure, the type of the result. For example,

    type
      FTYPE = **procedure** (REAL) : REAL ;
      PTYPE = **procedure** (INTEGER, INTEGER) ;

    are two procedure types, while the variables F and P are declared as two procedure variables:

```
var
  F : FTYPE ;
  P : PTYPE ;
```

These variables can be assigned other procedures which have been declared in the program and have the same number and types of parameters.

5. In Pascal when a change is made to part of a program the complete program must be recompiled. This can prove to be a time consuming and frustrating exercise with a large program. To avoid this problem Modula-2 provides the facility of separate compilation based on the new structuring facility, the module. Modules can be designed, constructed, compiled and tested by different programmers at different times. Any changes are thus confined to part of the program. Modules can be kept in a library in compiled rather than source form and made available to many users.

6. The input and output peripherals which are attached to each computer usually vary from computer to computer. As a result it is difficult to incorporate abstractions into a high level language which hide the details of the peripherals. Modula-2 does not provide input/output operations as part of the language but such operations can be provided as language extensions written in Modula-2 itself.

The next sections consider only those parts of Modula-2 which are concerned with parallel programming. First a description of the module is given, since it can be used to bring together all the necessary facilities for multiprogramming in a high level language. The features of Modula-2 specifically included for dealing with concurrency are then considered.

6.2   The module facility

One of the main criticisms of programming languages, like Pascal, which were developed in the seventies, was their inability to hide data objects. For example, if it is required to provide the facility of a stack in a language like Pascal it could be represented using an array and manipulated using procedures POP and PUSH as follows:

```
const STACKSIZE = 100 ;   (* maximum number of items *)
type ITEM = 0..1000 ;   (* type of items that can be stored *)
var ITEMS : array [1..STACKSIZE] of ITEM ;
  (* stack representation *)
  SP : 0..STACKSIZE ;   (* stack pointer *)
  FULL, EMPTY : BOOLEAN ;
  ---
  procedure PUSH(I:ITEM) ;
  begin
```

```
      if SP = STACKSIZE then
        FULL := TRUE
      else
      begin
        SP := SP + 1 ;
        ITEMS[SP] := I ;
        FULL := SP=STACKSIZE   (* stack full? *)
      end
    end   (* PUSH *) ;

    procedure POP(var I:ITEM) ;
    begin
      if SP = 0 then
        EMPTY := TRUE
      else
      begin
        I := ITEMS[SP] ;
        SP := SP − 1 ;
        EMPTY := SP=0   (* stack empty? *)
      end
    end   (* POP *) ;
      − − −
  begin
      − − −
    FULL := FALSE ; EMPTY := TRUE ;
    SP := 0 ;   (* initialization *)
      − − −
  end
```

where − − − has been used to represent other data declarations and statements which may in themselves be quite large sections of code.

If this stack facility is part of a larger program then it is easy to see how the definitions can get widely separated, in particular, the initialization of the stack pointer etc. Furthermore, it is possible for the statements of other subprograms to access the identifiers which have been designed specifically for the stack representation, since they are visible to those other sub-programs.

To solve this problem what is required is a language feature which can enable related definitions to be grouped together and which can restrict access to certain identifiers. The solution to this problem in Modula-2 is called a **module**, in Ada a **package**. The module is one of the most important new features that have been introduced to Modula-2 and has given the language its name.

In Modula-2 the structure of the module takes the following form:

```
module name ;
  import lists ;
  export list ;
```

```
  data declarations ;
  procedures ;
begin
  statements
end name ;
```

A program can be partitioned into several modules with each module containing its own constants, variables, procedures, types, import and export lists. These declarations are enclosed between the reserved words **module** and **end** with the module's given name repeated at the end of the definition.

The identifiers of the module that are available outside the module are those which are listed in the export list. All other identifiers are invisible outside the module. Conversely the only external identifiers which can be used inside the module are those which appear in an import list (and have been listed in some other module's export list). More specifically an object declared in a module A can be referenced in module B by listing that object in an import list in module B. At the same time module A must permit the object to be exported by listing it in its export list.

Using this new facility the earlier Pascal example of a stack can be rewritten as a Modula-2 module as follows:

```
module STACK ;
export FULL, EMPTY, PUSH, POP ;
  (* the objects available outside this module to other
     modules *)
const STACKSIZE = 100 ;
type ITEM = [0..1000] ;
var ITEMS : array [1..STACKSIZE] of ITEM ;
  SP : [0..STACKSIZE] ;
  FULL, EMPTY : BOOLEAN ;

  procedure PUSH(I:ITEM) ;
  begin
    if SP=STACKSIZE then
      FULL := TRUE
    else
      SP := SP + 1 ;
      ITEMS[SP] := I ;
      FULL := SP=STACKSIZE
    end
  end   (* PUSH *) ;

  procedure POP(var I:ITEM) ;
  begin
    if SP=0 then
      EMPTY := TRUE
    else
```

```
        I := ITEMS[SP] ;
        SP := SP − 1 ;
        EMPTY := SP=0
      end
    end   (* POP *) ;

  begin
    SP := 0 ;   (* initialization *)
    FULL := FALSE ; EMPTY := TRUE ;
  end STACK ;
```

The module provides a protective wall around the stack and the only objects which can be used outside the module by other modules are those listed in the export list: in this case the state of the stack as represented by the variables, EMPTY and FULL, and the operations that can be performed, namely, POP and PUSH.

Another user can import the objects listed in the export list, however the details of how the operations on the stack are implemented are unknown to this user. The implementation could be changed provided the user interface, that is, the procedure heading, was unchanged. More specifically, if the stack was changed so that it was represented using pointers rather than an array then the users of this stack would not have to change their programs to take account of this change.

Thus the advantages of modules are that they extend the language and they allow details of the implementation to be hidden. Another advantage, considered later, is that modules can be separately compiled.

A module's import list contains the dependence on other modules and should therefore contain only items which are actually needed. Such a list takes the form

  from NAME **import** OBJECT1, OBJECT2 ;

where the identifier following the **from** symbol is a module name and specifies the objects' source module. For example, a module which wishes to use the facilities of the module STACK should include the statement

  from STACK **import** EMPTY, FULL, PUSH, POP ;

If a module name is imported then all its identifiers are also automatically imported. For example,

  import STACK ;

means that all the identifiers in the export list of module STACK are imported and must be qualified when used, as in

  STACK.FULL.

Hence the **from** clause has the effect of unqualifying the imported identifiers. In this way there will be no confusion with identifiers of the same name in different modules which have been imported or declared in the importing module. The user can use the symbol **qualified** in an export list in which case the listed identifiers must be prefixed with the module's name when used outside the module.

If it is necessary for a module to be separately compiled, its description must be divided into two parts: a definition part which specifies what the module does and an implementation part which specifies how it does it. The definition part contains the declaration of exported identifiers, that is, those features of the module which are available outside the module. The explicit word **export** does not have to be used. If an exported identifier is the name of a procedure then only the heading is given with the procedure being defined in the implementation part. For example, in the case of the stack example, the definition part would be

```
definition module STACK ;
    var FULL, EMPTY : BOOLEAN ;
    procedure PUSH(I:ITEM) ;
    procedure POP(var I:ITEM) ;
end STACK ;
```

This definition part contains the exported information about the stack: the two possible states of the stack, EMPTY and FULL, plus the two possible operations that can be performed on the stack, PUSH and POP. A definition part can also contain import lists.

The implementation part contains the details of the operation of the objects listed in the definition part plus any other objects which are purely internal to the module. In the case of the stack example its structure is very similar to that given previously, except that no export list is required.

By splitting a module into definition and implementation parts there are advantages for the user. For example, the definition part provides a fixed interface to which other programmers must adhere and it can be designed and used before the implementation part is written.

Thus the Modula-2 module is a program structuring tool which enables the decomposition of a problem solution into more manageable sections with clearly defined interfaces. The modules can be worked on by different programmers, perhaps at different times. In addition, modules may be compiled and tested separately contributing to the better management and development of large programs. A user can build up a number of library modules which may be accessed by any program – they are major reusable software components that may be integrated into many programs.

6.3 Co-routines

As was stated previously, Modula-2 was designed primarily for implementation on a single processor system and therefore does not require sophisticated features to handle concurrency. On a single processor system the type of parallelism which is provided is more properly described as quasi-parallelism since the single processor is switched between different processes so that only one process is ever active at any time. Modula-2 assumes that a program is used to describe several processes that interact relatively infrequently and are therefore loosely coupled. As a result the problems of mutual exclusion and process synchronization are greatly simplified. A sufficient tool to handle this type of quasi-parallelism is the co-routine and that is what has been provided in Modula-2. Thus a process in Modula-2 is represented as a co-routine and both words are taken to mean the same thing in the following description.

A Modula-2 co-routine is a series of statements specifying its activities and a set of local variables. A co-routine is executed quasi-concurrently with other co-routines and control is passed between co-routines at explicit points in their statements. The points in a co-routine at which control is to be passed are indicated by means of a system procedure known as the transfer procedure. When a co-routine calls the transfer procedure it is suspended with its state variables being saved. When it is resumed, as a result of another co-routine calling the transfer procedure, it continues execution at the point and in exactly the same state as it was before suspension. Thus unlike a procedure call a co-routine call does not imply a subsequent return.

A Modula-2 program can consist of a number of different co-routines which execute independently, but not concurrently, with each co-routine represented by a process variable. All references to a process, such as a co-routine call, are made through its process variable. A process variable can therefore be thought of as a pointer to the actual process. In order to store any temporary variables used in the course of its execution each co-routine needs a workspace, for example the workspace contains details of the status of the co-routine between suspensions. The statements which a co-routine executes are specified as a Modula-2 parameterless procedure. A new process can be created if this information is available by means of a call to a system procedure as follows:

```
NEWPROCESS(P:PROC ; WSP:ADDRESS ; N:CARDINAL ;
          var NEW:PROCESS) ;
```

where type PROCESS denotes a co-routine and NEW is a process variable which is assigned to the newly created process and by which it is identified in future manipulations. The identifier P denotes a parameterless procedure that the new process will execute. PROC is a standard type, defined as **type** PROC=PROCEDURE, and it is used to indicate such a parameterless procedure. WSP and N specify the address and size of the workspace in which the process will execute; the size is to be chosen to reflect the number of local variables and calls used in the process (typical minimum value is 100 words); type ADDRESS denotes values used as addresses and it is defined as a pointer to a machine word and the type CARDINAL denotes the positive integer values.

For example, given the declarations

```
const LENGTH = 100 ;
type SPACE = array [0..LENGTH − 1] of WORD ;
var WSP:SPACE ;
    PLAYER:PROCESS ;
procedure MOVE ;
    (* statements *)
```

then the statement

```
NEWPROCESS(MOVE, ADR(WSP), SIZE(WSP), PLAYER) ;
```

creates, but does not activate, a new co-routine PLAYER which will execute the procedure MOVE. The workspace of a process is usually defined as an array variable. Its address can be determined by using the standard function ADR and the number of storage units it requires by the function SIZE.

After a co-routine is created it is activated or resumed by calling another system procedure, namely,

```
TRANSFER(var SOURCE, DESTINATION:PROCESS) ;
```

This procedure suspends the execution of the SOURCE co-routine and resumes execution of the co-routine DESTINATION.

The procedure TRANSFER identifies within each co-routine the points at which its execution can be suspended. When called it causes control to be transferred from one co-routine to another as determined by the parameters SOURCE and DESTINATION. The resumed co-routine continues execution at a point immediately after its last TRANSFER procedure call with the state of the computation being restored. In this way the activities of the co-routines are explicitly scheduled.

These two procedures are defined in a module SYSTEM and exported through the definition part which takes the following form:

```
definition module SYSTEM ;
  type ADDRESS ; WORD ; PROCESS ;
  procedure TRANSFER(var SOURCE, DESTINATION:
                     PROCESS) ;
  procedure NEWPROCESS(P:PROC ; WSP:ADDRESS ;
                       N:CARDINAL ;
                       var NEW:PROCESS) ;
end SYSTEM ;
```

SYSTEM is a standard module which also contains the data types and procedures which refer to low level operations required by a particular computer or implementation.

Hence, in summary, the procedure NEWPROCESS creates a process variable which is associated with a co-routine; it does not activate a co-routine. Any number of process variables or co-routines can be created. The procedure TRANSFER uses these process variables to enable the co-routines to pass control among themselves. A program is terminated if any of the co-routines reaches the end of its procedure body, when a program terminates all its co-routines are automatically terminated.

6.4   Concurrent processes

The last section illustrated how Modula-2 provides a primitive means of establishing and synchronizing processes by using co-routines and setting up explicit transfers between them. In this section we show how such facilities can be expanded to provide for the designation of concurrent processes and for controlling their interaction. In particular, we show how to define a monitor structure and its associated operations in Modula-2.

As explained in Chapter 3, shared variables can be used to transfer data among processes and the processes must only access such variables under conditions of mutual exclusion. A Modula-2 solution must encapsulate these shared variables in a module which guarantees mutual exclusion of processes, in other words, a module which performs the function of a monitor structure. Although, if there is more than one processor, only then is it necessary to implement mutual exclusion. A module is designated to be a monitor by specifying a priority in its heading.

A condition variable is used to identify a queue of waiting processes inside a monitor, and Modula-2 has a similar concept known as a signal. A signal is declared like a variable although it has no value nor can it have one assigned to it. It is used to synchronize processes, and apart from initialization the only other two operations which can be performed on a signal are identified by WAIT and SEND. These operations correspond to the operations of delaying and resuming a delayed process respectively.

A process may send a signal, and may also wait for some other process to send it a signal. Thus a Modula-2 signal is associated with a particular condition which if not true means a process should be delayed. A signal can be sent by another process when the associated condition is found to be true. This causes one of the delayed processes to be resumed, if no process is waiting this is considered to be a null operation. In a quasi-parallel system these operations correspond to a switch of the processor from the calling process to another (waiting) process, and these operations are the only occasions where such switches occur.

To synchronize concurrent processes by using a monitor with condition variables Wirth recommends the introduction of a module PROCESSES with five procedures, namely,

STARTPROCESS, SEND, WAIT, AWAITED, INIT

If these operations are listed in the definition part of the module they are made available to other users of the system as in

```
definition module PROCESSES ;
  type SIGNAL ;
    (* export the type signal *)

  procedure STARTPROCESS(P:PROC ; N:CARDINAL) ;
    (* start a concurrent process with program P and workspace N *)
  procedure SEND(var S:SIGNAL) ;
    (* one process waiting to receive S is resumed *)
  procedure WAIT(var S:SIGNAL) ;
    (* wait until S is received *) ;
  procedure AWAITED(S:SIGNAL) : BOOLEAN ;
    (* determines if at least one process is waiting for signal S *)
  procedure INIT(var S:SIGNAL) ;
    (* compulsory initialization of signals *)

end PROCESSES ;
```

STARTPROCESS(P,N) is used to start a process which is expressed as a parameterless procedure P ; N is the size of the workspace in which the process will execute and store its local variables; whether this process is executed in genuine or quasi-parallelism depends on the implementation. INIT(S) initializes the signal S; every signal must be initialized before it is used. SEND(S) sends a signal causing one of the processes waiting for signal S to resume execution; sending a signal for which no process is waiting is considered a null operation. WAIT(S) suspends the execution of the process which executes it until a signal S is received. AWAITED(S) is a Boolean function meaning that at least one process is waiting to receive the signal S.

Thus this module is sufficient to give more detailed control over parallel processing than is available with the use of just the TRANSFER procedure.

To illustrate the use of these features of Modula-2 we consider again a solution to the bounded buffer problem, namely, several processes (the producers) wish to communicate a series of items to other processes (the consumers). This is to be implemented by means of a buffer of finite capacity into which the producers deposit items and from which the consumers remove items when ready. The processes must be synchronized in such a way that the producers will not deposit items when the buffer is full and the consumers will not try to consume items when the buffer is empty.

A solution to this problem in Modula-2 is as follows:

```
module BOUNDEDBUFFER[1]   (* priority 1 *) ;
  from PROCESSES import
    SIGNAL, SEND, WAIT, INIT ;
  export DEPOSIT, REMOVE ;

const N = 20 ;   (* buffer size *)
var
  BUFFER : array [0..(N - 1)] of MESSAGE ;
  EMPTY, FULL : SIGNAL ;
```

```
POINTER : [0..N − 1] ;
(* position of next item to be consumed *)
COUNT : [0..N] ;   (* number of items in the buffer *)

procedure DEPOSIT(ITEM:MESSAGE) ;
begin
  if COUNT = N then WAIT(FULL) end ;
  BUFFER[(POINTER + COUNT) mod N] := ITEM ;
  COUNT := COUNT + 1 ;
  SEND(EMPTY)
end DEPOSIT ;

procedure REMOVE(var ITEM:MESSAGE) ;
begin
  if COUNT = 0 then WAIT(EMPTY) end ;
  ITEM := BUFFER[POINTER] ;
  COUNT := COUNT − 1 ;
  POINTER := (POINTER + 1) mod N ;
  SEND(FULL)
end REMOVE ;

begin
  COUNT := 0 ;
  POINTER := 0 ;
  INIT(EMPTY) ;
  INIT(FULL) ;
end BOUNDEDBUFFER ;
```

In this solution COUNT is the number of items in the buffer and POINTER indicates the position in the buffer from which the next item can be consumed. The signals required to synchronize the consumers and producers accessing the buffer are EMPTY, which will delay a consumer if there is nothing in the buffer to be removed, and FULL which will delay a producer if there is no more space left in the buffer in which to deposit an item. These conditions correspond to the Boolean expressions COUNT = 0 and COUNT = N respectively.

This module BOUNDEDBUFFER must import from the earlier module PROCESSES the features which it requires. It must also export those procedures which it will permit another process to use, in this case the procedures DEPOSIT and REMOVE.

This solution has been formulated in terms of a module BOUNDED-BUFFER which performs the role of a monitor. The shared variables have been declared within the monitor and should be protected by mutual exclusion. However if Modula-2 programs are specified for execution on a system with a single processor and the processor can only be switched between processes at specific points then it is not necessary to provide mutual exclusion.

6.5 Summary

Modula-2 has been designed primarily for implementation on a single processor system and as such the problems of mutual exclusion and process synchronization are greatly simplified. A process is implemented by means of a co-routine which is a set of local variables and statements specifying its activities. A co-routine is created by a call to a system procedure NEWPROCESS. It is activated by another system procedure TRANSFER. TRANSFER is used to identify within a co-routine explicit scheduling points, that is, the points at which one co-routine resumes another co-routine. A resumed co-routine continues execution in the same state as it was before it relinquished control. In this way control is transferred among the various processes of the system.

High level synchronizing facilities can be implemented by using the program structuring tool, the module, and the signal type with its special WAIT and SEND operations. These facilities can be used to construct a module which simulates the function of a monitor with condition variables.

EXERCISES

6.1 Construct a Modula-2 program which will output messages Hi and Ho alternately.

6.2 Construct a Modula-2 definition module which is to be used with a range of terminals. The module should provide the basic screen handling facilities of setting a position, getting a position, clearing a screen and drawing a line.

6.3 Devise a Modula-2 program which will simulate the game of chess.

6.4 Design a Modula-2 program using co-routines which will read characters from a file and output them. Every occurrence of a pair of asterisks in the input file is to be replaced by the single character upward arrow. All other characters are to be copied as they occur.

6.5 Construct a program using two co-routines that displays the letters X and Y on a screen. The letter X is plotted vertically until it collides with the letter Y in which case it shifts to another column. The letter Y is plotted horizontally and changes direction every 50 moves. Both letters appear to be moving simultaneously.

6.6 Explain why in Modula-2, waiting for a certain condition to arise must never be programmed in terms of an empty loop.

Chapter 7 **Pascal Plus**

7.1 Introduction

In this chapter some of the features of the concurrent programming language, Pascal Plus (Welsh and Bustard, 1979) are considered. Pascal Plus, as its name implies, is a superset of Pascal. The extensions that have been introduced to Pascal evolved from a series of language experiments which were carried out under the direction of C.A.R. Hoare at The Queen's University of Belfast in the mid-seventies. These experiments were concerned with operating systems and simulation modelling.

The extensions can be divided into two groups:

1. The envelope construct which is available for program decomposition and data abstraction. It defines:
   (a) a data structure;
   (b) the operations that can be applied to that data structure;
   (c) a control structure which brackets or envelops the execution of any block in which it is declared. In this way it can be guaranteed that any initialization and finalization of the data is performed in the correct sequence.

   Such a construct is similar to the module of Modula-2 and the package of Ada but because of its enveloping control structure it is more powerful.

2. Facilities for parallel programming. These consist of:
   (a) the process, which is used to identify the parts of a program which may be executed in parallel;
   (b) the monitor structure, which holds data shared by processes and guarantees that only one process at a time can modify that data;
   (c) the condition, which enables processes to synchronize their activities when using shared resources.

Pascal Plus is therefore similar in the parallel features that it offers to languages like Concurrent Pascal (Brinch Hansen, 1975) and Modula (Wirth, 1977). It represents a progression in parallel language evolution from Modula-2 described in Chapter 6.

82

The next section considers the envelope construct which, although it is essentially a sequential structure, can be used in conjunction with processes. The concurrent facilities of the language are then described and used to illustrate a solution to the bounded buffer problem. Other examples are also considered to illustrate how to use the envelope to give closer control over the activities of concurrent processes.

7.2   The envelope construct

The experience gained with programming languages like Pascal indicated that a more sophisticated tool than the subprogram is required for the construction of large programming systems. In the mid-seventies this led to the development of the module in Modula-2 and the envelope in Pascal Plus.

The structure of the envelope is similar to a Pascal procedure or function block and may appear in the same declaration position. It takes the following form:

```
envelope NAME ;
  (* local declarations *)
begin
  (* initialization statements *)
  *** ;
  (* finalization statements *)
end ;
```

The two sections of code serve to initialize and finalize the data of an envelope and the three asterisks, ***, represent what is known as the inner statement. The effect of the inner statement is to execute the rest of the block in which an instance of this envelope is declared.

An envelope is declared using the reserved word **instance** as follows:

```
instance
  ME : NAME ;
```

which means that the initialization statements (if any) of the envelope NAME are executed, then the statements of the block in which ME is declared, followed by the finalization statements (if any). Thus the block in which the instance of the envelope has been declared has been bracketed or enveloped. In this way the user is relieved of the responsibility for ensuring that the correct initialization and finalization are being performed and in the correct order. The inner statement has full statement status in Pascal Plus and therefore may be executed like any other statement, for example, as part of a conditional statement.

The example of programming a stack data structure which was used in Chapter 6 is repeated here only using the envelope construct. There is much similarity between the programs.

```
envelope STACK ;
const STACKSIZE = 100 ;
type ITEM = 0..1000 ;
var
  ITEMS : array [1..STACKSIZE] of ITEM ;
  SP : 0..STACKSIZE ;
  *FULL, *EMPTY : BOOLEAN ;

  procedure *PUSH(I:ITEM) ;
  begin
    if SP=STACKSIZE then
      FULL := TRUE
    else
      begin
        SP := SP + 1 ;
        ITEMS[SP] := I ;
        FULL := SP=STACKSIZE
      end
  end   (* PUSH *) ;

  procedure *POP(var I:ITEM) ;
  begin
    if SP=0 then
      EMPTY := TRUE
    else
      begin
        I := ITEMS[SP] ;
        SP := SP - 1 ;
        EMPTY := SP=0
      end
  end   (* POP *) ;

begin
  FULL := FALSE ; EMPTY := TRUE ;
  SP := 0 ;
  *** ;
  (* no finalization statements *)
end   (* STACK *)
```

Any identifier declared within an envelope may be starred, that is, preceded by an asterisk, *. This means that this identifier may be used outside the envelope in which it is declared. In the case of a procedure name it means that the procedure may be called from another envelope; in the case of a variable identifier it means that the variable is available, in read only mode, in another envelope. Such starred identifiers when used outside their envelope must be prefixed or qualified with the name of the envelope in which they are defined. Thus the starring mechanism is the means of indicating which identifiers may be exported. Conversely all unstarred identifiers are invisible outside their envelope and thus inaccessible to other envelopes.

More specifically, in the stack example the variables EMPTY and FULL and the procedures PUSH and POP are available outside the envelope since they have been starred. When these starred identifiers are used outside the envelope they must be prefixed by the envelope's name as in STACK.PUSH(I). All the other identifiers are not available outside the envelope and as a result can only be used within the envelope.

To use the above defined envelope STACK in a program an instance of it is declared as follows:

```
procedure P ;
instance
  S : STACK ;
  – – –
begin
  (* statements of P *)
end ;
```

The instance declaration creates a set of the envelope's variables and executes the body of the envelope as far as the inner statement, ***, that is, the variables FULL, EMPTY, and SP are initialized. The statements of P are then substituted for the inner statement. Only the identifiers of the envelope which are starred can be accessed by the statements of P, that is, FULL, EMPTY, POP, PUSH. When the execution of the statements of P is completed the finalization statements (none in this example) are executed.

An important property of this solution, similar to the Modula-2 solution, is that the representation of the stack is hidden from the user of the envelope. This means that provided the user interface, that is, the starred identifiers, are unchanged a different representation of the stack could be used. For example, a linked list representation rather than an array representation could be used provided the user interface, the procedure headings PUSH and POP, are unchanged.

When more than one envelope instance is declared in a block the order of enveloping is determined by the order of declaration – each instance envelops any instances declared after it, and the body of the block itself. For example, in the case where an array of stacks is required in a procedure such as

```
procedure P ;
instance
  S : array[1..2] of STACK ;
  – – –
begin
  (* statements of P *)
end ;
```

the order of execution of the statements of the envelopes and P is

initialization of S[1]
initialization of S[2]
statements of P
finalization of S[2]
finalization of S[1].

In practice, programs commonly use envelopes of which only one instance is required; in those situations the definition and declaration may be combined by the introduction of the reserved word **module** as in

```
envelope module ASTACK ;
(* definition of stack as before *)
```

which is equivalent to

```
envelope STACK ;
  (* definition as before *)
instance
  ASTACK : STACK ;
```

Thus the envelope provides a means of hiding information by allowing other envelopes to reference selected identifiers within an envelope. Such a facility is a necessary requirement in a modular programming language which enables program decomposition and data abstraction. In addition, an envelope may be defined with a formal parameter list, with the actual parameter list being defined in each instance declaration; envelope instances may themselves be passed as parameters; envelopes may be nested and envelopes may themselves be starred. Such possibilities considerably increase the range of application and usefulness of the envelope.

7.3 Processes

Processes in Pascal Plus are used to identify independent sequential actions whose execution may take place in parallel in a program. After a process has been defined, as many instances as required by the application can be declared. Once activated the processes proceed in parallel.

A process is defined as a block with a suitable heading which may if required include parameters. For example, a process PRODUCER can be defined as follows:

```
process PRODUCER ;
  (* local definitions and declarations *)
begin
  (* statements of producer *)
end   (* producer *);

instance
  BEE1, BEE2 : PRODUCER ;
```

The last declaration denotes two processes which may subsequently run in parallel. The order in which they are declared is not significant.

As with envelopes if only one instance of a process is required its definition and declaration may be combined by the introduction of the reserved word **module** as in

```
process module BEE ;
  (* local declarations *)
begin
  (* statements *)
end ;
```

Unlike an envelope, a process instance is never referred to directly and does not provide an interface of starred identifiers. A process name is therefore only a documentation aid.

The inner statement in the body of the block enclosing the declaration of the processes represents the activation point of those declared processes. This is illustrated in the following code fragment:

```
program BEES ;
  (* definition of PRODUCER as before *)
instance
  BEEHIVE : array [1..N] of PRODUCER ;
  – – –
begin
  (* initialization *)
  *** ;
  (* finalization *)
end
```

In this example N producer processes have been declared using an array of processes, the order implied by the array notation is not significant. All N processes become active when the inner statement is executed. The processes proceed independently and in parallel until they terminate, whereupon the code following the inner statement is executed.

7.4 Monitors

Since processes are not totally independent of one another they need to interact on occasions to pass information or to synchronize their activities. As we have seen previously (Chapter 3) if shared data is used it must be accessed by only one process at a time under the protection of mutual exclusion. In Pascal Plus shared variables can be placed in a monitor (which is regarded as a special kind of envelope) and accessed by means of a call to a procedure of the monitor. A monitor implements exclusion by allowing only one process at a time to execute its code.

The structure of a Pascal Plus monitor is as follows:

```
monitor BOUNDEDBUFFER ;
(* declaration of local data *)
  procedure *DEPOSIT(ITEM:MESSAGE) ;
  begin
    (* statements *)
  end ;
  (* declaration of other local procedures or functions *)
begin
  (* initialization *)
  *** ;
  (* finalization *)
end (* bound buffer *)
```

As in the envelope the body of the monitor consists of an inner statement surrounded by initialization and finalization code. On declaration the monitor first initializes its local data by executing the initialization code. Any subsequent calls to a procedure (or function) of the monitor use the current values of the local variables. Only the procedures of a monitor which are starred, such as DEPOSIT above, can be called from outside the monitor. Any other procedures are purely local to the monitor. To invoke a starred procedure the monitor name and the required procedure plus any actual parameters should be specified as in

```
BOUNDEDBUFFER.DEPOSIT(ITEM)
```

Other identifiers within a monitor, such as variable identifiers, may be starred in which case the data is available in read only mode outside the monitor.

Pascal Plus allows processes to be defined within a monitor in which case the local data of the monitor is available to them but in read only mode. Protection against simultaneous access to such data is guaranteed by considering such accesses as equivalent to a monitor function call.

If only one instance of a monitor is required its definition and declaration can be combined as in, for example:

```
monitor module ABUFFER ;
(* definition *)
```

which is equivalent to

```
monitor BOUNDEDBUFFER ;
(* as before *)
instance
  ABUFFER : BOUNDEDBUFFER ;
```

Pascal Plus insists that all data declared outside a process is associated with a monitor. This is achieved by means of the following language rules:

- monitor definitions and declarations may only appear in a monitor definition;

- process definitions may only appear in a monitor definition;
- the program block is itself a monitor definition.

Thus a concurrent program in Pascal Plus is equivalent to a monitor block and processes may be declared in either a monitor or the main program block. All processes are prepared for execution as each monitor is considered but only activated when the inner statement of the main program block is reached, that is, all processes start executing in parallel at the same time. This rule is necessary to avoid the data of a monitor being accessed by a process before it is initialized.

7.5 Process communication

If a process calls a monitor procedure it may have to be suspended within that procedure pending the action of another process or it may resume a previously delayed process. As shown in Chapter 4 this synchronization of processes can be achieved by means of a queue. Such a facility has been provided in Pascal Plus by means of a standard monitor called CONDITION, which has the following structure:

```
monitor CONDITION ;

    type RANGE = 0..MAXINT ;
    procedure *PWAIT(PR:RANGE) ;
    procedure *WAIT ;
    procedure *SIGNAL ;
    function *LENGTH : RANGE ;
    function *PRIORITY : RANGE ;

begin
end (* CONDITION *) ;
```

Associated with each instance of CONDITION is an ordered queue. The user can declare these queues in the same way that envelopes and monitors are declared, for example

```
instance
    FULL : CONDITION ;
```

declares a queue identified by the word FULL. Instances of this standard monitor can only be declared in a monitor.

To suspend itself on a CONDITION queue a process performs a WAIT operation expressed as FULL.WAIT. Such an action appends the process to the end of the queue identified by FULL. It also releases the exclusion on the monitor, otherwise another process would be prevented from entering the monitor. As a result of WAIT operations the processes are queued on a first come first served basis.

To release a process from a queue another process performs a SIGNAL operation indicating to the signalled process that the reason for its delay no longer holds. This operation is expressed as FULL.SIGNAL. When a process signals, it immediately passes control of and exclusive access to the monitor to the process at the front of the FULL queue. The signalling process is delayed until the signalled process releases the exclusion of the monitor, either by exiting the monitor or performing a WAIT operation. This form of enforced politeness is necessary in case the condition for resuming a delayed process is subsequently changed by the signalling process or perhaps another process intervening. A SIGNAL operation has no effect if there are no processes waiting.

To give closer control over the scheduling of the processes a PWAIT operation may be used to specify a priority in the form of a non-negative integer parameter, for example, FULL.PWAIT(I). The processes are then queued in the order of decreasing priority, that is, the suspended process is positioned behind all processes with a priority higher or equal to I. Hence the WAIT operation is equivalent to using the PWAIT operator with all processes having equal priority.

The length of a queue can be determined by using the operation, FULL.LENGTH, while the priority of the first process in a queue can be determined using FULL.PRIORITY. LENGTH and PRIORITY have been defined as functions in the standard monitor CONDITION.

If a process calls a monitor procedure which results in a call to a procedure in another monitor it will then have exclusive access to both monitors. If the process is suspended in the second monitor, exclusion is released on both monitors. If it is subsequently reactivated it has exclusive access to the second monitor and must gain access to the first monitor (if required) by competing for entry with any other processes wishing to gain entry to that monitor.

A solution to the bounded buffer problem where several producer processes are trying to send a number of items to several consumer processes by means of a finite buffer is now given. The necessary synchronization can be achieved by associating a queue with each possible waiting condition, namely, a full or an empty buffer. The structure of the monitor which protects the buffer takes the following form:

```
type MESSAGE = definition ;
monitor BOUNDEDBUFFER ;
const N = 20 ;   (* arbitrary value *)
var
  BUFFER : array [0..(N − 1)] of MESSAGE ;
  POINTER : 0..N − 1 ;   (* indicates next item to be consumed *)
  COUNT : 0..N ;   (* number of items in buffer *)
instance
  EMPTY, FULL : CONDITION ;
  (* queues for suspended consumers and producers respectively *)
```

```
procedure *DEPOSIT(ITEM:MESSAGE) ;
begin
  if COUNT = N then FULL.WAIT ;
  BUFFER[(POINTER + COUNT) mod N] := ITEM ;
  COUNT := COUNT + 1 ;
  EMPTY.SIGNAL
end ;  (* deposit *)

procedure *REMOVE(var ITEM:MESSAGE) ;
begin
  if COUNT = 0 then EMPTY.WAIT ;
  ITEM := BUFFER [POINTER] ;
  COUNT := COUNT - 1 ;
  POINTER := (POINTER + 1) mod N ;
  FULL.SIGNAL
end ;  (* remove *)

begin  (* initialization *)
  COUNT := 0 ; POINTER := 0 ;
  ***
end   (* bounded buffer *)
```

The procedures DEPOSIT and REMOVE are starred, indicating that they may be called from outside the monitor by the competing producer and consumer processes. The value of the variable COUNT determines whether a process should or should not be delayed. If the value of COUNT is zero then any consumer processes calling the procedure REMOVE should be suspended on the queue identified by EMPTY. Similarly, if the buffer is full, COUNT will have the value N and any further calls from the producer processes should be suspended on the queue FULL.

If a producer process is suspended on the FULL queue it will remain suspended until a consumer process calls the procedure REMOVE and takes an item from the buffer. It is the responsibility of the consumer process to signal the queue of producers that it is now possible to deposit an item in the buffer. Similarly when consumer processes are suspended it is the producer processes which cause their resumption.

This monitor can then be declared and used in a program with the starred procedures called as shown.

```
program PascalPlus ;
  (* BOUNDEDBUFFER definition *) ;
instance
  ABUFFER : BOUNDEDBUFFER ;

  process PRODUCER ;
  var
    ITEM : MESSAGE ;
  begin
```

```
      repeat
        (* produce item *)
        ABUFFER.DEPOSIT(ITEM) ;
      until FINISHED
    end ;  (* producer *)

    process CONSUMER ;
    var
      ITEM : MESSAGE ;
    begin
      repeat
        ABUFFER.REMOVE(ITEM) ;
        (* consume item *)
      until FINISHED
    end ;  (* consumer *)

  instance
    P : array [1..X] of PRODUCER ;
    C : array [1..Y] of CONSUMER ;
    (* X producers and Y consumers are declared *)
  begin
    (* program initialization *)
    ***
  end.
```

In this example X producer processes and Y consumer processes have been declared by using an array of processes. Each process consists of a loop which is dependent on the value of a Boolean variable FINISHED. A process's actions consist of a call to a procedure of the monitor ABUFFER and then some action on a data item. All the processes become active simultaneously when the inner statement of the main program is reached.

As another example, consider the definition of a monitor which will control the passage of simulated time. Associated with the monitor is an ordered queue, known as the time queue. A process may suspend itself on this queue for a certain period of time by calling a procedure. The time queue must be ordered so that processes with early wake up times are at the front. In addition, time must be advanced to the next significant event when all activity has stopped. At such time one or more processes are to be woken up. Such pseudo time features can be introduced to Pascal Plus by means of the following monitor:

```
monitor module SIMULATION ;
type *TRANGE = 0..MAXINT ;
var *TIME : TRANGE ;
instance
  TIMEQUEUE : CONDITION ;

  procedure *HOLD(PERIOD:TRANGE) ;
  begin
```

```
    TIMEQUEUE.PWAIT(TIME + PERIOD)
    (* append to the queue according to wake up time *)
  end   (* hold *) ;

  procedure ALARM ;
  begin
    TIME := TIMEQUEUE.PRIORITY ;
    (* time is advanced *)
    repeat
      TIMEQUEUE.SIGNAL
    until (TIMEQUEUE.LENGTH = 0) or
        (TIMEQUEUE.PRIORITY < > TIME)
    (* wake up all processes that should be awake at this
       time checking to make sure the queue is not empty *)
  end   (* alarm *) ;

  process module TICK ;
  begin
    ALLWAITING.WAIT ;
    (* wait until all other activity has stopped *)
    while TIMEQUEUE.LENGTH < > 0 do
      begin
        ALARM ;
        ALLWAITING.WAIT
      end
  end   (* tick *) ;

begin
  TIME := 0 ;
  ***
end (* simulation *)
```

Processes suspend themselves on the time queue until the event that they require takes place. They do this by calling the monitor procedure HOLD with an appropriate parameter from which their wake up time can be calculated. Their place on the time queue can then be determined using the priority wait operation. The process TICK has been declared local to the monitor and controls the progression from one event to another. TICK waits until all other processes have stopped and then calls the procedure ALARM. This waiting is achieved by using another standard Pascal Plus condition, ALLWAITING, which allows a process to await the state where all processes are either suspended on condition queues or have finished. The procedure ALARM when called advances time to the wake up time of the process at the front of the queue and wakes up all processes awaiting this time.

Hence the provision of simulation facilities can be easily introduced to Pascal Plus enabling users to test and evaluate programs ultimately intended for real time use.

As has already been demonstrated the basic structuring tools for programs involving parallelism are processes and monitors. However, the envelope also has a useful role to play in many parallel programs by providing additional interface security. This can be illustrated by the solution to the problem of the scheduling of a single resource among a number of competing processes. A Pascal Plus solution can be defined as follows:

```
monitor RESOURCE ;
var FREE : BOOLEAN ;
instance
  BUSY : CONDITION ;

  procedure *ACQUIRE ;
  begin
    if not FREE then BUSY.WAIT ;
    FREE := FALSE
  end   (* acquire *) ;

  procedure *RELEASE ;
  begin
    FREE := TRUE ;
    BUSY.SIGNAL
  end   (* release *) ;

begin
  FREE := TRUE ;
  ***
end   (* resource *)
```

If this monitor is to be used to schedule a lineprinter then an instance can be declared as follows:

```
instance
  LP : RESOURCE ;
```

and each process must bracket its use of the lineprinter by making calls LP.ACQUIRE and LP.RELEASE to the monitor. For the monitor to function correctly it is necessary that the processes are properly behaved, that is, that they never use the lineprinter before requesting it or subsequently forget to release it. The envelope construct can be used in conjunction with this monitor to effect this control. This control can be achieved by embedding the above monitor in a further monitor which administers the scheduling and use of the resource through an envelope interface as follows:

```
monitor module LPCONTROL ;
instance
```

```
LP : RESOURCE ;
envelope *INTERFACE ;
  procedure *PRINTLINE ;   (* statements *)
begin
  LP.ACQUIRE ;
  *** ;
  LP.RELEASE
end   (* interface *) ;

begin
  ***
end   (* LP control *)
```

Processes requiring the lineprinter do not acquire and release it explicitly. Instead they declare an instance of the interface envelope, for example **instance** MYLP : LPCONTROL.INTERFACE; after which the scheduling is implicit, that is, the envelope INTERFACE automatically brackets the user code with the correct calling sequence. The lineprinter is then used by means of a call MYLP.PRINTLINE in a user process, at which time the lineprinter has already been acquired.

Each declaration of the starred envelope creates a fresh set of variables for that user, however, any starred monitor procedures that are called as a result of using this envelope are subject to monitor exclusion.

Hence the use of an envelope in this manner provides a secure interface for each process using a shared resource. It both protects a resource by enforcing its correct acquisition and release and also simplifies its use by taking the task of scheduling it away from the processes.

7.6 Summary

Pascal Plus as its name implies is an extension of Pascal. The extensions include an envelope construct which can be used for program modularization and data abstraction and processes, monitors and conditions.

Processes represent independent actions which can execute in parallel. When they wish to compete for a shared variable or to co-operate on a task they must call a procedure of a monitor. A monitor contains the shared data which is protected by mutual exclusion. Conditions are used to identify queues of waiting processes. A process joins a queue by performing a WAIT operation; it remains on the queue until another process performs a SIGNAL operation. In this way the processes can co-operate to their mutual benefit. The monitor is a static structure in which items are deposited and removed by the dynamic processes.

EXERCISES

7.1 Devise a Pascal Plus envelope which can be used to provide a distinctive trace message at each entry and exit of a block in a program. If a precondition is to be associated with each block show how this can be incorporated into such an envelope.

7.2 Devise a Pascal Plus program which converts a file of text of a particular width to a different width while retaining its paragraph structure and any blank lines that are present.

7.3 Construct a monitor which enables the scheduling of resources among a number of competing processes under each of the following criteria:

(a) any one resource chosen from N identical resources;

(b) a particular resource chosen from N identical resources;

(c) a particular resource chosen from a subset M of N resources.

7.4 *The readers and writers problem* A database may be used either for reading or writing. Any number of users may read from it simultaneously, but any user who is writing must have exclusive access to database. Whenever a writer is ready to use the database, he should be allowed to do so as soon as possible. Construct a Pascal Plus solution to this problem.

7.5 *The spaghetti eaters* Five philosophers spend their lives eating or thinking. Each philosopher has his own place at a circular table in the centre of which is a large and continually replenished bowl of spaghetti from which he helps himself when seated at his own place. To eat the spaghetti requires two forks but only five forks are provided, one between each pair of plates. The only forks a philosopher can pick up are those on his immediate right and his immediate left. Construct a Pascal Plus solution to this problem.

Chapter 8 **Ada**

8.1 Introduction

In the early seventies the US Department of Defense carried out a survey of its software projects and discovered that in, for example, 1974 the Department had spent approximately 3000 million dollars. The major portion of this money had been spent on embedded systems, where an embedded system is one in which a computer is part of a larger system, such as a ship or missile. It was also discovered that the majority of these embedded systems tended to be large and often had a life cycle of over ten years. In addition, the requirements for the software were continually changing.

It was also confirmed that many software development projects were frequently behind schedule, over budget, unreliable and did not fulfil the original specification. In addition, other Department of Defense installations across America were engaged on very similar projects leading to a duplication of effort. Many of these similar projects were using the same programming language but had introduced local variants to the language to suit their particular environment. Thus the portability of programs was restricted. In other similar projects different languages were being used, sometimes high level languages, sometimes low level. Associated with all these projects were both the maintenance costs and the costs involved in training programmers.

In 1975 the Department of Defense established the Higher Order Language Working Group to draw up the requirements for a language which would enable standardization of the programming language to be used in the embedded systems application area. The first statement of the requirements for such a language was known as the Strawman document and was published in 1975. This document was widely circulated in academic and industrial communities for comments and was subsequently modified and known as the Woodenman document. This process of circulation for comment was repeated once more to produce a detailed document known as the Tinman document.

As a result of the Tinman document, several existing programming languages were examined to see if they were suitable as an embedded systems programming language. None of the existing languages proved satisfactory but it was felt that Pascal, Algol 68 or PL/1 would provide a suitable base for such a language.

An updated document was produced and referred to as Ironman. At this stage language design proposals were invited to meet the requirements of the Ironman document. Seventeen proposals were submitted from around the world and four of these were selected for further funding and investigation. The four proposals selected were submitted by CII Honeywell Bull (Green), Intermetrics (Red), Softech (Blue) and SRI International (Yellow). The colours were introduced to try to eliminate any bias in their assessment.

The four subsequent designs were submitted by early 1978 and circulated to groups all over the world for evaluation. All four designs used Pascal as their starting point. Eventually the four designs were reduced to two, Green and Red, as these were thought to show more promise.

A final revision of the requirements produced the document known as Steelman after which the two remaining proposers were given another year to finalize their designs.

The final choice was made in May 1979 when the proposal developed by the team led by Jean Ichbiah at CII Honeywell Bull, France was accepted. The language was then renamed Ada in honour of Augusta Ada Byron, Countess of Lovelace. She had worked with Charles Babbage and is regarded as the world's first programmer.

The next phase involved the testing and evaluation of the design by means of applications programmed at over 100 sites. This was followed by a conference in October 1978. The first definitive version of the language was then published in July 1980. It was then proposed to the American National Standards Institute as a standard and after two years this resulted in the ANSI Language Reference Manual (Reference Manual for the Ada Programming Language, ANSI MIL-STD-1815, United States Department of Defense, Washington DC). As well as the programming language Ada, a programming support environment known as APSE was also specified. This is a well coordinated set of useful tools to support the entire software life cycle.

8.2   Language criteria

Ada was designed to fulfil three main objectives:

1. a recognition of the importance of program reliability and maintenance;
2. a concern for programming as a human activity;
3. efficiency.

To realize these objectives the designers of Ada have introduced the following features:

- *Readability*   Emphasis was placed on program readability rather than ease of writing. The programming notation is explicit to aid with the documentation of the program. English-like constructs rather than cryptic forms are used.

- *Data abstraction*   In line with the developments introduced with Pascal the details of data representation are kept separate from the specification of the logical operations on the data.

- *Strong typing*   Each variable of the program must be explicitly declared and its type specified. Such information can then be used by the compiler to ensure that a variable has values compatible with the set of values defined by its type.

- *Programming in the large features*   As the size of programming projects increased and the number of programmers involved also grew it became obvious that language tools were required which enabled programs to be developed as a decentralized and distributed activity. Thus Ada provides a mechanism for encapsulation known as a **package** – essentially it enables a number of subprograms and the data which they manipulate to be grouped together and treated as a unit. It is similar in function to the module of Modula-2 and the envelope of Pascal Plus.

  The facility of separate compilation is also provided to enable isolated testing and debugging to be performed, as are facilities for library management. It is foreseen that programs will eventually be assembled from independently produced software components.

- *Exception handling*   In many situations an error may arise from which the programmer may not wish the program to terminate. Ada provides the user with the exception feature which enables the programmer to specify what action to take if an error occurs. Thus the consequences of errors in one part of a program may be contained.

- *Generic units*   With this feature a programmer can create a related piece of program from a single template. For example, he can define a stack which can be used as a stack for integers, reals and other data types. The unit is defined independently of the type of objects it manipulates and the type can then be defined at a later time by the programmer.

- *Tasking*   This enables a program to be conceived as a series of parallel activities. This is the main topic of this chapter.

8.3   Process/task definition

In Ada the word task rather than process is used to indicate a sequence of actions which are conceptually executed in parallel with other actions.

Every task is written in the declarative part of some enclosing program unit, which is called its parent. Different tasks proceed independently, except at points where they synchronize.

The definition of a task consists of two parts, its specification and its body. The task specification is the interface presented to other tasks and may contain entry specifications, which are a list of the services provided by the task. The task body contains the sequence of statements to be executed when any of its services are requested; it represents the dynamic behaviour of the task. For example, a task PRODUCER is defined as follows, where − − indicates a comment in Ada:

```
task PRODUCER is
  − − specification
end PRODUCER ;
task body PRODUCER is
begin
  − − body
end PRODUCER ;

begin − − active here
  − − parent
end ; − − terminates here
```

In the specification part is a list (possibly empty) of the services the producer is offering to other users. In the body is the (hidden) details of their implementation. The producer task automatically becomes active, that is, its body is executed, when the **begin** of the parent unit is reached. The task then executes in parallel with the statements of its parent. A task is said to have completed its execution when it has finished the execution of the sequence of statements that appears after its reserved word **begin**.

If several tasks are written in the same declarative part they are executed in parallel with one another and their parent. For example, introducing a CONSUMER task to the above example gives

```
task PRODUCER is
  − − specification
end PRODUCER ;
task body PRODUCER is
begin
  − − body
end PRODUCER ;

task CONSUMER is
  − − specification
end CONSUMER ;
task body CONSUMER is
begin
  − − body
end CONSUMER ;
```

```
begin – – parent
   – – all 3 tasks active here
end ; – – parent
```

Whenever the **begin** of the parent unit is reached all three tasks, the PRODUCER, the CONSUMER and the parent start to execute in parallel. The language does not specify the order in which the tasks are activated. They continue to execute and possibly interact until they reach the final **end**. The program unit in which a task (or tasks) is declared cannot be left until all tasks in that unit have terminated.

If several tasks are required with similar properties it is possible to define a task type and then to declare as many instances as are required. For example

```
task type PRODUCER__TASK is
   – – specification
end PRODUCER_TASK ;
task body PRODUCER__TASK is
begin
   – – body
end PRODUCER__TASK ;
```

defines a type called PRODUCER__TASK which is a task, and

```
BEE1, BEE2 : PRODUCER__TASK ;
```

declares two instances of the type PRODUCER__TASK. These tasks will be activated at the **begin** of the parent unit in which they are declared. If there is only one instance of a task, as in the earlier example, then we could alternatively have declared

```
PRODUCER : PRODUCER__TASK ;
```

Tasks may be declared as part of structured variables such as

```
BEEHIVE : array (1..N) of PRODUCER__TASK ;
```

with the tasks referred to as BEEHIVE(1), BEEHIVE(2), etc.

8.4   Entry procedures

In Ada tasks can be regarded as either active or passive. Passive tasks have the function of providing some service (or services) which are used by other active tasks.

To illustrate the use of these features of Ada we consider again a solution to the bounded buffer problem, namely, several tasks (the producers) wish to communicate a series of items to other tasks (the consumers). This is to be implemented by means of a buffer of finite capacity into which the producers deposit items and from which the consumers remove items when ready. The tasks must be synchronized in such a way that the producers will not deposit items when the buffer is full and the consumers will not try to remove items when the buffer is empty.

An example of a passive and several active tasks occurs in the bounded buffer problem. In Ada the buffer itself must be described as a task – a passive task – which will accept calls from the other active tasks, the producers and consumers.

The communication method used in Ada closely resembles that of Distributed Processes (Chapter 5); one task calls a procedure defined in another task and the parameter list is used to provide for the transfer of data.

The task specification is used to declare the procedures which other tasks can call, that is, the services available from this task. For this reason they are referred to as entry procedures. For example, the specification of a task BOUNDED_BUFFER which allows items to be deposited and removed from a buffer could have its specification part defined as:

```
task BOUNDED_BUFFER is
  entry DEPOSIT(ITEM : in MESSAGE) ;
  entry REMOVE(ITEM : out MESSAGE) ;
end BOUNDED_BUFFER ;
```

indicating that it will accept calls to the procedures DEPOSIT and REMOVE from other tasks; the reserved words **in** and **out** indicate input and output parameters respectively.

Thus the specification contains a list of entry procedures which are the parts of a task which are available to other tasks to call and thus use. If the task provides no services then it requires no entry procedures in its specification.

In the body of the task BOUNDED_BUFFER more details of the entry procedures must be given in the following form:

```
accept DEPOSIT(ITEM : in MESSAGE) do
  -- statements
end ;
-- statements

accept REMOVE(ITEM : out MESSAGE) do
  -- statements
end ;
```

The **accept** statement must use the same identifier name and a list of parameters of the same number and type as appeared in the specification part. The statements between the **do** and **end** (if any) perform the service associated with the entry procedure; these statements correspond to a critical section.

To use any of the entry procedures another task must make a call of the form

```
BOUNDED__BUFFER.DEPOSIT(ITEM) ;
```

that is, an entry procedure heading qualified with a task name.

Thus the overall structure of a solution for the bounded buffer problem takes the following form:

```
task BOUNDED__BUFFER is
  entry DEPOSIT(ITEM : in MESSAGE) ;
  entry REMOVE(ITEM : out MESSAGE) ;
end BOUNDED__BUFFER ;
task body BOUNDED__BUFFER is
  -- depends on the representation used for the buffer
begin
  -- statements
  accept DEPOSIT(ITEM : in MESSAGE) do
    -- statements
  end ;
  accept REMOVE(ITEM : out MESSAGE) do
    -- statements
  end ;
  -- statements
end BOUNDED__BUFFER ;


task type PRODUCER is
  -- no entry procedures required
end PRODUCER ;
task body PRODUCER is
  ITEM : MESSAGE ;
begin
  loop
    -- produce item
    BOUNDED__BUFFER.DEPOSIT(ITEM) ;
    exit when FINISHED ;
  end loop ;
end PRODUCER ;


task type CONSUMER is
  -- no entry procedures required
end CONSUMER ;
task body CONSUMER is
  ITEM : MESSAGE ;
begin
  loop
    BOUNDED__BUFFER.REMOVE(ITEM) ;
    -- consume item
    exit when FINISHED ;
  end loop ;
end CONSUMER ;
```

An infinite loop construct is available in Ada as shown above in the body of the producers and consumers. To leave such a construct requires an **exit** statement which specifies the condition under which an exit should be made.

Several instances of these task types can be declared, as follows:

P : **array** (1..X) **of** PRODUCER ;
C : **array** (1..Y) **of** CONSUMER ;

so that the X producers, the Y consumers and the BOUNDED__BUFFER task are all operating independently and in parallel. The tasks are activated when the **begin** of the parent block is reached.

8.5 Process/task communication

As stated previously the communication method used in Ada closely resembles that of Distributed Processes, one task calls a procedure defined in another task and the parameter list is used to provide for the transfer of data. This mechanism is reflected in the specification part of a task by means of the entry procedures. For example, the calls accepted by the BOUNDED__BUFFER task are those of a deposit or a removal of an item as indicated in the specification part. The statements of the task body following the appropriate reserved word **accept** are executed whenever another task calls the entry procedure that it requires and that call is accepted by the called task.

Thus whichever task reaches its communication statement first must wait for the other task, that is, either the calling task calls an entry procedure such as BOUNDED__BUFFER.DEPOSIT(ITEM) or the called task reaches the appropriate accept statement, in this case:

accept DEPOSIT(ITEM: **in** MESSAGE) **do**

When both tasks are ready to communicate we have a rendezvous. At the rendezvous the parameters are transferred and the body of the **accept** statement executed. The calling task is delayed and can only proceed when the execution of the **accept** statement has been completed. The two tasks then proceed independently. Thus the synchronization of the tasks is implicit.

As in Distributed Processes the synchronization is asymmetric, the called task is named by the caller but not vice versa as, for example, in BOUNDED__BUFFER.REMOVE(ITEM), the BOUNDED__BUFFER task does not know which of the consumer tasks has called it.

If there are several calls to a particular entry procedure they are queued. To allow for this situation a single queue is associated with each entry procedure and waiting tasks are processed on a first come first served basis. Execution of an **accept** removes one task from the queue.

As an illustration consider the problem of passing a single character between two tasks, that is, a producer task inputs a character into a single element buffer which is then output to a consumer task. This can be represented as follows:

```
task SINGLE__BUFFER is
  DEPOSIT(CH : in CHARACTER) ;
  REMOVE(CH : out CHARACTER) ;
end SINGLE__BUFFER ;

task body SINGLE__BUFFER is
  C : CHARACTER ;
  - - local variable
begin
  loop
    accept DEPOSIT(CH : in CHARACTER) do
      C := CH ;
    end ;
    accept REMOVE(CH : out CHARACTER) do
      CH := C ;
    end ;
  end loop ;
end SINGLE__BUFFER ;
```

The task body consists of an infinite loop containing two accept statements, the order of these two statements dictates the order in which a rendezvous can be established with either of the two calling tasks. The solution expresses the deterministic sequence of DEPOSIT and REMOVE calls which are required. The producer task makes a call SINGLE__BUFFER.DEPOSIT(C) and as a result may join a queue associated with this entry procedure. When its call is accepted, that is, the SINGLE__BUFFER task reaches the first **accept** statement, the parameter is passed. Both tasks then proceed independently and in parallel. Only after a character has been input to the local variable C will it be possible for a call to the REMOVE entry procedure to be accepted. This will ensure that there is always a character available to be passed on to the consumer task. Hence in this simple example there are only two queues with the possibility of only one task being placed on either of the queues at any time.

Non-determinism has been introduced into Ada by means of the **select** statement. This statement consists of a number of alternatives, only one of which can be selected at any time. It therefore enables a choice from among several entry procedure calls to be specified. For example, in the bounded buffer problem the buffer task can be programmed to accept producer and consumer task calls by placing the details of the appropriate entry procedures in the select alternatives. When the BOUNDED__BUFFER task is ready to select a task call the order of selection is non-deterministic since neither producers nor consumers are given priority. This can be programmed as follows:

```
select
  accept DEPOSIT(ITEM : in MESSAGE) do
    - - statements
  end ;
or
  accept REMOVE(ITEM : out MESSAGE) do
    - - statements
  end ;
end select ;
```

If neither of the entry procedures has been called the BOUNDED__BUFFER task waits. If one of them has been called it is executed. If both have been called then either one is selected and executed. It is not known which call will be selected, the choice is at random and the programmer cannot rely on the selection algorithm used when programming other parts of the system.

A conditional execution of a **select** alternative can be introduced by means of a **when** clause, this is equivalent to a guarded command. For example,

```
when COUNT < N =>
  accept DEPOSIT(ITEM : in MESSAGE) do
    - - statements
  end ;
```

will ensure that the value of COUNT is less than N before the **accept** statement is executed.

The guards are evaluated when the task reaches the beginning of the **select** statement in order to determine which guards are open. A guard is open if its Boolean expression is true otherwise the guard is closed. If an alternative of the **select** statement does not have a guard then it is regarded as being open. Selection of one of the open alternatives takes place immediately if a corresponding rendezvous is possible, that is, if there is a corresponding entry call issued by another task and waiting to be accepted. If several alternatives can thus be selected, one of them is chosen arbitrarily (the language does not define which one). When such an alternative is selected, the corresponding **accept** statement and any other statements of the alternative are executed. In the case where all the guards are closed an error is reported. It is possible for a **select** statement to have an else part which will be executed if other alternatives are closed. If no rendezvous is immediately possible and there is no else part, the task waits until an open alternative can be selected.

A solution for the bounded buffer problem is now given incorporating the **select** statement.

```
task BOUNDED__BUFFER is
  entry DEPOSIT(ITEM : in MESSAGE) ;
  entry REMOVE(ITEM : out MESSAGE) ;
end BOUNDED__BUFFER ;
```

```
task body BOUNDED__BUFFER is
  N : constant INTEGER := 20 ; -- arbitrary value
  BUFFER : array (INTEGER range 0..N - 1) of MESSAGE ;
  POINTER : INTEGER range 0..N - 1 := 0 ; -- subrange variable
  COUNT : INTEGER range 0..N := 0 ;
begin
  loop
    select
      when COUNT < N =>
        accept DEPOSIT(ITEM : in MESSAGE) do
          BUFFER((POINTER + COUNT) mod N) := ITEM ;
        end ;
      COUNT := COUNT + 1 ;
    or
      when COUNT > 0 =>
        accept REMOVE(ITEM : out MESSAGE) do
          ITEM := BUFFER(POINTER) ;
        end ;
      POINTER := (POINTER + 1) mod N ;
      COUNT := COUNT - 1 ;
    end select ;
  end loop ;
end BOUNDED__BUFFER ;
```

When the buffer is empty only a DEPOSIT call is accepted; when it is full
only a REMOVE call is accepted. When the buffer is neither full nor empty
either call can be accepted, it is not known which. The **accept** statements
are the critical sections and a calling task is delayed while an **accept**
statement is executed. The updating of the variables POINTER and COUNT
is not part of the critical sections which was the case in the monitor
solution. The calling tasks are able to proceed when these updating
operations are taking place.

The PRODUCER and CONSUMER tasks are as defined previously, that is,

```
task type PRODUCER is
end PRODUCER ;

task body PRODUCER is
  ITEM : MESSAGE ;
begin
  loop
    -- produce item
    BOUNDED__BUFFER.DEPOSIT(ITEM) ;
    exit when FINISHED ;
  end loop ;
end PRODUCER ;

task type CONSUMER is
end CONSUMER ;
```

```
task body CONSUMER is
  ITEM : MESSAGE ;
begin
  loop
    BOUNDED_BUFFER.REMOVE(ITEM) ;
    -- consume item
    exit when FINISHED ;
  end loop ;
end CONSUMER ;


P: array (1..X) of PRODUCER ;
C: array (1..Y) of CONSUMER ;
```

Each of the X producer tasks and Y consumer tasks proceed independently and in parallel interacting with the buffer task whenever they need to deposit or remove a data item. The interaction is achieved by means of a rendezvous whenever the buffer task accepts one of the entry calls. The reader should compare this solution with that given in Section 7.5 using a monitor and conditions.

Another problem considered in the last chapter was the scheduling of a single resource among a number of competing processes. A solution which can be used for comparative purposes is now given in Ada.

```
task RESOURCE is
  entry ACQUIRE ;
  entry REMOVE ;
end RESOURCE ;

task body RESOURCE is
  FREE : BOOLEAN := TRUE ;
begin
  loop
    select
      when FREE =>
        accept ACQUIRE do
          FREE := FALSE ;
        end ;
    or
      accept RELEASE do
        FREE := TRUE ;
      end ;
    or
      terminate ;
    end select ;
  end loop ;
end RESOURCE ;
```

Each time round the loop the task is willing to accept a call to ACQUIRE or a call to RELEASE or to **terminate**. The ACQUIRE possibility is preceded by a guard which must be open for such a call to be considered. No guard condition has been placed upon the entry procedure RELEASE since the releasing of the resource is always welcome. The **terminate** possibility is included to enable the task to indicate its willingness to finish. A **terminate** alternative cannot be selected while there is a queued entry call. There is also a more powerful termination statement, the **abort** statement, which unconditionally and immediately terminates a task.

A family of entries can be used to distinguish between Ada tasks. This is achieved by using an entry declaration that includes a discrete range where each member of the range is associated with one task. For example, the declarations

```
type ID is new INTEGER range 1..N ;
  - - defines a new subrange type ID
entry RELEASE(ID'FIRST..ID'LAST) ;
  - - ID'FIRST is the first integer in the subrange etc.
```

creates a family of entries one for each value in the range ID.

This can then be used to give each task in a resource scheduler a unique identity as follows:

```
type ID is new INTEGER range 1..N ;
task RESOURCE is
  entry ACQUIRE(D : in ID) ; - - an entry with a parameter
  entry RELEASE(ID'FIRST..ID'LAST) ;
end RESOURCE ;

task body RESOURCE is
  USER : ID ;
begin
  loop
    accept ACQUIRE(X : in ID) do
      USER := X ;
    end ;
    accept RELEASE(USER) ;
  end loop ;
end RESOURCE ;
```

When a task acquires the resource it must supply its identity number. When this task is finished using the resource it must call the corresponding member of the RELEASE family to relinquish the resource. The scheduler will only accept a call on this RELEASE entry. Hence this solution will detect inadvertent misuse of the scheduler, but cannot detect deliberate misuse such as one user usurping another's identity.

As a final example consider the problem of ensuring that the highest priority waiting process is always given a resource. In Pascal Plus this was easily achieved by means of the PWAIT operation when delaying a process so that a subsequent SIGNAL operation activated the highest priority process. However, in Ada, the only queues available are attached to entry procedures which are served on a first come first served basis and are not under programmer control.

A solution to this problem can be achieved by using a family of entry procedures and declaring an entry procedure for each value in the required priority range.

A resource allocator for this problem can be programmed as in

```
type PRIORITY is (HIGH, MEDIUM, LOW) ;
  – – three priority values

task RESOURCE is
  entry ACQUIRE(PRIORITY) ;
end RESOURCE ;

task body RESOURCE is
begin
  loop
    select
      accept ACQUIRE(HIGH) do
      – – statements
      end ;
    or
      when ACQUIRE(HIGH)'COUNT = 0 =>
        accept ACQUIRE(MEDIUM) do
        – – statements
        end ;
    or
      when ACQUIRE(HIGH)'COUNT = 0 and
           ACQUIRE(MEDIUM)'COUNT = 0 =>
        accept ACQUIRE(LOW) do
        – – statements
        end ;
    end select ;
  end loop ;
end RESOURCE ;
```

The requests for the resource are now placed on three queues according to their priority. The top priority is HIGH and requests from processes with this priority will always be considered first. A process with priority MEDIUM will only be considered if there are no top priority processes waiting, this is reflected in the guard in the second select alternative. The attribute COUNT when applied to the entry ACQUIRE(HIGH) determines the number of tasks on the queue for that entry. The lowest priority processes are only considered if no high or medium priority processes are waiting. Such an approach is feasible if the number of priority values is small. If the number of priority values is large some type of looping construct needs to be used.

8.6 Summary

In a concurrent programming environment a programmer requires not only program and data structures to represent those parts of the program which can conceptually proceed in parallel but also a means of controlling the interaction of such parts. The need to control such interaction arises when information is to be exchanged or the progress of one process depends on another.

The first major step forward in this area was the introduction of the semaphore to regulate parallel activity. However, semaphores can lead to programs which are difficult to write and to understand and which are sensitive to minor change. To avoid such difficulties critical regions and conditional critical regions were introduced. These, in turn, evolved into the monitor with conditions. Such a structure gathers together the critical sections and the operations upon the critical sections into one structure. The monitor is best suited to a configuration in which the processors share a common memory.

A second approach to the synchronization of processes is that of message passing. In this approach the processes rendezvous to exchange information and then continue their activity in parallel and independently. Such a technique is best suited to a system in which each processor has its own local memory.

The Pascal Plus and Ada solutions to the bounded buffer problem illustrate the essential differences between these two synchronization methods. In Ada the transfer of data is direct and synchronized while in Pascal Plus it is through a passive abstract data structure. As a result these two different communication techniques require different program design methods.

In Ada the buffer is represented as a task with the synchronization specified in terms of **entry**, **select** and **accept** statements while in Pascal Plus the CONDITION, WAIT and SIGNAL features are used to control the buffer. In both cases the buffer is accessed in a mutually exclusive manner. In Ada the tidying up operations, for example, the adjustment of the value of the variable COUNT can be performed without delaying the calling process. In a monitor only one procedure may be executing at a given time while in Ada only one task entry may be executing at a given time.

EXERCISES

8.1 Construct an Ada program which can be used to search an already sorted database of items based on the principle of linear search applied in parallel.

8.2 Construct a parallel program which reads a text file, capitalizes all the lower case letters, and writes the transformed text to the output file.

8.3 Construct a solution to the bounded buffer problem which is based on a last in first out order rather than a first in first out order, that is, the last data item deposited in the buffer is the first to be removed.

8.4 Construct a resource allocator task which will allocate N identical resources.

8.5 Construct an Ada task type which can be used to represent a binary semaphore.

8.6 *The readers and writers problem*   A database may be used either for reading or writing. Any number of users may read from it simultaneously, but any user who is writing must have exclusive access to the database. Whenever a writer is ready to use the database, he should be allowed to do so as soon as possible. Construct an Ada solution to this problem.

8.7 *The spaghetti eaters*   Five philosophers spend their lives either eating or thinking. Each philosopher has his own place at a circular table in the centre of which is a large, continually replenished bowl of spaghetti from which he helps himself when seated at his own place. To eat the spaghetti requires two forks but only five forks are provided, one between each pair of plates. The only forks a philosopher can pick up are those on his immediate right and his immediate left. Construct an Ada solution to this problem.

Chapter 9 Occam: a Distributed Computing Language

9.1 Introduction

The ideas represented in Communicating Sequential Processes have been used as the basis for the concurrent programming language Occam. Occam is a high level language which is intended to be used for programming many interconnected or distributed computers. It takes its name from William of Occam who lived in England in the fourteenth century. One of his main philosophical beliefs was that things should be kept as simple as possible. The main objective of the language Occam is that it should remain simple while at the same time provide a set of programming features sufficient for programming distributed systems. For example, Occam lacks many high level programming language features such as recursion, data types and pointers. It is not, therefore, a competitor for a language like Ada which addresses a much wider application area. However, it does include similar concepts of concurrency and communication as those which are found in Ada.

Occam was developed by the Inmos Company whose main activity is the design and implementation of chips called transputers. A transputer is a single chip computer with a processor, local memory, and four dedicated input/output links. A transputer is either a 16- or 32-bit processor providing 10 million instructions per second processing power with 2 Kbytes of memory. Each link is capable of transferring 10 Mbits/second. The links enable transputers to communicate with each other, as shown in Figure 9.1. Because of these links any number of transputers can be joined together to form a network of computers with all the transputers capable of operating concurrently. An Occam program can be easily mapped onto any number of these transputers, which can run in parallel and communicate by exchanging messages using the input/output links. The number of transputers in the network can be increased or decreased (to a single transputer) and the Occam program can still be executed without changing its description. It is interesting to note that the word transputer is derived from transistor and computer, since the transputer is both a computer on a chip and a silicon component like a transistor.

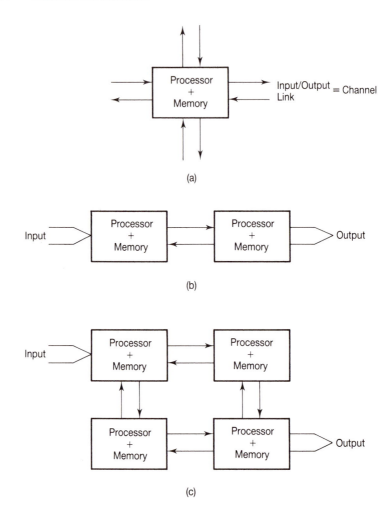

Figure 9.1   Transputers: (a) a single transputer; (b) a two pipeline transputer system; (c) an array of transputers.

The main vehicle for the specification of an action which can take place in parallel with other actions in Occam is the process. There are three primitive processes: namely, assignment, which changes the value of a variable; input, which receives a value from a channel; and output, which sends a value to a channel. A channel is thus the means by which two processes can communicate with each other when they are both ready to do so. A channel in Occam corresponds to a link on the transputer.

By combining these processes with the use of constructors a program in Occam is put together. There are three constructors available for forming more complex processes, namely,

1. the sequential constructor indicated by **seq**, which causes its component processes to be executed one after another, terminating when the last component terminates;

2. the parallel constructor indicated by **par**, which causes its component processes to be executed concurrently, terminating when all its components have terminated;

3. the alternative constructor indicated by **alt**, which chooses one of its component processes from among several processes for execution, terminating when the chosen component terminates.

In addition, there is a conditional process which selects the first component process whose Boolean expression is true for execution and then terminates, and a repetitive process which executes the component process for as long as the Boolean expression is true.

9.2 Sequential processes

Each of the primitive processes of Occam can be defined without the need for a process heading. An assignment process is indicated as

    X := X + 1

which increments the value of X.
    An input process is indicated as

    IN ? X

where the symbol ? is used to indicate an input operation. The effect of this process is to input from the channel IN a value for the variable X.
    An output process is indicated as

    OUT ! EXPRESSION

where the symbol ! is used to indicate an output operation. The effect of this process is to output the value of the EXPRESSION to the channel OUT.
    If it is required to input or output more than one value then they are listed in the required order. For example

    IN ? X1 ; X2

assigns the first value from the channel IN to X1 and the second value to X2.
    These three primitive processes are the building blocks or components from which all other processes are constructed. As the later sections illustrate they can be combined sequentially or concurrently to create more complex processes.
    To demonstrate the use of these primitive processes consider the construction of an adder process which spends its life receiving values from

one channel, forming their sum, and then passing the values to another channel. Such a process requires a local variable which can be used to hold a value which is input; this can be declared in Occam as

var ITEM :

Notice that the variable ITEM has been declared without type, and will be associated with the process that follows. It cannot be accessed outside the scope of that process.

Since the activities of the adder process are sequential in nature it must be declared as a sequential process in Occam using the sequential constructor (**seq**) as follows:

```
var ITEM:
seq
```

Every declaration in Occam is introduced by a keyword such as **var** and each syntactic entity requires a separate line. Indentation also plays an important role as it is the means of indicating entities which are components. In this example since the next component is a process it must be indented and appear on a new line. Any number of component processes can follow **seq** with each component appearing on a new line and indented by the same amount. These component processes are then executed one after the other since they are part of this sequential process. The sequential process terminates when the last component process has terminated.

Since the adder process is to receive a value from a channel this channel must be declared before it is used by means of the keyword **chan** as in

```
chan IN:
var ITEM:
seq
  IN ? ITEM
```

The value from the input channel IN will be stored in the variable ITEM. The input process is indented to indicate that it is a component of the sequential process.

The sum of the input values can be calculated using an assignment process and using the variable SUM to store the result, for example.

```
chan IN:
var SUM:
seq
  SUM := 0
  var ITEM:
  seq
    IN ? ITEM
    SUM := SUM + ITEM
```

The variable SUM has been declared and initialized in an enclosing sequential process and indentation introduced to take account of this.

The introduction of an output process will enable the input values to be passed to another process by means of the channel OUT as follows:

```
chan IN, OUT:
var SUM:
seq
  SUM := 0
  var ITEM:
  -- start of adder process
  seq
    IN ? ITEM
    SUM := SUM + ITEM
    OUT ! ITEM
  -- end of adder process
```

where -- indicates a comment.

As the program is currently defined it deals with a single input value. To enable the program to deal with a series of input values a loop should be introduced. This can be achieved by the use of a repetitive process preceding the adder process to form an infinite loop as follows:

```
chan IN, OUT:
var SUM:
seq
  SUM := 0
  while TRUE
    var ITEM:
    seq
      IN ? ITEM
      SUM := SUM + ITEM
      OUT ! ITEM
```

Since the addition is now a component of the repetitive process all its components have been indented by the same amount.

Alternatively and more usefully the loop can be made to terminate by forming an expression which is dependent on some other input variable, CONTINUE, as follows:

```
chan IN, OUT, LINK:
var SUM, CONTINUE:
seq
  SUM := 0
  LINK ? CONTINUE
  while CONTINUE
    var ITEM:
    seq
      IN ? ITEM
      SUM := SUM + ITEM
      OUT ! ITEM
      LINK ? CONTINUE
```

A value for the Boolean variable CONTINUE is input from another channel, LINK, before the repetitive process is executed and after the treatment of each data value. Whenever the value FALSE is input on the channel LINK the summation of the values will stop.

Thus Occam has a simple regular syntax. Each primitive process and each constructor occupies a line by itself and the components of a constructor are indented. Declarations are introduced by keywords such as **var** which are prefixed to processes. Any declared variables have the scope of the process to which the declaration is prefixed.

9.3 Parallel processes

It is possible to have more than one process acting in parallel in an Occam program and the means of achieving this are considered in this section. For example, if we have two adder processes with similar characteristics which are to operate in parallel they could be declared as follows:

```
chan IN1, IN2:
chan OUT1, OUT2:
var SUM1, SUM2:
seq
  SUM1 := 0
  SUM2 := 0
  par
    -- first adder process
    while TRUE
      var ITEM1:
      seq
        IN1 ? ITEM1
        SUM1 := SUM1 + ITEM1
        OUT1 ! ITEM1
    -- second adder process
    while TRUE
      var ITEM2:
      seq
        IN2 ? ITEM2
        SUM2 := SUM2 + ITEM2
        OUT2 ! ITEM2
```

The constructor **par** indicates that any following processes can be executed in parallel, in this example, the two adder processes. The extent of each process is determined by its indentation and the order in which the processes are specified does not matter. Both processes proceed independently and receive values from different channels, they sum these values and output them to other channels.

Hence **par**, like **seq**, can be followed by any number of component processes, each starting on a new line and each indented by the same amount. In this example the two outer processes are executed in parallel while their component processes are executed sequentially. The program terminates when all the component processes terminate. Thus the words **seq** and **par** are the main constructors used for indicating the sequential and parallel execution of processes respectively.

There is also available a prioritized parallel construct which gives each component process a different priority depending on its textual position; the first component has the highest priority and the last component the lowest priority. It is indicated by the words **pri par**. If several parallel processes are at the same priority and able to run they are considered in turn.

If several processes are required to be of the same type then a name can be associated with a process definition and this name used at a later time. For example, considering the adder process which was described above as a template for a definition, a process can be defined as follows:

```
proc ADDER(chan SOURCE, SINK, var SUM) =
  while TRUE
    var ITEM:
    seq
      SOURCE ? ITEM
      SUM := SUM + ITEM
      SINK ! ITEM
```

SOURCE and SINK are two formal parameters representing channels and SUM is a formal parameter representing a variable. Instances of this named process ADDER can be declared as follows:

```
chan IN1, IN2:
chan OUT1, OUT2:
var SUM1, SUM2:
seq
  SUM1 := 0
  SUM2 := 0
  par
    ADDER(IN1, OUT1, SUM1)
    ADDER(IN2, OUT2, SUM2)
```

The text of the defined process is substituted for all occurrences of the name with actual parameters being substituted for formal parameters. Thus this example is equivalent to the two adder example considered above.

9.4   Communicating processes

In the above example the two adder processes do not communicate with one another since each operates on its own variables which are not shared with or required by the other parallel process. If they wish to communicate then the same channel must be used by both processes to form a communication link between them. One of the processes may output to the channel while the other may input from the same channel. A process may communicate with any number of channels.

If one process is ready to communicate with another then it waits until this second process is ready to communicate with it, thereby establishing a rendezvous after which they pass information along the channel and then continue on their separate independent ways. Thus a channel allows one-way communication between two parallel processes, it connects two processes so that one process can send a value onto the channel and another process can receive that value from the same channel.

In Occam to establish a communication link between the two adder processes requires the declaration of a channel which is then used by both processes. To illustrate this situation the two adder example has been changed to establish a need for communication, using a channel LINK as in:

```
chan LINK:
chan IN, OUT:
var SUM1, SUM2:
seq
  SUM1 := 0
  SUM2 := 0
  par
    while TRUE
      var ITEM1:
      seq
        IN ? ITEM1
        SUM1 := SUM1 + ITEM1
        LINK ! SUM1
    while TRUE
      var ITEM2:
      seq
        LINK ? ITEM2
        SUM2 = SUM2 + ITEM2
        OUT ! ITEM2
```

The first process inputs the values which it sums, after which the partial sums are sent to the second process which sums the partial sums. The communication between the processes is established by means of the channel LINK which has been declared and associated with both processes.

More specifically, one process sends the values stored in SUM1 to the second process via the channel LINK. Since LINK has been used in the first process as an output channel the value of SUM1 will be sent to the second process which has used LINK as an input channel, the value input is stored in its local variable ITEM2. If we required two-way communication between these two processes then a second channel would be required with values being passed in the opposite direction, that is, the second process would use the channel to output a value and the first process to input a value.

An input process will not complete execution until an output process on the same channel is executed. Whichever process reaches its communication statement first waits for the other process to reach its communication statement, the value is then passed along the channel after which both processes continue on their separate execution paths.

9.5 Alternative processes

To allow for the situation where a process has a number of channels associated with it and wants to select one of a number of actions depending on which channel sends it a message first the alternative constructor (**alt**) has been provided. When a process encounters such a construct it means that one of several alternative actions or processes may be chosen at that stage of the process' execution.

A guard is associated with each component of the alternative construct to introduce a different choice criterion for each component. The guard can consist of an optional Boolean expression followed by an input. The Boolean expression must be true for that component to be selected; if there is no Boolean expression then the guard is regarded as true. Hence only if the condition is true and input is possible will that component be selected. For example

    (NUMBER > 0) & LINK ? ITEM

requires that the value of NUMBER is positive and that a value is ready to be input from the channel LINK. A guard without a Boolean expression is ready if an output process is waiting to output to that channel.

An alternative process waits until at least one of the guarded processes is ready to execute. One of the ready processes is then selected at random and executed. The construct then terminates.

The following example illustrates the use of an **alt** constructor which has two component processes:

```
– – other declarations here
alt
  – – first process
  (NUMBER > 0) & LINK1 ? ITEM1
    seq
      NUMBER := NUMBER − 1
      SUM := SUM + ITEM1
  – – second process
  LINK2 ? ITEM2
    SUM := SUM + ITEM2
```

Each component process requires an output process to be wishing to communicate with it before it can be selected. In addition, the first guard has a Boolean expression which must be true before it is chosen. If both guards are ready, one of the processes is chosen at random and executed. If only one guard is ready that alternative is chosen. If neither of the guards is ready then the alternative process waits. After execution of the chosen component process the construct then terminates.

It is also possible to associate a priority with an alternative process so that if more than one guard is ready the first one in textual sequence is selected. The priority is indicated by the words **pri alt**.

In order to synchronize the activities between processes the **any** primitive is provided. If it is used as part of an input process such as

LINK ? **any**

the value coming in on the channel L!NK will be disregarded – thus it has the effect of delaying the receiving process until it is signalled by another process. This could be used to stop a process if it was inserted as the guard of one of the component processes of the alternative process as, for example,

```
chan STOP:
chan IN, OUT, LINK:
var SUM, CONTINUE:
seq
  SUM := 0
  CONTINUE := TRUE
  while CONTINUE
    var ITEM:
    alt
      LINK ? ITEM
        SUM := SUM + ITEM
      STOP ? any
        CONTINUE := FALSE
```

To stop this process a value needs to be sent on the channel STOP so that when this component process is selected the Boolean flag CONTINUE will be set to FALSE after which the process terminates.

Another useful feature is the **skip** command which terminates with no effect. For example

```
if
  (CHAR >= '0') and (CHAR <= '9')
    skip
  TRUE
    CHAR := 'X'
```

converts all characters which are not digits to the character 'X'. The **skip** is always ready and therefore available for selection, its only effect is to terminate. This example also illustrates the use of a conditional process indicated by **if**. The conditional process executes the first component (textually) which is able to execute and then terminates. If there is no component able to execute, then the construct terminates with no other effect.

9.6   Replicated processes

A replicator is provided to enable a process to be duplicated a fixed number of times. It can be used in conjunction with either of the three constructors and takes the following forms:

1. **seq** I = [0 **for** N]
2. **par** I = [0 **for** N]
3. **alt** I = [0 **for** N]

The starting value for I is zero and it is increased by 1, N times, where N is a constant expression. The process which is required to be replicated is described after the chosen heading. For example:

```
def  N = 4:
  -- definition of a constant
chan  IN, OUT:
var  SUM:
seq
  SUM := 0
  seq  I = [0 for  N]
    while  TRUE
      var  ITEM:
      seq
        IN ? ITEM
        SUM := SUM + ITEM
        OUT ! ITEM
```

will create N adder processes which will execute sequentially, that is, in the order they are created.

If the replicator **par** I = [0 **for** N] is used it will create an array of N parallel processes which execute concurrently. If **alt** is used instead of **par** in the replicator it means that one of the N component processes is selected according to the rules described earlier for the **alt** constructor.

If N channels are required they can be declared using

chan LINK[N]:

which creates the channels LINK[0], LINK[1] ... LINK[N − 1]. This is referred to as a vector of channels.

Other features of Occam have been introduced to facilitate parallel programming such as the **wait** process. It is used to delay execution until a period of time has passed. A wait process is defined to be ready to execute if its following expression evaluates to true. The expression must be a clock comparison. For example

wait ALARM > TIME

delays the process until the value of ALARM is greater than TIME. The keyword **after** can be used for comparing two time values. For example

wait now after ALARM

means the process continues execution when the time provided by the local clock is after the time stored in ALARM; **now** provides the value of a clock which is local to each process; **after** ensures that the two time values derived from the clock are compared.

If it is necessary to determine the time taken by a process then this can be achieved by consulting the local clock at appropriate times as in:

```
chan LINK, FINISH:
var START, STOP, ELAPSED, SUM, ITEM, CONTINUE:
seq
  SUM := 0
  START := now
  while CONTINUE
    alt
      LINK ? ITEM
        SUM := SUM + ITEM
      FINISH ? any
        CONTINUE := FALSE
  STOP := now
  ELAPSED := STOP - START
```

In this example the clock is consulted before and after the main computational part of the process by means of the **now** primitive.

9.7 Summary

The transputer is a small but complete computer which can be used as a building block with other transputers to construct a distributed computer network. It is its ability to be incorporated into a network that distinguishes it from other microcomputers. Each transputer has four input/output links which enable it to communicate with other transputers.

Occam has been designed as a programming language to handle sequential and concurrent processes. Processes co-operate with each other by passing messages directly over channels. When transputers are programmed in Occam each transputer implements an Occam process and each link implements an Occam channel in each direction between two transputers.

The range of features provided in Occam has been kept deliberately small, but sufficient, to enable the specification of solutions to concurrent programming problems. The features are such that they map closely onto the transputer hardware to increase efficiency of execution.

Case study: matrix multiplication using Occam

This case study illustrates the multiplication of two matrices A and B using a square array of transputers. Each transputer performs a simple calculation such as multiplying two input values and adding them to a third value. These input values are then passed on to neighbouring transputers using the output links. For example, assume we have a 4-transputer system and the following data:

$$A = \begin{pmatrix} 5 & 6 \\ 7 & 8 \end{pmatrix} \qquad B = \begin{pmatrix} 1 & 2 \\ 3 & 4 \end{pmatrix}$$

The algorithm works by inputting the values of one array from the north and the other from the west as follows:

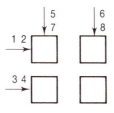

Figure 9.2

The top left transputer calculates the product of its input values, stores the product and outputs the input values to its south and east neighbours as shown.

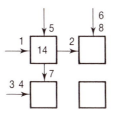

Figure 9.3

Now three transputers can operate in parallel by multiplying their input values from their north and west neighbours, adding the result to whatever value is currently in their local store and outputting values to their south and east neighbours. These calculations are continued until all the input data is exhausted as shown in Figure 9.4.

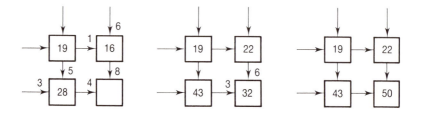

Figure 9.4

The problem now is to translate this into an Occam program. The basic action for each transputer can be represented as

```
chan NORTH, SOUTH, EAST, WEST:
var A, B, T:
seq
  par
    NORTH ? A
    WEST ? B
  T := T + (A * B)
  par
    SOUTH ! A
    EAST ! B
```

where the input and output of values can be performed in parallel. Values A and B are input from the NORTH and WEST channels respectively. They are multiplied and added to the local value T. After which the values are output (in parallel) on the channels SOUTH and EAST.

To represent all the transputers in an array of transputers of size N * N requires the use of a sequential replicator as in:

```
def N = 2:
chan NORTH, SOUTH, EAST, WEST:
var A, B, T:
seq
  T := 0
  seq I = [0 for N]
    seq
      par
        NORTH ? A
```

```
      WEST ? B
      T := T + (A * B)
      par
        SOUTH ! A
        EAST ! B
```

This creates N processes, which execute sequentially. Each process inputs two values, in parallel, multiplies these values, and then, in parallel passes them on. This can be made into a process definition by introducing a process heading such as

proc MULT(**chan** NORTH, SOUTH, EAST, WEST)

The channels required for the passing of the results between transputers and to allow for the output of final results can be declared as a vector of horizontal and vertical channels as in:

```
chan row[N*(N + 1)]:
chan column[N*(N + 1)]:
```

These are then used as actual channel parameters in the above process MULT.

Having defined the actions and the channels for an individual transputer it is now necessary to express this for all the transputers in the array. This can be done by using the procedure MULT in parallel as in:

```
par
  par I = [0 for N]
    par J = [0 for N]
      MULT(COLUMN[((N + 1) * I) + J],
           COLUMN[((N + 1) * I) + (J + 1)],
           ROW[(N * I) + J], ROW[N * (I + 1) + J])
```

so the whole program looks like:

```
def N = 2:
proc MULT(chan NORTH, SOUTH, EAST, WEST)=
  var A, B, T:
  seq
    T := 0
    seq I = [0 for N]
      seq
        par
          NORTH ? A
          WEST ? B
        T := T + (A * B)
        par
          SOUTH ! A
          EAST ! B:

chan COLUMN[N * (N + 1)]:
chan ROW[N * (N + 1)]:
par
```

```
par I = [0 for N]
  par J = [0 for N]
    MULT(COLUMN[((N +1) * I) + J],
         COLUMN[(((N + 1) * I) + (J + 1))],
         ROW[(N * I) + J], ROW[(N * (I + 1)) + J])
```

Although perhaps not immediately obvious that two matrices are being multiplied together, the solution has a high degree of parallelism.

EXERCISES

9.1 Construct an Occam program representing a simple buffer which repeatedly inputs a value and then outputs it.

9.2 Design an automatic tea maker in Occam which wakes you up in the morning with a message and offers a cup of hot tea. It also has a clock and will make tea at any other time, on request.

9.3 A high technology digital radio replaces an analog volume control with two buttons one marked louder, the other marked softer. Design an Occam volume controller process which will accept messages and will transmit a message to the amplifier controller to indicate how loud the volume should be.

9.4 Devise an Occam program which will estimate the square root of a value using the Newton-Raphson approximation technique. An initial guess at the square root is used to produce a better estimate using the formula $X_n = (X_{n-1} + (X_0/X_{n-1})) / 2$. This formula is reapplied until the final estimate is sufficiently close to the real square root.

9.5 Devise an Occam program which will represent the bounded buffer problem as described in Section 4.1.

PART THREE

SYNCHRONOUS PARALLEL PROGRAMMING

As each new generation of computers was implemented it enabled the users of these machines to solve much larger and more demanding problems. The engineering and scientific communities have consistently required machines which could execute even more operations per second than those currently available. An example is the solution of aerodynamic flow problems which are governed by the Navier Stokes equations. These equations were discovered in the early years of this century. Although scientists know how to solve these equations they have lacked the computing power to achieve a solution within a reasonable time or in its full generality. The equations can be solved by using a grid of data points whose spacing over the region of interest determines the amount of data required and the accuracy of the results obtained. The availability of a sufficiently powerful machine to solve these equations would enable the elimination of unpromising aircraft and spacecraft designs by computer simulation rather than the use of expensive wind tunnel experiments. This

129

provided a strong economic argument in favour of more powerful machines.

Another representative example is numerical weather forecasting where a grid is used to encompass the earth and information is collected at each of the grid points. This data can then be used to solve the equations which govern the interaction of the elements, using a technique based on finite differences. The grid data points can be processed from one pole to the other pole. Since the same set of instructions is to be applied to the data along a particular processing direction it is possible to perform much of the processing in parallel. In the course of the calculation some mechanism must be available to enable communication between adjacent data points. By utilizing the parallelism inherent in the problem the required results can be produced much faster than using a sequential computer. This, in turn, can mean the difference between predicting or not predicting the occurrence of a hurricane, storm or major abnormality in the weather. In many situations numerical weather simulation is the only tool available since controlled experiments cannot be carried out. This provided a strong time critical argument in favour of more powerful machines.

Because of these increasing demands by the engineering and scientific communities involved with such problems, hardware designers implemented computers which departed from the traditional architecture as proposed by von Neumann. These machines are now widely known as array and vector processors.

In an array processor an arithmetic unit, roughly equivalent to that used in a serial computer, is duplicated a number of times. In addition, there is a single control unit which directs the activities of the duplicated arithmetic units. These units have a full instruction set and can only operate in synchronous or lockstep mode by executing the instruction broadcast by the control unit. There is some flexibility in the system since any combination of the arithmetic units can be enabled (or disabled) meaning that they execute (or do not execute) the broadcast instruction. Examples of array processors are the Illiac IV (Barnes *et al.*, 1968), the ICL Distributed Array Processor (Parkinson, 1983) and the Massively Parallel Processor (Batcher, 1979).

In a vector processor each arithmetic operation is assigned to a functional unit which consists of a number of stages; a pair of operands is required to pass through all the stages for a particular operation to be completed. However, after a pair of operands has passed through the first stage another pair of operands can be introduced to the first stage. Hence, when all the stages are filled, many operand pairs are being operated upon in parallel with a resultant improvement in performance over a serial computer. This technique is usually referred to as pipelining. It is not a concept which is unique to computers nor in fact was it discovered by computer scientists. Henry Ford used this conveyor belt approach in the construction of his model T car back in the 1920s. Examples of vector processors are the CDC Cyber 205 (Lincoln, 1982) and the Cray-1 (Russell, 1978).

The net effect of this revolution in computer architecture has been that the number of instructions executed per second is greatly increased and that numerical experiments which previously had been uneconomical or too time consuming became feasible.

Thus in the parallel processors, represented by array and vector processors, the processing is performed in a lockstep or overlapped fashion. We refer to this as the synchronous parallel programming environment. As a result these machines do not have the mutual exclusion or synchronisation problems associated with multiprocessor or distributed systems. This, in turn, is reflected in the high level languages available for these machines. Thus array and vector processors are best suited for grid or mesh type problems in which the processing of data in regular patterns is the dominant feature. The problems of communication are now concerned with the movement of data between the various parallel or overlapped processing streams.

The properties of these grid type problems indicate that dynamically varying data structures are not essential, but rather arrays with primitive, enumerated, subrange or record data items as defined in Pascal are necessary. Program constructs are required which enable this type of parallel processing to be specified and varied in the course of program execution. In addition, a means of communicating between the parallel processing streams is required.

It would appear that history is repeating itself as the developments in synchronous parallel programming technology have not kept pace with the architectural advances. The result is that many programmers and researchers are expected to use very sophisticated hardware with primitive and inadequate software tools. The current situation is similar to that which faced programmers of the early sequential machines.

The historical analogy with the development of sequential programming languages becomes even more apparent when the languages which are currently available for array and vector processors are considered.

These programming languages can be separated into two groups (Perrott, 1979a):

- *Detection of parallelism*   In this group the programmer uses a sequential programming language for the application and it is the responsibility of a compiler to determine which parts of the application can be executed in parallel. The major motivation for such an approach is to utilize existing sequential programs and consequently save the development costs. However, to gain any substantial benefit the user must restructure the code or design it to suit the compiler. Examples of such languages are CFT (Reference Manual, 1981) for the Cray-1 and Ivtran (Millstein, 1973) for the Illiac IV.

- *Expression of machine parallelism*   In this group the languages provide either a syntax which directly reflects the architecture of the machine or demand that the programmer must explicitly encode hardware instructions in separate subroutine calls. This effectively turns these languages into higher level assembly languages. However, the implementation problems which are a major challenge are considerably simplified. Examples of such languages are CFD (Stevens, 1975) for the Illiac IV and DAP Fortran (Reference Manual, 1980) for the ICL Distributed Array Processor.

In both cases the concept of abstract programming has not been fully realized.

The existing languages in these groups have ignored many of the recent developments in sequential program and data structuring which are relevant in this new environment. In addition, the knowledge accumulated in language design and compiler construction techniques has not been utilized.

A third approach has recently been taken which aims to exploit the parallelism in a problem. The data and program structures of these languages enable a programmer to express directly the parallel nature of a problem without reference to the hardware or the detection mechanism of the compiler. This makes the language suitable for implementation on both array and vector processor configurations. This, in turn, should enable some measure of program portability to be achieved. An example of this language type is Actus (Perrott, 1979b).

The following chapters consider approaches which have been used in the synchronous parallel programming environment by examining representative examples of each language group.

DETECTION OF
PARALLELISM LANGUAGES

Chapter 10 Cray-1 FORTRAN Translator: CFT

In this language group a programmer uses a sequential programming language for the application and it is the responsibility of a compiler to determine which parts of the application can be executed in parallel.

The major motivation for such an approach is to utilize existing sequential programs and consequently to save development costs. However, to gain any substantial benefit the user must restructure the code or design it to suit the compiler's detection mechanism.

Thus the languages in this group have ignored many of the recent developments in program and data structuring which are relevant in this type of parallel environment. In addition, much of the knowledge accumulated in language design and compiler construction has not been utilized.

10.1 Hardware considerations

In order to illustrate the advantages and disadvantages of this language group the CFT language (Cray Fortran Translator version 1.09) which is available on the Cray-1 computer is first considered. The objective of this compiler is to examine a program written in sequential FORTRAN and to detect which parts of the program can be executed in parallel and which cannot.

A brief digression at this point is appropriate to outline the architecture of the Cray-1 since a knowledge of some of its hardware features can help improve the performance of a CFT program.

The Cray-1 was designed by Seymour Cray in the early seventies and the first machine was delivered to the Los Alamos Scientific Laboratory, New Mexico in 1976. It is a vector processor machine based on the principle of pipelining. An overview of the memory and the computation section is given in Figure 10.1.

The memory, which can consist of up to 1 million 64-bit words, is organized into 16 banks. The banks are phased so that a reference to a word in one memory bank does not interfere with a reference to a word in another memory bank. As a result the number of words that can be accessed in the memory and sent to the rest of the system is greatly increased. This is referred to as the memory bandwidth and the Cray-1 has

134

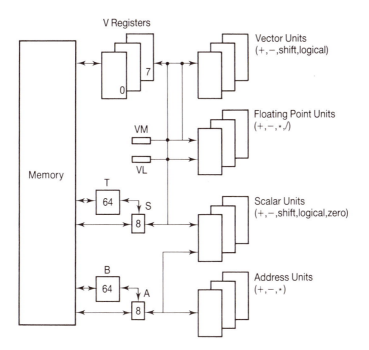

Figure 10.1 The Cray-1 computer system.

a maximum rate of 80 million words per second. This rate can be capitalized upon if a vector of operands is stored in different memory banks.

The main processing power of the machine lies in the 12 pipelined functional units. These units take their operands from a number of registers which, in turn, receive them from the memory. This intermediate register storage between the memory and the functional units is one of the main differences between the Cray-1 and other such machines. Its effect is to reduce the time required to set up a functional unit for operation.

The register storage has been divided into scalar, vector and address registers as follows:

- There are 8 *scalar* or S registers of 64 bits each. They are used for storing and providing operands for scalar processing as on most serial computers. There are also 64 backup or T registers which are used as temporary storage for the S registers. A functional unit can access the S registers directly but not the T registers; the only operations possible on the T registers are move operations, to and from memory or the S registers.

- There are 8 primary *address* or A registers which are used for memory references and as index registers. They are only 24 bits in length and are backed up by 64 B registers also of 24 bits.

- The most significant registers of the Cray-1 are the 8 *vector* or V registers. Each of these registers has 64 elements with each element being of 64 bits in length. Any vector which is required to be processed must first be placed in these vector registers before being fed to the appropriate functional unit. After the operation is performed the results are returned to a vector register.

There are two other registers which add flexibility to the computational power of the machine:

- the *vector mask* or VM register which is 64 bits in length. Each bit of the VM register corresponds to an element of a vector register. It is used in test instructions involving vector registers to identify particular elements.

- the *vector length* or VL register which is a 7-bit register. It contains the number of elements that are to be processed in a vector operation, that is, the length of the vectors held in V registers.

In total there are over 4 Kbytes of register storage and how these registers are used is one of the main factors which influences the performance of the Cray-1. There is no direct means by which the CFT programmer can program these registers. However, a programmer can improve the performance of a program if aware of these hardware characteristics; this is demonstrated in the following sections.

Each of the 12 functional units is pipelined and performs a specific operation; they have been divided into the following 4 groups:

- *vector functional units* which perform integer addition, logical and shift operations on vectors;

- *floating point functional units* which perform addition, multiplication and reciprocal approximation operations on vectors and scalars. There is no divide functional unit, division is performed by multiplying the reciprocal of the divisor with the dividend;

- *scalar functional units* which perform integer addition, logical, shifting and population (or leading zero) count on scalars. The population count functional unit counts the number of 1 bits in an operand while the leading zero counts the number of 0 bits preceding the first 1 bit in the operand;

- *address functional units* which perform addition and multiplication operations on addresses.

The functional units can receive data from their respective register types, with the floating point functional units receiving data from either of the scalar or vector registers. Each functional unit operation is divided into a number of stages and each stage takes 1 clock period (12.5 nanoseconds). The clock period is the heartbeat of the system and all activity is measured in terms of clock periods. After the first pair of operands has completed the first stage of a functional unit a second pair of operands may be introduced into the pipeline. In this way the operation on a vector of operands can be overlapped. After the first pair of operands has passed through all the stages the results are produced at the rate of one every clock period. This means it is possible to attain a computational rate of 80 million floating point operations per second. Over a sustained period of time the performance rate is less. The time taken to execute an instruction is known as the functional unit time. It varies depending on the particular functional unit and is measured in terms of clock periods. For example, the vector integer addition unit has a unit time of 3 clock periods while for floating point addition it is 6 clock periods.

The functional units act independently and under certain circumstances several of them can act in parallel. This is referred to as chaining in Cray-1 terminology. This occurs when the output from one functional unit is used as the input of another functional unit, thus avoiding the delay caused by storing and retrieving data in memory. In other words, intermediate results do not have to be stored to memory and can be used even before the vector operation that created them runs to completion. In this way the computational speed of the machine, theoretically at least, can be pushed to 240 million floating point operations per second for a short period of time. Chaining, therefore, depends on using different functional units and V registers and it is not something which the CFT programmer can influence directly.

Since the two main parts of the Cray-1 computation section consist of scalar and vector functional units a program's statements must be divided up for execution on these different functional units. Thus if a program written in sequential FORTRAN is presented to the CFT compiler it will attempt to vectorize or parallelize it as much as possible, that is, generate code which will execute on the vector (rather than the scalar) functional units.

In certain circumstances the compiler can easily detect which parts of the program can be executed in parallel. However, to increase the percentage of the program executed in parallel it is necessary for a programmer to rearrange the statements of the program to match the detection mechanism of the compiler. If a new program is being written then the programmer should facilitate the easy detection of parallelism when constructing the program. This is achieved by being aware of what the compiler can detect and having some understanding of the machine's architecture. In either situation there will always be some code which must be executed sequentially where no vectorization is possible.

There are no well established principles which can be expounded to guide programmers when programming in this environment since the detection mechanism is associated with the particular compiler being used. The techniques have been widely described as *ad hoc* as the next sections illustrate.

10.2   Assignment statements

The data structure which can be most easily vectorized is the array or dimensioned variable (in one dimension only) and the program structure which best facilitates vectorization is the DO loop. In effect, a DO loop referencing dimensioned quantities only has the best chance of being vectorized.

As a simple example consider the addition of two real vectors A and B with the results to be stored in a vector C, assuming that the number of elements in each vector is 64. In sequential FORTRAN a solution can be specified as

```
        DO 1 I = 1, 64
          C(I) = A(I) + B(I)
1       CONTINUE
```

Such a loop can be easily vectorized on a machine like the Cray-1.

Considering this program in terms of the hardware is useful in appreciating what takes place. Each of the 8 vector registers on the Cray-1 can hold 64 values hence the vectors A and B could be loaded in registers V1 and V2, for example, as shown in Figure 10.2.

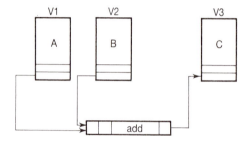

Figure 10.2

After register loading the elements of V1 and V2 can be fed to the addition functional unit in a continuous data stream of 64($\times$2) values. After a delay the result of the addition of the first elements of A and B will be produced and the remaining 63 additions appear at regular intervals. In this case the results are stored in a third vector register V3.

The delay before the production of the first result depends on which functional unit is being used. In the case of the floating point addition functional unit it is 6 clock periods, where 1 clock period is 12.5 nanoseconds. The clock period is also the time between the production of the results in a functional unit once the process has commenced.

Thus the time to produce the 64 results is 69 clock periods, whereas, if vectorization was not used, the corresponding time would be 6 × 64 clock periods. The speed-up in this case is roughly a factor of 6. This calculation ignores the overheads involved in setting up the pipeline, such as the calculation of addresses and the time to transfer operands between the memory, the registers and the functional unit.

If there are more than 64 elements in the vectors being manipulated then this will affect the performance of the machine, as only 64 elements (or less) can be fed into a functional unit at a time. Thus an overhead will be introduced as each batch of 64 elements is loaded into a vector register. It is sometimes useful for a programmer to be aware of this fact when choosing the size of the program's data structures.

Another aspect of the above code which enabled its easy vectorization was that the elements to be manipulated were all independent of each other. If there is a dependence between elements it sometimes means that vectorization is not possible. This particular situation is examined in more detail in a later section.

Each of the functional units of the Cray-1 is capable of delivering one result every clock period. Also each vector functional unit can act independently and as a result if the program statement demands it, several functional units can act in parallel. For example, in the following loop:

```
        DO 1 I = 1, 64
          D(I) = A(I) * B(I) + C(I)
1       CONTINUE
```

the multiplication and addition functional units can act in parallel. If the 64 values of A, B and C are stored in vector registers V1, V2 and V3 respectively and the results are to be stored in V4 the above loop can be represented pictorially as in Figure 10.3

After the result of the multiplication of the first elements of A and B is produced it is placed in a vector register and then fed into the addition functional unit together with the first element of C. Once this process is

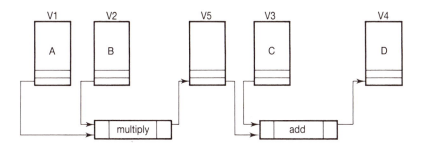

Figure 10.3

established it continues for the remaining 63 elements of the arrays. Thus chaining has been established and the overhead of having to store and retrieve the results of the multiplication operations from memory before using them again in the addition functional unit has been avoided. The addition and multiplication functional units are operating in parallel with a resultant improvement in the program's performance.

A very rough approximation to the improvement in performance for this example can be shown by considering three different situations; the functional unit times for vector floating point addition and multiplication are 6 and 7 clock periods respectively.

	Clock Periods
Scalar	
64 additions	$= 64 \times 6 = 384$
64 multiplications	$= 64 \times 7 = \underline{448}$
	832
Vectorization without chaining	
64 additions	$= 63 + 6 = 69$
64 multiplications	$= 63 + 7 = \underline{70}$
	139
Vectorization with chaining	
64 additions	
64 multiplications	$= 6 + 7 + 63 = 76$

These calculations ignore the overheads involved in setting up the functional unit; they are meant to give an indication of the improvements that can be effected. As can be seen by this simple example vectorization can be an order of magnitude faster than the equivalent scalar computation in certain circumstances.

It is seldom the case that a program consists of such straightforward DO loops which can be so easily vectorized; more often a program will consist of nested DO loops. In such circumstances only the innermost DO loop will be vectorized by the CFT compiler. Consequently the programmer must ensure that it is within the innermost DO loop that the major part of the computation takes place or that the loop indices facilitate vectorization.

This situation occurs in the multiplication of two matrices to produce a third, as in

```
        N = 50
        DO 2 I = 1, N
        DO 2 J = 1, N
          AA(I,J) = 0.0
        DO 2 K = 1, N
          AA(I,J) = AA(I,J) + BB(I,K) * CC(K,J)
2       CONTINUE
```

This code will not be vectorized since the array AA is independent of the innermost loop index, K.

However, such a program fragment can be vectorized if the programmer rearranges the loops such that the innermost statement depends (as much as possible) on the innermost loop index as in the following code:

```
        N = 50
        DO 21 J = 1, N
        DO 22 I = 1, N
          AA(I,J) = 0.0
22      CONTINUE
        DO 21 K = 1, N
        DO 21 I = 1, N
          AA(I,J) = AA(I,J) + BB(I,K) * CC(K,J)
21      CONTINUE
```

Both innermost loops can now be vectorized with a resulting improvement in the performance of the program.

However such an inversion of loops could have a considerable effect on a program's structure. In this particular case there are alternate ways of specifying matrix multiplication but this example is representative of one possible programming situation that can occur frequently and must be reorganized to improve performance.

If all situations were as easily recognized as this then vectorization would be straightforward. But a program segment may have one major loop with many nested loops; the rearranging of all these loops may not be desirable or even possible.

The occurrence of statements in a DO loop which involve scalar variables may prevent vectorization taking place. In the following example the loop will not be vectorized because of the variable TEMP.

```
        DO 3 I = N, M
          TEMP = B(I) * C(I)
          D(I) = E(I)/TEMP + TEMP
3       CONTINUE
```

The circumvention of this problem requires the replacement of scalar variables by array variables. The extra storage required enables an increase in processing speed.

With the more recent compilers the statements of a DO loop can contain scalar variables or constants in an expression, provided they change by fixed increments each time round the loop. In practice this means they must adhere to the following conditions:

• they are invariant, that is, a constant or variable which is unmodified by changes of the loop variable;
• they are constant increment integers (CII), that is, integers which are changed only once by an invariant expression. The defining expression must not contain parentheses or operators other than plus or minus.

For example, in the following FORTRAN loop:

```
DO 4 I = N, M
  K = K - DELTA
  A(I) = X1 * DD(L,M) * B(I)
  J = 100 - I
4       CONTINUE
```

I, K, J are constant increment integers whereas DELTA, 100, X1, DD(L,M) are invariants. These entities will therefore not prevent vectorization of the loop.

Thus there are several rules that a programmer must be aware of and not violate if program loops are to be vectorized. These are therefore an additional problem which the programmer has to contend with while writing optimized programs for the Cray-1.

Another situation which presents difficulties for a vectorizing compiler arises when it is required to apply an operation across the elements of an array, for example, to sum the elements of an array. This is an example of a more general situation where the number of dimensions on the left side of the assignment operator is less than on the right side.

A summation can be vectorized by using additional storage and combining the array elements in steps of 64. However to make this type of operation worthwhile on the Cray-1 requires the number of elements to be in excess of 100. The efficiency of such an operation depends on the number of iterations of the loop and the complexity of the loop. In order to assist the programmer in this situation several optimized routines have been provided in the CFT library. So whenever possible, simple loops that calculate a single scalar result should be replaced with a call to an optimized routine. For example, to sum the elements of an array

```
        SUM = 0.0
        DO 5 I = 1, 100
          SUM = SUM + A(I)
5       CONTINUE
```

is better written as

```
SUM = SSUM(100,A(1),1)
```

which uses the standard library function SSUM.

As each version of the compiler is released more restrictions are removed on the statements of a DO loop. However the user must be aware of what can or can not be used in the statements of a DO loop and when it is better to use a specially optimized subroutine or function.

10.3 Conditional statements

A conditional statement within a DO loop causes problems for a vectorizing compiler; such a statement usually requires an immediate jump to another statement or the updating of certain array elements only. This is not the type of operation which a pipelined functional unit is good at performing. For example, the statements

```
        DO 6 I = N, M
          X(I) = A(I)
          IF (B(I).GT.C(I)) X(I) = D(I)
6       CONTINUE
```

in a FORTRAN program indicate that the value of some elements of X are determined by the relative values of B and C. In a vector processor, such as the Cray-1, this would mean that the data stream fed to a functional unit would have to be split depending on the values of B and C. Unfortunately such a situation is anathema to a pipelined functional unit which prefers a uniform uninterrupted data stream.

To circumvent this problem special utility functions are provided in CFT. There are five such vector functions which are available for handling conditional statements, namely, CVMGT, CVMGP, CVMGZ, CVMGN and CVMGM. The first four letters indicate Conditional Vector MerGe functions. Each function requires 3 arguments and it is the last letter of the function's name which indicates the condition on which the other two arguments are selected. The possible conditions which can be applied to the last argument correspond to the letters as follows: T-TRUE, P-POSITIVE, Z-ZERO, N-NONZERO, M-MINUS. For example, the following function

```
    CVMGT (P, Q, R)
```

means P is returned if R is true, Q is returned if R is false.

The vector function CVMGM is one which can be substituted in place of the above conditional statement which allows vectorization to continue; the parameters determine which updates are performed. The programmer should write the following to enable vectorization to take place

```
        DO 6 I = N, M
          X(I) = CVMGM(D(I), A(I), C(I) − B(I))
6       CONTINUE
```

where D(I) is returned if C(I) − B(I) < 0,
and A(I) is returned if C(I) − B(I) >= 0.

Another example of the use of these vector functions is the transformation of

```
        DO 7 I = N, M
          X(I) = C(I)
          IF (B(I).GT.C(I)) X(I) = B(I)
7       CONTINUE
```

which must be rewritten as follows to obtain a vectorized loop

```
        DO 7 I = N, M
          X(I) = CVMGT(B(I), C(I), B(I).GT.C(I))
7       CONTINUE
```

Depending on the statements other arrangements are possible; the last example could alternatively have been written as

```
        DO 7 I = N, M
          X(I) = AMAX1(B(I), C(I))
7       CONTINUE
```

to produce a vectorizable loop where the vector function AMAX1 returns a vector consisting of the larger of the elements of its two vector arguments. There is also a function AMIN1 which returns the smaller of its arguments.

The net effect of using these functions is that the original code has been changed considerably with the introduction of non-standard features so that vectorized code can be produced.

There can, however, be disadvantages in coding IF statements in this way. The computer may perform extra work by evaluating both true and false expressions before deciding which value to use. For example, in the loop

```
        DO 8 I = 1, 1000
          IF(X(I).GE.0.9999) C(I) = ASIN(C(I))
8       CONTINUE
```

the expression would never invoke the ASIN routine if all X(I) were less than 0.9999. However the equivalent vector loop

```
        DO 8 I = 1, 1000
          C(I) = CVMGT(ASIN(X(I)), X(I), X(I).GE.0.9999)
8       CONTINUE
```

requires 1000 evaluations of ASIN.

Whether or not there is a speed advantage in vectorizing IF statements in this manner depends in a complicated way on the complexity of the expressions and on the probability of their evaluation being required.

The second disadvantage is concerned with illegal operations. A loop such as

```
        DO 9 I = N, M
          IF(X(I).NE.0) X(I) = 1.0/X(I)
          IF(Y(I).GE.0) Y(I) = SQRT(Y(I))
9       CONTINUE
```

should not be rewritten using the preceding methods. In the rewritten loop

```
        DO 9 I = N, M
          X(I) = CVMGN(1.0/X(I), X(I), X(I))
          Y(I) = CVMGP(SQRT(Y(I)), Y(I), Y(I))
9       CONTINUE
```

both division and use of the intrinsic function SQRT would produce errors when processing unneeded cases.

Hence when a conditional statement occurs within a DO loop the decision as to whether it is advisable to vectorize the loop or not must be considered carefully. If vectorization is to be introduced then one of the special utility functions must be used. These functions may change the structure of the original loop and also introduce a non-standard feature to the program.

10.4   Index interdependencies

There are certain circumstances in which it may not be possible to vectorize the FORTRAN code at all. Such situations usually occur when there is a dependency between the indices of array references. For example, given the following loop in a sequential FORTRAN program

```
      DO 10 I = 2, 4
        B(I) = A(I − 1)
        A(I) = C(I)
10    CONTINUE
```

the following assignments are intended to take place

B(2) = A(1), A(2) = C(2),
B(3) = A(2), A(3) = C(3),
B(4) = A(3), A(4) = C(4).

However, if this code is vectorized it means the first assignment statement is treated by a functional unit before the second one is started, that is, all values of A are first assigned to B before any of the values of C are assigned to A. Hence the order of the assignments is as follows:

B(2) = A(1), B(3) = A(2), B(4) = A(3),
A(2) = C(2), A(3) = C(3), A(4) = C(4).

A comparison of the underlined assignments indicates that the intended effect is not being achieved, the value assigned to B is the old rather than the new value of A. This is a consequence of vectorization. It is important to emphasise that this occurs because all the values that are to be assigned are fed into the pipelined unit at the same time.

A factor which influences the assignment order is the relationship between the indices of the elements of A. For example, if the loop was changed to the following

```
      DO 11 I = 2, 4
        B(I) = A(I + 1)
        A(I) = C(I)
11    CONTINUE
```

then in the sequential case the following assignments would take place

B(2) = A(3), A(2) = C(2),
B(3) = A(4), A(3) = C(3),
B(4) = A(5), A(4) = C(4),

while if the loop is vectorized the following assignments would take place

B(2) = A(3), B(3) = A(4), B(4) = A(5)
A(2) = C(2), A(3) = C(3), A(4) = C(4).

The effect is the same since the assignments to A in both cases take place after the use of that value of A.

An index interdependency can also occur within a single assignment statement as well as across a group of assignment statements as above. For example, given the loop:

```
      DO 12 I = 2, 4
        A(I) = A(I −1) + A(I +1)
12    CONTINUE
```

in the sequential case this means the following assignments are performed:

A(2) = A(1) + A(3), A(3) = A(2) + A(4), A(4) = A(3) + A(5).

whereas with vectorization it is the old values of A which are used in the assignments. This can be illustrated by considering actual values for A.

A		1	2	3	4	5
values	before	100	200	300	400	500
sequential	after		400	800	1300	
vectorized	after		400	600	800	

In general, a dependency exists if the evaluated subscript of the reference on the right of the assignment operator is less than the evaluated subscript on the left side. However, in some cases such as A(I + N) = A(I) if N is negative there is no dependency but this cannot be determined at compile-time. Therefore to prevent indeterminate results such a loop is not vectorized. Similarly, for a loop such as

```
      DO 13 I = N, M, 2
        A(I) = A(I − 1)
13    CONTINUE
```

the difference between the subscripts is examined but not the magnitude. Even though no dependency exists the loop is not vectorized. Similar dependencies prevent vectorization occurring with negative increments, negative subscript expressions and with equivalenced arrays because of the storage overlap.

Hence it is the relationship between the indices on both sides of the assignment operator which determines if it is safe to vectorize or not. In the following loop

```
        DO 14 I = N, M, L
          A(I) = A(I + K)
14      CONTINUE
```

the conditions under which it will be vectorized are either

1. L and K are positive or
2. L and K are negative.

If either or both of these conditions is broken vectorization will not be attempted.

The inhibiting of vectorization because of such dependencies may be relaxed in the case of multi-dimensional array processing. If the compiler can determine that the specified array elements are in different vectors (i.e. rows, columns, planes, etc.) of the array then vectorization is possible. For example, the loop

```
        DO 15 I = 2, 100
          AA(I,J) = AA(I,J − 1) + B(I)
15      CONTINUE
```

can be vectorized since different columns of the matrix AA are being used on either side of the assignment operator. However, the loop

```
        DO 16 I = 2, 100
          AA(I,J) = AA(I,J1) + B(I)
16      CONTINUE
```

will not be vectorized since the compiler cannot determine whether J and J1 are equal.

Hence index interdependencies pose very complex analysis problems for a vectorizing compiler since it must analyse the range of the subscripts, the order of references and the sign of the control variable. As a result the conditions under which the compiler will vectorize such code are severely restricted. There is however a compiler directive IVDEP which can be placed in front of a DO loop which forces the compiler to ignore any index interdependency.

10.5 Independent indexing

When vectorizing a FORTRAN program CFT allows only one subscript in an array reference to vary, this means that loops referencing the diagonal elements of an array will not be vectorized. This is illustrated in the following code:

```
       DIMENSION AA(N,N)
       DO 17 I = 1, N
         AA(I,I) = B(I)
17     CONTINUE
```

Although this loop involves the assignment of a contiguous set of values, the elements of AA to which they are to be assigned are not contiguous. The Cray-1 regards a vector as data which is regularly spaced; the data does not have to be in contiguous memory locations but there must be the same number of locations between the elements. The references to the elements of AA in the above loop do in fact fulfil this criterion since they are N + 1 elements apart. Thus the above loop can be vectorized by changing it to:

```
       DIMENSION AA(N,N)
       J = 1
       DO 18 I = 1, N
         AA(J) = B(I)
         J = J + N + 1
18     CONTINUE
```

However as can be seen by examining the new loop this does require a considerable re-working of the original code to effect vectorization.

Another case which is difficult to vectorize is the updating of the off diagonal elements of a matrix as in the loop

```
       DO 19 I = 2, N
         AA(I,I − 1) = AA(I,I − 1) + B(I)
19     CONTINUE
```

This will not be vectorized because both indices of AA are varying each time round the loop.

The general case of this last situation is known as independent indexing, that is, the selection of a non-uniform series of array elements. This occurs when an integer array is used to specify the required indices of a second array. This is illustrated in the following loops.

```
       DO 20 I = 1, N
         INDEX(I) = B(I)
20     CONTINUE

       DO 21 I = 1, N
         AA(INDEX(I),I) = AA(INDEX(I),I) + B(I)
21     CONTINUE
```

Again it is not possible to vectorize this last loop directly because one of the indices is specified by means of an array which references a non-contiguous set of data values.

This last example includes a situation generally referred to as a scatter operation where the elements of a contiguous vector are scattered throughout a second vector (or matrix). This can be illustrated by the next example where contiguous elements of B are distributed into the vector A using some other vector to establish the index pattern for A.

```
C       scatter
        DO 20 I = 1, 100
           A(INDEX(I)) = B(I)
20      CONTINUE
```

The complementary operation to the scatter operation is the gather operation where the elements of some vector are rearranged as a contiguous vector of the same operands. For example,

```
C       gather
        DO 20 I = 1, 100
           B(I) = A(INDEX(I))
20      CONTINUE
```

However, both types of operation are unsuitable for a machine like the Cray-1 since there is not a contiguous data stream which can be fed into a pipelined functional unit. More recent vector processors provide hardware instructions to deal with scatter/gather operations.

10.6 Subprograms

At a functional level, the same vectorizing techniques can be applied to the statements of a subprogram. However, if a function or subroutine is called from within a DO loop, vectorization will stop. The body of the subprogram could be inserted in a loop to enable vectorization to continue. Such an approach destroys any structure in the original program and encourages monolithic programs – somewhat against the beneficial practice of structured programming.

In CFT the input/output facilities are those available in FORTRAN. However, loops containing any input/output statements, GOTO, IF, or CALL statements are not vectorizable. In addition, any procedures named in an EXTERNAL statement inhibit vectorization of an inner DO loop referencing them.

10.7 Summary

The main advantage of the CFT vectorizing compiler is that existing sequential programs can be moved relatively inexpensively to a parallel architecture. However, it does condemn a project to the use of sequential FORTRAN.

The disadvantages are that to gain substantial vectorization help from a programmer is required. The vectorization modifications can destroy the structure of the original program and thus make the program more difficult to understand, correct or modify. The ability to enhance an existing program is a necessary criterion in a developing scientific discipline.

The programmer when constructing a new program must ensure that the data structures and the nesting of DO loops facilitates vectorization; this may not be the most natural or direct expression of a problem's solution. Hence the programmer's attention is directed away from the representation of the problem. Also the techniques and algorithms used to write a program for a sequential machine may not be the best techniques to use when constructing a parallel program.

The following are the recommended CFT guidelines to promote vectorization of DO loop operations:

- Keep subscripts simple and explicit; do not use parentheses in subscripts.
- Do not use IF, GOTO, or CALL statements.
- Use the Cray-1 FORTRAN intrinsic functions where appropriate.
- Make judicious use of the Cray-1 FORTRAN utility procedures CVMGT, CVMGP, CVMGM, CVMGZ, CVMGN, and the AMAX and AMIN functions in lieu of IF statements.
- Rewrite large loops that contain a few unvectorizable statements as two or more loops, one or more of which will vectorize.

These are just some of the techniques which are required, and practices which must be avoided, in order to assist the vectorization process and thus improve the performance of a program written for a sequential machine architecture on a vector processor. All these techniques are applied at the statement level and do not represent a strategy for the production of large programs for vector processors.

Case study: Laplace's equation

In this case study we consider a numerical problem, namely, the solution of the Laplace partial differential equation:

$$d^2U / dX^2 + d^2U / dY^2 = 0$$

on a rectangular grid R. The values of U on the boundary of the grid R are given and it is required to find values (approximate) of U at each interior point of the grid. The grid R is divided up into an M by N array of points which are identified by the indices i and j. The Laplace equation can be approximated by the difference equations

$$U_{i-1,j} + U_{i+1,j} + U_{i,j+1} + U_{i,j-1} - 4U_{i,j} = 0$$

which means that the value of U at any point is the average of the values of its four neighbouring north, south, east and west points. Thus a solution for point i,j can be expressed as

$$U_{i,j} = 0.25 \times (U_{i-1,j} + U_{i+1,j} + U_{i,j+1} + U_{i,j-1})$$

It is necessary to apply this solution to each point within the grid R. When considered together it gives a system of linear equations to be solved. The question is can this problem be solved efficiently on a vector processor such as the Cray-1?

A method which can be used to solve this system is the Gauss-Seidel iteration method where the formula for deriving the $(N + 1)$st approximation of $U_{i,j}$ from the Nth is

$$U_{i,j}^{(N+1)} = 0.25 \times (U_{i-1,j}^{(N+1)} + U_{i,j-1}^{(N+1)} + U_{i,j+1}^{(N)} + U_{i+1,j}^{(N)})$$

where the old data is used for the southern and eastern neighbours and new data for the western and northern neighbours. Part of the code to solve this type of equation can be expressed in FORTRAN as

```
REAL U(M,N)

DO 1 I = 2, M − 1
DO 1 J = 2, N − 1
    U(I,J) = 0.25 * (U(I − 1,J) + U(I + 1,J) +
                     U(I,J + 1) + U(I,J − 1))
1       CONTINUE
```

If this code is compiled under CFT it will not be vectorized because there are index interdependencies; the Jth element in row I depends on the updated value of the $(J - 1)$th element thus preventing vectorization.

This dependency can be illustrated by a closer examination of part of the grid, for example, the points surrounding the point (i,j) can be represented as

$$(i - 1j - 1) \quad (i - 1j) \quad (i - 1j + 1)$$
$$(i \quad j - 1) \quad (i \quad j) \quad (i \quad j + 1)$$
$$(i + 1j - 1) \quad (i + 1j) \quad (i + 1j + 1)$$

which demonstrates the dependency.

A vector solution can be obtained by considering the points under what is known as a red-black ordering scheme. In this scheme all the points which satisfy the equation

$$(i + j) \bmod 2 = 0 \text{ are classified black,}$$

while the points that satisfy

$$(i + j) \bmod 2 = 1 \text{ are classified red.}$$

Assuming that i and j each has an odd value, then the red points are underlined in the following:

$$
\begin{array}{ccccc}
(i-2j-2) & (i-2j-1) & (i-2j) & (\underline{i-2j+1}) & (i-2j+2) \\
(\underline{i-1j-2}) & (i-1j-1) & (\underline{i-1j}) & (i-1j+1) & (\underline{i-1j+2}) \\
(i \quad j-2) & (\underline{i \quad j-1}) & (i \quad j) & (\underline{i \quad j+1}) & (i \quad j+2) \\
(\underline{i+1j-2}) & (i+1j-1) & (\underline{i+1j}) & (i+1j+1) & (\underline{i+1j+2}) \\
(i+2j-2) & (\underline{i+2j-1}) & (i+2j) & (\underline{i+2j+1}) & (i+2j+2)
\end{array}
$$

One possible technique is to work within the red points and then the black points. For example the point (i,j), a black point, is updated using the four red points $(i,j-1), (i+1,j), (i,j+1), (i-1,j)$. All of the black points on the same diagonal as (i,j) can be updated in this manner. However, to avoid interaction of the updates the points are divided into two vectors of alternate points, that is, points $(i+2,j-2), (i,j), (i-2,j+2)$ and points $(i+1,j-1), (i-1,j+1)$. This same technique can be applied to all of the black diagonals. Similarly for the red points. Hence a solution to Laplace's equation can be coded in CFT as

```
        REAL U(M,N)

CDIR$ IVDEP
C       RED POINTS
        DO 1 J = 2,N − 2,2
        DO 2 I = 2,M − 2,2
            U(I,J) = 0.25*(U(I − 1,J) + U(I,J − 1) + U(I + 1,J) + U(I,J + 1))
            U(I + 1,J + 1) = 0.25* (U(I + 2,J + 1) + U(I + 1,J + 2) +
                             U(I + 1,J) + U(I,J + 1))
2       CONTINUE
1       CONTINUE

CDIR$ IVDEP
C       BLACK POINTS
        DO 3 J = 2,N − 2,2
        DO 4 I = 3,M − 1,2
            U(I,J) = 0.25*(U(I,J − 1) + U(I + 1,J) + U(I − 1,J) + U(I,J + 1))
            U(I − 1,J + 1) = 0.25* (U(I − 2,J + 1) + U(I − 1,J + 2) +
                             U(I − 1,J) + U(I,J + 1))
4       CONTINUE
3       CONTINUE
```

The Cray-1 compiler would not vectorize the above code because of the potential index interdependencies. However, since we know from an examination of the problem that there is no interaction between the referenced points it is safe to force vectorization using the IVDEP directive.

Thus by reconsidering the problem it has been found possible to restructure the solution to produce a vector of operands which can be efficiently processed on a machine like the Cray-1.

EXERCISES

10.1 Given the following FORTRAN loop

```
       DO 1 I = 1,128
          A(I) = B(I) * C(I) + D(I) * C(I) + F(I) * G(I)
1      CONTINUE
```

draw a timing diagram to show how a pipelined execution of this loop would be executed.

10.2 Devise a sequence of four vector instructions which can benefit from chaining on the Cray-1. Illustrate your answer with diagrams.

10.3 Determine if the following loop can be vectorized if expressed in CFT.

```
       A(0) = X
       DO 1 I = 1,N
          A(I) = A(I − 1) * B(I) + C(I + 1)
1      CONTINUE
```

10.4 Determine if the following loop can be vectorized in CFT

```
       DO 1 I = 1,N
          IF (A(I).NE.0) A(I) = A(I) − 1
1      CONTINUE
```

10.5 How should the following loops be converted to enable parallel processing on a vector processor?

(a)
```
       DO 1 I = 1,N
          A(I) = B(I − 1)
          B(I) = 2 * B(I)
1      CONTINUE
```

(b)
```
       DO 1 I = 1,N
          A(I) = B(I) + C(I)
          B(I) = 2 * A(I + 1)
1      CONTINUE
```

(c)
```
       DO 1 I = 1,100
       DO 1 I = 1,  20
          AA(I,J) = BB(I,J) + CC(I,J)
1      CONTINUE
```

10.6 Devise a fast algorithm for the following arithmetic operations on a vector processor:

(a) the dot product of two N element vectors;

(b) the searching of the maximum among N elements of a vector.

Chapter 11 CDC Cyber FORTRAN

11.1 Hardware considerations

One of the main rivals of the Cray-1 computer is the Control Data Corporation Cyber 205. The Cyber 205 has been available in its present form since 1981 and evolved from an earlier CDC vector processor known as the Star-100; STring and ARray processor. The architecture of the Cyber 205 is similar to the Cray-1 in that it is based on functional units which are pipelined. However, the number and the arrangement of the functional units are different. Another major difference is that the Cyber 205 does not contain the vector intermediate registers that are part of the Cray-1's computation section. Hence any data required to be processed is transferred directly from the memory to the designated Cyber vector functional unit; the data is not grouped in batches of 64 operands as is required by the Cray-1. Any results produced are sent to the memory. This means that the time to set up a pipeline for processing vectors is longer than a similar process on the Cray-1, however, once the operation is established there are no interruptions as each multiple of 64 operands is encountered.

The high level language provided on the Cyber 205 is based on FORTRAN and is known as Cyber 200 FORTRAN (version 1). The compiler for this language will attempt to detect which parts of a sequentially written FORTRAN program can be executed by the pipelined functional units. In addition, several extensions have been provided which enable a programmer to express parallelism directly, and there are special call statements which provide access to machine instructions. It is not essential for a FORTRAN programmer to be familiar with the architecture of the Cyber 205, although there are certain circumstances in which such a knowledge can improve the performance of a program.

To enhance the description of Cyber 200 FORTRAN a brief overview of the Cyber 205 architecture is given in Figure 11.1.

The Cyber 205 can have a main memory of up to 4 million 64-bit words organized into a number of memory banks. This interleaved organization of the memory enables a maximum bandwidth of 8 words per clock period to be delivered. Since the clock period is 20 nanoseconds this gives a maximum bandwidth rate of 400 million words per second. The

154

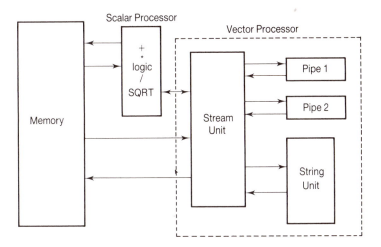

Figure 11.1   Cyber 205 two pipe system.

computation section of the Cyber 205 consists of a scalar processor and a vector processor. The scalar processor receives and decodes all instructions from the memory. It executes scalar instructions itself and directs decoded vector and string instructions to the vector processor for execution. The scalar processor can execute scalar instructions in parallel with most vector instructions if there are no memory references generated by the scalar instruction. Thus, the scalar processor can evaluate the array subscript expression for the next vector instruction while the current vector instruction is being executed.

The scalar processor consists of five independent functional units which perform addition/subtraction, multiplication, logical, shift and division/square root operations. All units except the division unit are pipelined and may take a new set of operands every clock period. This gives a potential peak scalar processing rate of 50 million floating point operations per second. There is also a load/store unit which controls access to the memory.

The vector processor of the machine consists of either one, two or four floating point arithmetic pipes and a string unit; the string unit performs all bit logical and character string operations on strings, where a string is a vector of bits or bytes. These units are fed with data by a stream unit which manages the traffic between the floating point pipes and memory. Each floating point pipe is in turn made up of five separate pipelined functional units which include addition, multiplication and shifting operations. Division and square root operations are performed in the multiplication unit. A floating point unit can produce one result each clock period. This is equivalent to executing 50 million floating point operations per second. It can also produce 32-bit results increasing the performance to 100 million floating point operations per second, per pipelined unit for short time periods.

In the Cyber 205 there are no vector registers so that each vector pipeline is directly connected to the main memory and all vector operations are memory to memory based. This means that it takes much longer to start up a pipelined unit on the Cyber 205 than on the Cray-1. However it does mean that once processing has started there is no overhead associated with each batch of 64 operands. Also because of the Cyber's higher bandwidth rate it outpaces the Cray-1 when the length of a vector exceeds a certain size. In fact, the Cyber 205 can handle a continuous stream of operands up to 65 535 in length.

Thus it is not necessary for the Cyber 200 FORTRAN programmer to size the program's data structures to suit the machine's characteristics in order to improve performance. Rather the programmer should try to make the size of the data structures as large as possible.

It is only possible to access consecutively stored operands in the memory of the Cyber 205. If it is required to access non-consecutively stored operands then all the surrounding elements must also be fetched from the memory. A control vector of bits is then used to select the relevant operands. Such a control vector has one bit for each word of the vector and an operation can only be applied to a particular element if the corresponding control bit is set to one. The manipulation of these bit vectors is performed by the string unit. Alternatively, if the control vector is very sparse the elements may be compressed and stored consecutively. Any operations which are then performed will be more efficient on the compressed vector. In addition, several frequently required operations, such as scatter and gather, have been implemented using microcode in the stream unit to improve their efficiency.

There is a restricted form of chaining available on the Cyber 205. It corresponds to the situation where two different vector instructions use different units and one of the operands is a scalar. The output from one unit is fed as the input of the second unit with no intermediate access to memory. In this way two units are operating in parallel. Examples of such a situation are the following operations

vector + scalar × vector

and

(vector + scalar) × vector

which enable the multiplication and addition units to act in parallel. The performance of a pipelined unit will be doubled for such an operation, that is, a 100 and 200 million floating point operations per second for 64-bit and 32-bit arithmetic respectively. Thus on a 4-pipe machine the maximum performance is 800 million floating point operations per second under very special certain circumstances.

11.2   Automatic vectorization

The principles on which the Cyber 200 FORTRAN compiler tries to detect which parts of a program can be vectorized are similar to those used in the Cray CFT compiler. However the details of each compiler's method of detection are different and therefore affect the efficiency of operation of the same program executing on these two machines.

As in CFT a DO loop with statements manipulating dimensioned variables has the best chance of being vectorized. Such loops should be as long as possible because of the overhead involved in setting up a pipelined operation. A simple example of a vectorizable loop is:

```
      DO 1 I = 1,N
        C(I) = A(I) + B(I)
1     CONTINUE
```

where N may be a constant or variable.

More loops can be vectorized in Cyber 200 FORTRAN since it can handle nested DO loops, provided the nested loops can be vectorized. Hence matrix multiplication expressed as

```
      DO 1 I = 1, N
      DO 1 J = 1, N
       AA(I,J) = 0.0
      DO 1 K = 1, N
       AA(I,J) = AA(I,J) + BB(I,K) * CC(K,J)
1     CONTINUE
```

will be vectorized without rearranging the statements. There are, however, restrictions such as the iterative count of the nested DO loops must be less than or equal to 65 535, that is, $N \times N \times N <= 65\ 535$ in this example. Also N or any of the control parameters of any nested DO loops must be constants. If a loop cannot be vectorized, then a loop which contains the non-vectorizable loop cannot be vectorized either. There are other restrictions placed on such a loop, for example, the form of an array subscript expression must be one of the following

$V, V + C, V - C, V \times C$

where V is a control variable and C an integer constant. The use of relational operators within a loop also renders the loop non-vectorizable.

If the references to an array increase by a constant value each time round the loop then the loop will be vectorized. However, if this loop is nested the outer loop will not be vectorized. For example, given the loops

```
      DO 1 I = 1,5
      DO 2 J = 1,5,2
       AA(J,I) = BB(J,J)
2     CONTINUE
1     CONTINUE
```

the subscripts of AA are increasing in increments of 2 and the subscripts of BB are increasing by 12. Thus the inner loop will be vectorized but not the outer loop.

The left side of an assignment statement in a vectorizable loop must be a loop dependent array reference or a scalar reference as illustrated in the following loop:

```
      DO 3 I = 1, N
        TEMP = B(I) * C(I)
        D(I) = E(I)/TEMP + TEMP
3       CONTINUE
```

However, there are some restrictions which apply to DO loops in Cyber 200 FORTRAN which contain scalars, namely,

1. a scalar reference must not appear before its definition,
2. if a scalar is defined within a loop, and appears in a nested loop, the loop is not vectorized,
3. if a scalar is an array element, every reference to that array in the loop must have the same subscript.

Hence the programmer must be aware of these loop restrictions which may appear arbitrary and inconvenient at times.

A conditional statement appearing within a loop will prevent vectorization; there are no conditional merge functions provided as is the case in Cray CFT. A different approach is used in Cyber 200 FORTRAN with a new language construct being provided, this is treated along with the other explicit vectorization features of Cyber 200 FORTRAN in the following section. If these new features are used in a loop it will prevent the automatic vectorization of that loop.

Cyber 200 FORTRAN, like CFT, has the same problems with index interdependencies and independent indexing as were illustrated in Sections 10.4 and 10.5. As a result if there is any doubt about the result, vectorization does not take place.

The following statements will prevent vectorization in a Cyber 200 FORTRAN program loop:

- an input/output statement,
- an IF or GOTO statement,
- calls to other than standard subprograms,
- explicit vectorization statements.

There is some similarity with the list of statements which prevent vectorization in Cray CFT but even so moving programs from one machine to another would be a non-trivial task.

Hence as far as the detection of parallelism within a program is concerned Cyber 200 FORTRAN can handle more loops than CFT.

However, the restrictions that have been placed on a loop are not the same restrictions as in CFT. As a result Cyber 200 FORTRAN does not represent a logical progression in the evolution of this type of language.

Another difference between CFT and Cyber 200 FORTRAN occurs when constructing a new program; the Cyber 200 FORTRAN user does not have to be aware of the factor 64 in choosing the program's data structures. However, because of the longer time involved in setting up a functional unit the user should, where possible, ensure that the iteration count of the loop is as large as possible.

11.3 Explicit vectorization

The Cyber 200 FORTRAN compiler as well as detecting which parts of a program can be executed in parallel also provides features which enable a user to express explicitly the parallelism inherent in a problem. These features should be more properly considered when dealing with the expression of problem parallelism languages. However, they are included here to give a consistent treatment of the Cyber 205's main programming language.

These new features include both parallel data structures and statements and as a result are more appropriate when constructing new programs rather than adapting existing programs. FORTRAN 200 provides two new data types to deal with the declaration of vectors in a program, namely:

1. a vector, which is an ordered set of scalar elements;
2. a descriptor, which is a pointer to a vector.

A vector can be defined using a previously declared scalar array and by selecting a base address and a length. For example

VECTOR(BASE; LENGTH)

where VECTOR is the name of an array whose elements are of type integer, half precision, real, double precision, complex or bit (not logical or character); BASE is the subscript which designates the vector's first element; and LENGTH is a non-negative integer expression with certain limits imposed depending on the type of the vector.

Thus the elements in the array VECTOR, starting with the element VECTOR(BASE) and continuing for LENGTH contiguous elements belong to the newly defined vector VECTOR(BASE; LENGTH). The length of the vector must be written within the bounds of the declared array because no compile-time or run-time checks are performed.

More specifically, given the declaration DIMENSION V(30) then V(1;10) and V(21;10) are the vectors corresponding to the first 10 and last 10 elements of V respectively. Thus an array element can belong to more than one vector, as in V(1;4) and V(2;5) which corresponds to the elements

V(1) V(2) V(3) V(4)

and

V(2) V(3) V(4) V(5) V(6)

respectively.

Vectors can also be constructed from multi-dimensional arrays, for example, given DIMENSION BB(2,5) then BB(2,1;4) refers to the vector made up from the elements

BB(2,1) BB(1,2), BB(2,2), BB(1,3).

Since the array is stored column first in memory the length, 4 in this example, refers to the above elements.

In addition to the DIMENSION statement there is also a ROWWISE statement which can be used to declare an array. In this case the subscript significance is the reverse of an array that has been declared in a DIMENSION statement. For a two-dimensional array it is the second rather than the first subscript which varies fastest.

Vectors can be constructed from such arrays using the same technique. For example, given ROWWISE BB(2,5) then BB(2,1;4) refers to the vector made up from the elements

BB(2,1) BB(2,2) BB(2,3) BB(2,4).

A descriptor is defined as a pointer to a vector and is identified by a symbolic name. It has the same type as the vector to which it points. Every descriptor must appear in a DESCRIPTOR specification statement and must be defined before it is used. At compile-time, a descriptor can be initialized to point to a particular vector using the DATA statement. For example, the declarations

```
DESCRIPTOR POINTR
DIMENSION V(100)
DATA POINTR / V(1;50)/50 * 1.0 /
```

mean that POINTR refers to the vector made up of the first 50 values of the array V. The 50 elements of the vector V have been initialized to the value 1.0; the number of constants in the value list must be the same as the number of elements in the vector.

It is also possible to form an array of descriptors. For example, in the declarations

```
DESCRIPTOR PTRS
DIMENSION V(100), PTRS(2)
DATA PTRS(1) / V(1;100) / ,PTRS(2) / V(51;100) /
```

PTRS is declared as a descriptor with 2 elements. The first element PTRS(1) points to the current values of the 100 contiguous elements of the array V and PTRS(2) points to the current values of the last 50 elements of V. This is the main method by which vectors can be organized into arrays of vectors. Other examples are

```
INTEGER A
REAL B(5)
DESCRIPTOR A,B,C(10)
```

where A is an integer descriptor, B is a real descriptor array of 5 elements, and C is a real descriptor array of 10 elements.

11.4 Expressions

The language has been extended so that an expression can be formed using vector operands of the same length, the operands are combined by matching the corresponding elements of the vectors in the expression, that is, element by element processing. Using the above declarations

```
V(1;50) * V(51;50)
```

multiplies the 1st and the 51st, 2nd and 52nd, etc. elements of the array V. If one of the operands in an expression is a scalar then it is matched with every element of the vector. For example, in the expression

```
V(1;100) + N
```

the value N is added to each of the 100 elements of V. Equivalent expressions can be formed using the descriptors which point to the same vectors. For example, given the declarations

```
DESCRIPTOR POINTR, PTRS
DIMENSION V(100), PTRS(2)
DATA POINTR / V(1;50) / , PTRS(1) / V(1;100) / , PTRS(2) / V(51;50) /
```

then

```
POINTR * PTRS(2) and PTRS(1) + N
```

are equivalent methods of specifying the two expressions considered above. In this case, however, because of the use of descriptors, the code is more difficult to understand since one level of indirection has been introduced.

Expressions involving the relational operators produce a string of bits with a one representing a true result and zero representing a false result. For example, the relation

```
V(1;5) > V(6;5)
```

will produce a string of five bits whose values are determined by the comparisons. As will be illustrated in the next section this is an important method for the selective updating of a vector.

11.5 Assignment statements

There are effectively two types of assignment statement, one of which deals with the creation of descriptors and the other with the updating of the elements of a vector.

As well as being able to establish a descriptor at compile-time it is possible by means of the ASSIGN statement to create a descriptor at run-time. Such a descriptor can be assigned part of a vector or another descriptor. For example, given the declarations

```
DESCRIPTOR POINTR, PTRS
DIMENSION V(100), PTRS(2)
```

and the statements

```
ASSIGN POINTR, V(1;50)
ASSIGN PTRS(1), POINTR
```

then the descriptor POINTR points to the first 50 elements of V as does the descriptor PTRS(1); it is the current values of V which are used to create the vector. The type of the descriptor must agree with the type of the vector or descriptor it is being assigned.

The FORTRAN assignment statement has been expanded to include vectors and descriptors on both sides of the assignment operator. For example,

```
REAL R(100), X(30)
R(1;30) = X(1;30)
```

means that the first 30 elements of R are assigned the corresponding values of X. The length of the vectors on both sides of the assignment operator must be the same. These new extensions are, in effect, a shorthand notation for writing sequential FORTRAN DO loops since

```
C(1;64) = A(1;64) + B(1;64)
```

is equivalent to

```
        DO 1 I = 1, 64
          C(I) = A(I) + B(I)
1       CONTINUE
```

The same effect can be achieved by using descriptors to represent the required vectors. For example

```
DESCRIPTOR RPTR, XPTR
REAL R(100), X(30)
DATA RPTR/R(1;30) / , XPTR/X(1;30)
RPTR = XPTR
```

is an alternative way of assigning the 30 values of X to part of the vector R. Another example of an assignment statement using descriptors is

```
DESCRIPTOR P1, P2
DATA P1 / X(1;30) /
– – –
P2 = –(P1 + N) / 2.0
```

which causes the descriptor P2 to point to the vector formed from the elements of X in the above expression.

Consider the multiplication of two matrices BB and CC to produce a third matrix AA. Since the Cyber 205 defines a vector as the contents of a set of contiguous memory locations in memory an efficient solution can be devised by treating the matrices as long vectors made up of the columns (or rows) of each matrix as follows:

```
        PARAMETER (N = 100 ; NSQ = N * N)
        REAL AA(N,N), BB(N,N), CC(N,N)

        AA(1,1;NSQ) = 0.0

        DO 1 I = 1,N
        DO 1 J = 1,N
          AA(1,J;N) = AA(1,J;N) + BB(I,J) * CC(1,I;N)
1       CONTINUE
```

In this solution each column of CC is processed only once but each of the columns of AA is processed N times. Also the computation of the elements of the product matrix is a linked triad of the form vector + scalar × vector so that the operation can be chained improving the performance of the algorithm.

If a ROWWISE declaration had been used then the linked triad code would be replaced by

```
AA(I,1:N) = AA(I,1:N) + CC(I,J) * BB(J,1:N)
```

As this example demonstrates these vector extensions are a more compact means of expressing parallel data structures and their manipulation.

11.6   Control statements

In order to provide for the situation where a vector condition dictates the updating of a vector of operands FORTRAN 200 provides a conditional statement which takes the form

```
WHERE (EXP) Statement
```

EXP is a vector bit expression and Statement is a vector assignment statement. A vector bit expression is formed by applying a relational operator to vector operands, a bit is set 1 or 0 depending upon whether the relation is true or false for the vector elements involved.

All vector operands in either the expression or the statement must have the same length and must be of type integer, real or half precision. The vector expression in the statement can contain only addition, subtraction, multiplication and division operators and references to certain vector functions.

On execution the vector bit expression is evaluated to produce a control vector. This control vector determines which values are stored in a vector when the assignment statement is executed. Hence, in an assignment a result is stored only if the corresponding element in the control vector contains a 1 bit. Otherwise no assignment takes place. For example, given the declarations

```
REAL A(5), B(5), C(5)
DATA A/3.0, 9.0, 12.0, 2.0, 16.0/
DATA B/6.0, 6.0, 10.0, 5.0, 4.0/
DATA C/9.0, 3.0, 0.0, 7.0, 7.0/
```

then in the statement

```
WHERE (A(1;5).LT.B(1;5)) C(1;5) = A(1;5) + B(1;5)
```

only the values of 1st and 4th elements of C are changed, since only the 1st and 4th elements of A are less than B.

Thus to handle the conditional statements used for illustration purposes with CFT (Section 10.3) the user should write in Cyber 200 FORTRAN

```
X(1;N) = A(1;N)
WHERE (B(1;N).GT.C(1;N)) X(1;N) = D(1;N)
```

and

```
X(1;N) = C(1;N)
WHERE (B(1;N).GT.C(1;N)) X(1;N) = B(1;N)
```

which is a much more precise and readable representation.

There is also a block WHERE statement in which the control vector is applied to the vector assignment statements which appear between the WHERE statement and the next END WHERE statement. An OTHERWISE statement can be used with a block WHERE statement to reverse the effect of the control vector established in the block WHERE statement, as in

```
WHERE (A(1;5).LT.5.0)
  C(1;5) = 0.0
OTHERWISE
  C(1;5) = A(1;5)
END WHERE
```

If the values of A are 3.0, 9.0, 12.0, 2.0 and 16.0 then the values 0.0, 9.0, 12.0, 0.0, 16.0 are assigned to C.

When using the WHERE statement all the vectors must be of the same length and must be of type integer, half precision or real. Expressions must be composed of addition, subtraction, multiplication and division operations and in addition to vectors only references to vector functions are allowed.

11.7 Subprograms

Vector functions are defined in a manner similar to FORTRAN functions except that the function name must appear in a DESCRIPTOR statement. A vector function is referenced when the name of the function followed by the actual argument(s) appears in an expression. There are a number of vector intrinsic functions which can be used for commonly required tasks. Such intrinsic functions can be usefully employed to perform operations such as scatter and gather which are difficult on a vector processor. For example, there is an intrinsic vector function

    Q8VGATHER (V, I; U)

that creates a vector consisting of selected elements of the input argument V. The vector I indicates the elements of V which are to be assigned to the function result U. An element of V may be assigned to more than one element of the function result and not all the elements of the input argument must be assigned to the function result. If V is a vector that consists of 2.0, 4.0, 6.0, 8.0 and I consists of 1, 4, 4, 2 the values 2.0, 8.0, 8.0, 4.0 are assigned to the result U.

Another function Q8VSCATR (V,I;U) scatters the values of V as determined by the vector I. For example, if the input argument V is a vector that consists of the elements 2.0, 4.0, 6.0, 8.0 and the vector I consists of 1, 4, 4, 2 and the vector U consists of 9.0, 9.0, 9.0, 9.0 then after the execution of the function, U consists of 2.0, 8.0, 9.0, 6.0. The fourth element of the output argument is assigned the value 4.0 but is then reassigned the value 6.0. The third element of the output argument is never assigned a value and therefore retains its original value.

In addition to these high level language facilities FORTRAN 200 provides a series of special subroutines which enable the user to specify machine instructions in the object code. As a result code is generated in line. By using these instructions the programmer has more control over the hardware of the Cyber 205. Such control is not possible for a programmer using the Cray-1.

These instructions are utilized as follows: CALL m(a_1, a_2 -- a_n) where m is a special name beginning with the characters Q8 and a_i is an argument corresponding to one of the fields of the instruction format. The arguments are either label references, symbolic references or literals and require a knowledge of the hardware for their proper use.

There is also a Q7 series of subroutine calls which enable concurrent input and output to be performed. These routines allow overlapping of computation with input and output of large data arrays, thus maximizing the use of system resources.

11.8 Summary

Cyber 200 FORTRAN, like CFT, enables existing FORTRAN programs to be executed directly by detecting which parts of a sequentially written program can be vectorized. However, to gain any substantial vectorization, help from a programmer is usually required. The Cyber 200 FORTRAN compiler does perform vectorization in certain situations which are not possible with the CFT compiler. In both languages the situations which can be vectorized are a reflection of the techniques used in the construction of the compiler. A programmer should therefore be familiar with the detection of parallelism techniques employed in order to improve a program's performance.

In these languages there is no agreement or consistency in the features which should be vectorized or how they should be represented. For example, to vectorize a loop which contains a conditional statement in CFT requires a conditional merge function, while to do the same task in Cyber 200 FORTRAN requires a completely different statement, the WHERE statement. Such substantial differences mean that the moving of programs between these machines is a non-trivial task.

A knowledge of the hardware can also improve the performance of a program. For example, on the Cray-1 a data structure of size 64 can be manipulated more efficiently than one of size 65. While on the Cyber 205 a user should try to ensure that the data structures are as large as possible.

Thus these languages provide a useful tool for the utilization of existing software, however since they are based on a sequential language and require special knowledge of the compiler and to a limited extent the hardware, they do not represent a straightforward method for the construction of programs for vector processors. Cyber 200 FORTRAN has tried to solve this problem by introducing explicit features to represent the declaration and manipulation of data in parallel.

EXERCISES

11.1 Express the following FORTRAN loops in Cyber FORTRAN using explicit vectorization statements:

(a)
```
            DIMENSION X(5,3), Y(2,5)
            DO 1 I = 1,5
              X(I,3) = Y(2,I)
    1       CONTINUE
```
(b)
```
            DIMENSION X(5,3), Y(10,3,2)
            DO 1 I = 1,3
            DO 2 I = 1,5,3
              X(I,J) = Y(I,J,2)
    2       CONTINUE
    1       CONTINUE
```

11.2 Determine if it is possible to vectorize the following using the Cyber FORTRAN compiler:

(a)
```
            DIMENSION A(10,10), B(10,10)
            DO 1 I = 1,10
            DO 2 J = 1,10,2
              A(J,I) = B(J,J)
    2       CONTINUE
    1       CONTINUE
```
(b)
```
            DIMENSION A(10,10), B(10,10), C(10,10)
            DO 1 I = 1,10
              T = A(I,1) + B(I,1)
              C(I,1) = C(I,1) * T + A(I,1)/T
            DO 2 J = 1,10
              T = A(J,I) + B(J,I)
              C(J,I) = A(J,I) * T + B(J,I)/T
    2       CONTINUE
    1       CONTINUE
```

11.3 Convert the following sequential FORTRAN loops to Cyber FORTRAN:

(a)
```
            A(0) = X
            DO 1 I = 1,N
              A(I) = A(I − 1) * B(I) + C(I + 1)
    1       CONTINUE
```
(b)
```
            DO 1 I = 1,N
              IF (L(I).NE.0) A(I) = A(I) − 1
    1       CONTINUE
```
(c)
```
            DO 1 I = 1,N
              A(I) = B(I − 1)
              B(I) = 2 * B(I)
    1       CONTINUE
```
(d)
```
            DO 1 I = 1,N
              A(I) = B(I) + C(I)
              B(I) = 2 * A(I + 1)
    1       CONTINUE
```

11.4 If X and Y are square matrices of order N write vector code to perform the addition of these matrices.

11.5 Construct a Cyber FORTRAN program which will efficiently search for the maximum among N elements of a vector.

11.6 If A is a square matrix write vector code which will transpose this matrix.

11.7 Given the matrices X and Y of order N stored by columns, show how the last row of Y can be stored in the last row of X using one vector instruction.

EXPRESSION OF MACHINE
PARALLELISM LANGUAGES

Chapter 12 Illiac IV CFD FORTRAN

Expression of machine parallelism languages provide either a syntax which directly reflects the architecture of the machine or demand that the programmer explicitly encode hardware instructions in separate subroutine calls. This effectively turns these languages into higher level assembly languages. However, the implementation problems which are a major challenge for such machines are considerably simplified. To demonstrate some of the features of these languages and to try to identify the principles on which they are based, two languages have been selected for illustration purposes: CFD FORTRAN (Stevens, 1975) which is one of the earliest languages of this type and DAP FORTRAN (Reference Manual, 1980) which is one of the more recent languages. Both languages were designed for particular array processors, namely, the Illiac IV and the ICL Distributed Array Processor, respectively.

12.1 Hardware considerations

The Illiac IV was the result of a series of array processor systems which were developed under the auspices of the US Department of Defense Advanced Research Project Agency at the University of Illinois in the early 1960s. The objective was to develop a highly parallel computer with a large number of arithmetic units to perform vector or matrix computation at the rate of 10^9 operations per second. What emerged was a machine with 64 arithmetic units capable of executing approximately 200 million operations per second. This required a major technological effort in the late sixties and early seventies and proved the viability of the array processor concept. As a result the Illiac IV has had a profound influence on many subsequent array processors and for this reason warrants special consideration.

The Illiac IV was eventually sited at the NASA Ames Research Center in California where one of its main uses was in the solution of problems concerning computational fluid dynamics.

During the development of the Illiac IV more attention was paid to the hardware than the software with the result that when it was delivered the programming languages available were primitive in their parallel features.

In order to rectify this anomaly the Computational Fluid Dynamics Branch of the NASA Ames Research Center set about designing a language similar to commonly used versions of FORTRAN but incorporating the parallel hardware features of the Illiac IV. This language is known as CFD.

In general, this approach has been used for the languages available for array processors, that is, they have been designed on the principle that the architecture of these machines is unique and that the language should reflect this directly. In order to understand this philosophy in the case of CFD a brief overview of the architecture of the Illiac IV is given in Figure 12.1.

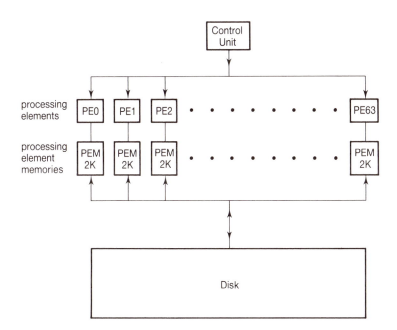

Figure 12.1   The Illiac IV system.

The Illiac IV consists of a control unit (CU) and 64 processing units. Each processing unit consists of a processing element (PE) and a memory (PEM) of 2K 64-bit words. This gives a total memory of 128K which is fed by a disk capable of holding 16 million words.

All program instructions are interpreted by the control unit which after decoding an instruction can either execute the instruction itself or broadcast it to the 64 processing elements. The control unit is limited in the type of instructions it is capable of performing, namely, integer arithmetic instructions which are primarily used for loop control and address calculation. If the control unit requires a floating point calculation to be performed it must be delegated to one of the processing elements.

The major computing power of the machine resides in the processing elements which have a repertoire of conventional instructions and a number of operating registers. The processing elements which execute an instruction can take their operands either from their own memory or one of the operands may be broadcast from the control unit. In addition, a processing element may be disabled so that it does not execute a broadcast instruction. For example, if an add instruction is broadcast by the control unit, any combination of the processing elements may execute it or ignore it; they are then referred to as enabled and disabled processing elements, respectively. It is not, however, possible for processing elements to execute different instructions.

Thus there is one instruction stream directed by the control unit and 64 data streams, hence the designation of the Illiac IV as a SIMD machine, that is, a Single Instruction Multiple Data machine. The ability to enable and disable processing elements provides the machine with its main parallel processing flexibility.

All 128K words of the memory can be accessed by the control unit but only 2K by each processing element. Each processing element contains a local index register which can be used to access into its own memory. If one processing element requires a value in another processing element's memory then that value must be routed or transferred. To facilitate this operation the processing elements are connected in a closed circular fashion and a total 64 words are routed if a route instruction is applied (see Section 12.4).

This is a brief summary of the main hardware characteristics of the Illiac IV which are reflected in the high level language considered in the next sections.

12.2   Assignment statements

The syntax of CFD directly reflects the 64 processing element/control unit dichotomy. When declaring a variable the user must decide on which processor or processors it should be manipulated. The means of achieving this are by prefixing each variable declaration with either CU or PE. For example

```
CU INTEGER I, J, K
CU REAL N, Y, Z
CU LOGICAL M
PE INTEGER A(*), B(*,6)
PE REAL C(*,10)
```

The asterisk * is used as an implicit index of 1 to 64 in a PE declaration; it can only be associated with the first dimension. The asterisk abbreviation then becomes a means of expressing 64 simultaneous operations in the program text. For example A(*) = 0 will initialize all 64 elements of the array A. Since the control unit does not have a floating point capability any real variables declared with prefix CU will be manipulated by one of the processing elements.

Thus the data structures and program statements directly reflect the parallelism of the machine and this, in turn, enables the generation of efficient object code.

Such a syntax enables problems which can be represented with 64 or a multiple of 64 in one dimension to be easily expressed. For other array sizes the user must increase the array declaration sizes to the next multiple of 64 and take account of this during the program's construction. For example, an array of 180 elements must be expressed and manipulated in batches of 64 elements as

```
        PE REAL AA(*,3), BB(*,3), CC(*,3)
        CU INTEGER I
        - - -
        DO 1 I = 1,3
          AA(*,I) = AA(*,I) + BB(*,I) * CC(*,I)
  1     CONTINUE
```

The multiplication and addition operations are performed by each of the processing elements on an element by element basis, 64 elements at a time. The natural one-dimensional structure of the problem has had to be described as a two-dimensional structure to accommodate the fixed size of the first index. In fact, the new data structure is larger than what is required. The danger now is that in certain circumstances the computation may not always be defined for the surplus elements giving rise to erroneous results. To avoid this problem the user should tailor the data structures and program constructs to the dimension of the machine; however, as in the above example, this may not always be the most appropriate representation of the solution. The fact that the implicit loop is always associated with the first index may also cause conceptual problems.

As further illustration of these concepts consider the multiplication of two matrices BB and CC to produce a third matrix AA. This can be expressed as

```
        PE REAL AA(*,50), BB(*,50)
        CU REAL CC(50,50)
        CU INTEGER J,K
        - - -
        DO 2 J = 1,50
          AA(*,J) = 0.0
        DO 2 K = 1,50
          AA(*,J) = AA(*,J) + BB(*,K) * CC(K,J)
  2     CONTINUE
```

In this solution each element of a column of BB is multiplied by a single element of the array CC. The result of these 64 multiplications is then added to 64 elements which form a column of AA. This calculation is performed for each element of CC and each column of BB to produce the required matrix AA. Any scalar variables in a parallel expression such as CC(K,J) are duplicated to give the same number of elements as the parallel variables, 64 in this case. Conversely it is not possible to assign an expression containing array references to a scalar variable. This must be handled by introducing a temporary parallel variable.

To vary the number of array elements being manipulated in parallel the user can directly enable and disable any of the processing elements by means of a special logical variable called MODE. MODE is a 64-bit word with each bit corresponding to a processing element. The bits can be selectively turned on and off corresponding to processing elements being enabled or disabled. MODE therefore describes the current state of the machine. For example, the assignment statement

MODE = ON .TURN OFF. 51.TO.64

will enable the first 50 processing elements only. ON is a logical constant representing 64 ones. TURN OFF is a logical operator which sets bits 51 to 64 to zero. The mode remains set until changed by a later statement. If the above MODE statement preceded the statements of the matrix multiplication example, then only the minimum number of processing elements required for the example would be used to execute the instructions. Individual processing elements can be enabled as follows

MODE = OFF .TURN ON. I

where OFF is a logical constant representing 64 zeros, TURN ON is a logical operator which resets bit I meaning that only processing element I is enabled.

12.3 Conditional statements

In order to provide more flexibility when setting the state of the machine the MODE variable can be assigned the result of a test expression which contains parallel variables. For example

PE INTEGER A(*), B(*)
MODE = A(*).LT.0

will test the 64 values of A and for those values which are negative the corresponding MODE bits are set to one with the other bits being set to zero. The pattern of processing elements as determined by the mode variable are enabled and then applied to the statements which follow.

This pattern remains effective until a new processing pattern is established. For example, in the following statements if $A(1) = -1$ and $A(64) = -1$ with all other values of A positive then in the statements

```
MODE = A(*).LT.0
A(*) = - A(*)
B(*) = A(*)
```

only processing elements 1 and 64 will be enabled and only elements 1 and 64 of A and B will be changed.

The same processing pattern can be established by means of an IF statement without the use of the MODE variable, however the range of statements to which the processing pattern is applied may be different. For example, executing the statements

```
IF (A(*).LT.0) A(*) = - A(*)
B(*) = A(*)
```

using the above values for A would ensure that all the values of A were positive by changing only elements 1 and 64. However, all the values of B would be changed since the processing pattern is only established for the range of the IF statement.

The earlier examples which were used to illustrate the difficulties of conditional statements for the detection of parallelism languages such as Cray FORTRAN can be expressed in CFD using the IF statement. For example, updating the elements of an array X as a result of a comparison between other array values can be expressed as:

```
        PE INTEGER X(*,4), A(*,4), B(*,4), C(*,4), D(*,4)
        - - -
        DO 3 I = 1,4
          X(*,I) = A(*,I)
          IF (B(*,I).GT.C(*,I)) X(*,I) = D(*,I)
3       CONTINUE
```

All the elements of X are assigned their corresponding value of A after which only certain elements of X are updated as a result of the test expression. The statements are applied to 64 elements each time round the loop, again two-dimensional arrays have been used to accommodate the fixed size of the first dimension.

In addition to the logical connections .AND., .OR., .NOT., the CFD language also provides the quantifiers .ANY. and .ALL.. This enables a test to be applied across the elements of an array. For example, given the declaration PE REAL Y(*) the statement IF(.ANY.(Y(*).LT.0.0)) Y(*) = 0.0 means that if at least one of the elements of Y is negative then all of the elements of Y will be assigned the value zero.

12.4   Index interdependencies

In the detection of parallelism languages considered previously, index interdependencies prevent vectorization since the values required were already in a functional unit. In the expression of machine parallelism languages under consideration in this section index interdependencies also require special treatment by the user. This arises even though array processors do not have the pipelining problems which are associated with vector processors and corresponds to data being moved between processing elements whenever an index interdependency occurs.

As a result, a dependency between the indices of a parallel variable in CFD must be explicitly catered for by the programmer. As far as the Illiac IV is concerned it corresponds to the movement of a data value from one processing element memory to another processing element memory. This is referred to as routing or intercommunication of the values.

Routing between the elements of the same or a different array is specified in CFD by associating the distance the data values should be moved with respect to the implicit index. For example, in the case of different arrays the statement

   $B(*) = A(* + 1)$

means that the elements of A will be moved one position to the left before being assigned to B, that is, the following assignments take place in parallel

   $B(1) = A(2), B(2) = A(3), ---, B(64) = A(1).$

Note, the value A(1) has been shifted off one end and appeared at the other end.

All routing is performed before the assignments take place thus avoiding the updating problems which can occur with vector processors when they are performing a similar operation.

In general a positive expression attached to the implicit index means that the values are moved to the left and then the assignment is carried out. Elements which are moved off one end of the array reappear at the other end, thus it is a cyclic rotation. A negative expression attached to the implicit index means that the values are moved to the right before the assignment is performed. For example, the statement

   $A(*) = A(* - 1)$

is equivalent to the 64 assignments

   $A(1) = A(64), A(2) = A(1), A(3) = A(2), ---, A(64) = A(63)$

and corresponds to all the values of the array being moved to the right neighbouring position with the value of A(64) being assigned to A(1).

The solution of Laplace's equation, as considered in the last chapter, is another example in which index interdependencies occur. The solution requires each point in a grid to be updated using its immediate north, south, east and west neighbours. In CFD this must be expressed explicitly by associating routing values with the implicit indices for the east and west neighbours as in the following statements:

```
        PE REAL U(M,N)

        MODE = ON.TURN OFF. 1,64
        DO 1 J = 2,63
            U(*,J) = 0.25 × (U(*,J + 1) + U(*− 1,J) +
                            U(*+ 1,J) + U(*,J − 1))
 1      CONTINUE
```

this causes 62 elements of the array U to be simultaneously updated using their north, south, east and west neighbouring point values. All the routing operations are performed before the assignment takes place thus guaranteeing that the correct values are being used.

As stated above the routing of data in the Illiac IV corresponds to the moving of values among the processing element memories. How the processing elements are connected together affects the efficiency of such an operation. In the case of the Illiac IV a nearest neighbour connection scheme is used. To illustrate this connection scheme a 16 processing element system is shown in Figure 12.2; the numbers 0 to 15 are used to indicate the processing elements and the letters are used to indicate the connections.

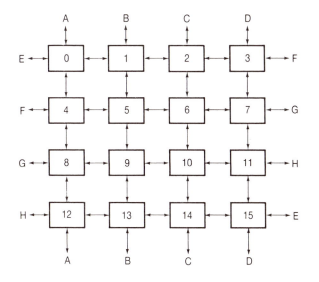

Figure 12.2   The Illiac IV interconnection scheme.

The immediate neighbours of the processing element i are given by the formula

(i + 1) MOD 16, (i − 1) MOD 16, (i + 4) MOD 16, (i − 4) MOD 16

where the operator MOD gives the remainder after division.

More specifically, the immediate neighbours of processing element 10 are 11, 9, 14, 6 while for processing element 1 the neighbours are 2, 0, 5, 13. Thus a routing distance of 1 or 4 is performed most efficiently on this scaled down Illiac IV. Since the processing elements are connected in this configuration any data values routed off the end of the array appear at the other end. On the Illiac IV itself, since it is of size 64 the most efficient routes are for distances of 1 and 8. Any other distance has to be performed in terms of the distances 1 or 8.

The user has to be careful if the problem solution requires an array with dimension greater than 64 and involves routing operations since the data will always be routed in units of 64.

In general the interconnection scheme has a direct influence on the successful exploitation of parallelism. Ensuring that the right data is available to the right processor at the right time is necessary to keep as many processing elements as busy as possible. Thus if the user is aware of how the processing elements are connected the efficiency of some programs may be improved.

As an example consider the problem of summing 64 elements, each of which is resident in a different processing element memory. Such a problem gives an insight into the kind of techniques which are required when programming an array processor and how routing can be used.

Without any attempt to perform the sum in parallel the calculation would require 63 additions. However if neighbouring values were added, then values a distance 2 apart, then values a distance 4 apart, the sum could be obtained after $\log_2 64$ additions. For example, on an 8-processor system, the addition stages are as follows:

	P1	P2	P3	P4	P5	P6	P7	P8
Add elements 1 apart	1	2	3	4	5	6	7	8
Add elements 2 apart	3	5	7	9	11	13	15	9
Add elements 4 apart	10	14	18	22	26	22	18	14
	36	36	36	36	36	36	36	36

Since the values have been rotated across all the processing elements the answer to the summation is contained in each processing element's memory.

This can be coded in CFD by employing a routing distance which increases by a factor of 2 each time round a loop as in

```
J = 1
DO 6 I = 1,6
    A(*) = A(*) + A(*+ J)
```

```
            J = J * 2
  6      CONTINUE
```

Each element is added to a neighbouring element each time round the loop; the neighbours are $2^n (n = 0,1,2,3,4)$ distance away on each iteration. At the end of the loop all the elements of A contain the sum of the elements.

When programming an array processor it is therefore useful to be aware of, first the number of processing elements available, and second how the data is allocated in the memory. Recall that each processing element has its own local memory in which data can be placed and easily accessed.

Thus if we are considering a matrix then the way in which it is arranged in memory and how it is to be manipulated are important considerations. If the rows of the matrix are laid out across the local memories of the processing elements then accessing and manipulating the array by rows in parallel is straightforward. It is also possible to select any combination of elements provided the selection is one per column, since each processing element has its own index register. For example, on a 4-processing element system with the matrix arranged as follows:

$P1$	$P2$	$P3$	$P4$
a_{11}	a_{12}	a_{13}	a_{14}
a_{21}	a_{22}	a_{23}	a_{24}
a_{31}	a_{32}	a_{33}	a_{34}
a_{41}	a_{42}	a_{43}	a_{44}

the selection of the row

$a_{11} \ a_{12} \ a_{13} \ a_{14}$

or any row is easily established.

It is also straightforward to reference the diagonal

$a_{11} \ a_{22} \ a_{33} \ a_{44}$

or any combination of elements such as

$a_{21} \ a_{42} \ a_{13} \ a_{44}$

where one element is selected from each column.

However to select a column of this array means that all the processing elements except one would be idle and this would lead to memory bank conflicts with resulting poor program performance. Thus any program which consists of row and then column manipulations would require a matrix transformation between manipulations to improve its efficiency. The programmer should be aware of this problem when constructing the program.

If the data is skewed, that is, each row is shifted one place compared to the previous row then some of these problems can be solved. For example, if the matrix is skewed as follows:

P1	P2	P3	P4
a_{11}	a_{12}	a_{13}	a_{14}
a_{24}	a_{21}	a_{22}	a_{23}
a_{33}	a_{34}	a_{31}	a_{32}
a_{42}	a_{43}	a_{44}	a_{41}

each row can be easily referenced as can each column. However the diagonal has been placed in only two processing element memories and it is therefore not so efficiently manipulated.

Hence the storage allocation scheme is something which a programmer should be aware of when using the Illiac IV to avoid introducing major inefficiencies to a program.

12.5   Independent indexing

The selection and manipulation of a contiguous series of elements is straightforward to specify in the existing languages for array and vector processors. Such a group of elements is easy to fetch from memory and easy to manipulate. However the selection and manipulation of a series of random elements as required with independent indexing is sometimes difficult to perform in parallel. The usual means of indicating such a random selection of elements from a two- or higher-dimensional array is to use a second integer array to specify the required index positions in the first array.

A simple example is to update the diagonal elements of a matrix which can be expressed in CFD as

```
PE INTEGER INDEX(*)
DATA INDEX/1,2,3,- - - 64/
- - -
A(*,INDEX(*)) = A(*,INDEX(*)) + 1.0
```

Since each processing element has its own index register this operation can be performed in parallel.

A more general indexing pattern can be established by assigning the appropriate values to the indexing array INDEX and providing the data has been arranged so that each processing element has to fetch only one operand from its local memory the operation can be performed in parallel. If this last condition is not fulfilled then the operation of independent indexing cannot be performed in parallel.

Examples of this situation are gather and scatter operations. These operations can be represented in sequential FORTRAN as

```
      DO 12 I = 1, 64
        A(I,INDEX(I)) = B(I)
12    CONTINUE
```

where the values of B(I) are scattered throughout the array A.

The complementary operation is the gather operation, namely,

```
      DO 12 I = 1, 64
        B(I) = A(I,INDEX(I))
12    CONTINUE
```

where the values of A are gathered into the contiguous elements of the array B. When translated into CFD these operations involve the routing of many values by different distances and cannot therefore be performed in parallel.

12.6 Subprograms and input/output

Several standard functions have been provided in CFD to enable operations to be applied across the 64 elements of an array. These functions can be used for example to find either the maximum, minimum or sum of the elements. CFD also enables a programmer to construct subroutines and functions using any of the previously described program and data structures.

One of the major defects of the language is the availability of only primitive facilities for handling the input and output of data. The Illiac IV has a very small main store compared with its backing store. The data must be carefully arranged on the backing store by the user in such a way that when it is moved into the main store it is spread uniformly across the processing elements. The arrangement of the data on the backing store can have a crucial effect on the efficiency of a program.

WRITE, READ and DISK statements are the means available to a user to move the data between the main and backing stores. A WAIT statement is also available to enable synchronization between a transfer of data from the memory and its subsequent use. The programming required to handle input/output requires careful consideration and serves to distract the programmer from the main programming objective.

12.7 Summary

The advantage of a language like CFD is that the syntax is based on the parallelism of the underlying hardware and enables the generation of efficient object code.

The disadvantage is that if the problem parallelism does not match the parallelism of the machine the user must change the data structures. This can add significantly to the complexity of the problem solution and cause a programmer to restructure the program. This, in turn, can lead to difficulties if the program is required to be modified.

EXERCISES

12.1 Consider a scaled down Illiac IV with only 4 processing elements. Devise a CFD program which will multiply

(a)   a vector of size 3 with a 3 × 3 matrix ;

(b)   two 3 × 3 matrices.

12.2 Devise a CFD program for finding the inverse of an 8 × 8 triangular matrix on the Illiac IV.

12.3 Using the Newton-Raphson formula

$$X_n = 0.5 \times (X_{n-1} + X_0 / X_{n-1})$$

determine the square root of 64 values stored in the one-dimensional array A.

12.4 Devise a CFD program which will sum the 64 values, one value in each PE memory, such that the result is to be found in the first PE memory only.

12.5 Construct a CFD program which will sort

(a)   the values of a 64-element array;

(b)   the values of a 64 × 64-element matrix.

Chapter 13 Distributed Array Processor FORTRAN

13.1 Hardware considerations

A second example of the expression of machine parallelism languages is the language available on the ICL DAP (Distributed Array Processor) and known as DAP FORTRAN. This language, unlike the Illiac IV language considered in the last chapter, enables a second dimension of parallelism to be associated with a data declaration which matches that available on the machine.

A brief divergence to consider the main characteristics of the DAP is useful before considering the main features of the language. The DAP consists of an array of identical processors or processing elements. The size of the array is 64 × 64 giving a total of 4096 processing elements. Each processor is very simple in that it consists of three registers and can perform a set of simple instructions. The instructions operate on the registers and the available store. The store available to a processing element is 4K bits and each processor is a bit rather than a word processor. Apart from the larger number of processing elements this is one of the major differences with the Illiac IV. However such a difference is transparent to a user of the machine.

There is in addition a Master Control Unit (MCU) which acts as a co-ordinator for the processing elements. The MCU selects the next instruction to be executed and either executes it itself or broadcasts it to the processing elements. One of the registers, known as the activity register, determines whether a processing element participates in a broadcast instruction. Thus any pattern of the 4096 processing elements can participate in a broadcast instruction as determined by the status of their activity register. The MCU can perform some scalar operations such as the control of DO loop variables and certain centralized functions, however like the Illiac IV the main processing power lies in the processing elements. Thus, the DAP is also a single instruction multiple data stream machine. The major differences between the DAP and the Illiac IV are that the number of processing elements has been increased substantially and that each processing element has reduced processing power.

The DAP is hosted by an ICL 2900 series machine and does not act as a back end processor. It is an integral part of the 2900 and if it is not being used as an array processor it can be used as a store module of the host computer. Each processing element is allocated to a semiconductor store chip in the module. Hence once data has been loaded into the store it may be processed by the 2900 or the DAP. There is no overhead associated with loading the DAP and the DAP user has access to all the host machine's features.

Thus the overall architecture of the DAP itself is similar to the Illiac IV, a control unit with many processing elements, however the languages used to program each machine, although based on FORTRAN, have little in common in their parallel features.

13.2   Data types and statements

As in CFD on the Illiac IV the architecture of the DAP is reflected in its principal programming language. It contains three basic data types: scalars, vectors and matrices where a vector is an array of size 64, and a matrix is a two-dimensional array of size 64×64. Vectors and matrices may be treated either as sets of individual items or more efficiently as entire arrays.

The declaration of variables of these types is introduced to a program as follows:

```
DIMENSION A( ), BB( , )
INTEGER II( , )
LOGICAL F( )
```

Since the dimensions of a vector and a matrix are constrained to be 64 and 64×64 respectively they are omitted in a declaration statement. In DAP terminology they are referred to as constrained dimensions. In the above example there are two matrices BB and II of type real and integer, respectively, and two vectors A and F of type real and logical respectively. A matrix may also be regarded as a one-dimensional set of 4096 values, obtained by joining successive columns of the matrix end to end; it is then referred to as a long vector.

Arrays of vectors and matrices can be declared by introducing higher dimensioned variables. For example,

```
REAL AA( ,3), BBB( , ,5)
```

declares an array AA of 3 vectors and an array BBB of 5 matrices. A maximum of 7 dimensions may be specified with at most two constrained dimensions.

An individual element of a vector is selected by specifying the required index. For example, given

```
REAL AVEC( )
```

then AVEC(I) selects the Ith element of the 64-element vector AVEC. The complete vector is referenced by writing AVEC( ) or AVEC.

A similar means is used when referencing parts of a matrix. For example, given the declaration

REAL AMAT(,)

then   AMAT(I,J)   references an individual element,
        AMAT(I,)   references the Ith row,
        AMAT(,J)   references the Jth column, and
        AMAT(,)   or AMAT references all 64 × 64 elements.

A null subscript is interpreted as the selection of a complete dimension whenever it occurs in an array reference.

The same techniques can be applied to higher dimensioned variables. For example, given the declaration of the four matrices

REAL AAA(, ,4)

then   AAA(I,J,2)   selects the IJth element of the second matrix,
        AAA(3, ,2)   selects the third row of the second matrix,
        AAA(,3,2)   selects the third column of the second matrix, and
        AAA(, ,2)   selects the entire second matrix.

Vectors and matrices can be indexed either directly as above or by using a logical array to mask out those values that are not required. For example, given the declarations

REAL AVEC( ), AMAT(,)
LOGICAL LV( ), LM(,)

then AVEC(LV) selects the element of AVEC for which LV has the value TRUE. The logical vector LV must have one, and only one, value TRUE. The expression AMAT(LM) references the elements for which the values of the logical matrix LM are TRUE. In addition, a logical vector in one of the index positions of a matrix references either a row or a column of that matrix, that is, AMAT(LV,) references the Ith row if the value of LV(I) is TRUE.

A programmer can form expressions using either vectors or matrices and specify an assignment to a variable of a similar type. For example, given the declarations

REAL AA(,), BB(,), CC(,)
REAL VEC1( ), VEC2( ), VEC3( )

then the statements

VEC3( ) = VEC1( ) + VEC2( )
AA(,) = BB(,) + CC(,)

correspond to the addition of vectors VEC1 and VEC2 to give VEC3. The addition is performed on an element by element basis. Similarly the

64×64 matrices **BB** and **CC** are added to give **AA**, the 4096 additions are performed in parallel.

A vector or matrix can alternatively be specified without the parentheses thus the assignments

    VEC3 = VEC1 + VEC2
     AA = BB + CC

are equivalent to the above statements.

If a scalar is assigned to a vector or matrix, the scalar will be expanded the required number of times so that each element of the vector or matrix is assigned the scalar value. Assignment of a vector to a matrix or vice versa is not allowed since there is an incompatibility of types across the assignment operator. However a row or column of a matrix can be assigned to a vector since they are both of the same type.

If the above indexing techniques are used on the left side of an assignment statement they determine which elements of a vector or matrix are to be updated. In effect certain elements are masked out and not updated. For example, the statement

    VEC1(LV) = VEC2

sets VEC1(I) equal to VEC2(I) if and only if LV(I) has the value TRUE. This is equivalent to the statements VEC1(I) = VEC2 or VEC1(I) = VEC2(I). The left side of the assignment statement determines which element is updated.

If the logical vector LV has several values TRUE then all the corresponding elements of the vector VEC1 are updated. Thus it is the left side of the assignment operator which determines which elements of the vector are updated.

Similarly for the case of matrices, the statement

    MAT1(LM) = MAT2

updates only those elements of the matrix MAT1 for which the logical matrix LM has the value TRUE.

There is considerable flexibility in the processing patterns which can be established by using scalars, logical vectors or matrices in the index positions of a matrix. For example, the assignment

    AMAT(,LV) = AVEC

assigns the vector AVEC to those columns selected by the logical vector LV while

    AMAT(,IS) = AVEC

selects just one column corresponding to the value of the scalar IS and assigns the vector AVEC to that column.

The above technique can be used to handle the case which was referred to in previous chapters as independent indexing. For example, given the declarations

```
REAL AMAT( , )
INTEGER IV( )
```

then AMAT(,IV) on the left side of the assignment operator can be used to select components of the matrix from consecutive columns and from rows determined by IV, that is, the elements AMAT(I,IV(I)) for I from 1 to 64. If IV contains the values 1 to 64 this corresponds to the selection of the main diagonal of the matrix.

Thus there is considerable flexibility in the way in which the elements of a matrix can be accessed in DAP FORTRAN.

13.3   Data alignment

The problems of routing which corresponds to moving values from the memory of one processing element to another memory is more involved on the DAP than the Illiac IV. On the DAP not only do we have the problems associated with routing the values of a vector but also the problems of routing the values of a matrix.

The processing elements of the DAP are arranged in an array and connected with a nearest neighbour interconnection scheme, that is, each processing element is connected to its north, south, east and west neighbours. The connections at the sides of the array are connected to those on the opposite side of the array. This hardware connection scheme is reflected in the language features which are concerned with data alignment.

A different notation is used depending on whether the shift is of distance one or greater. The nearest neighbour shifts are specified by using + or − as the default index and interpreted as follows: given

```
REAL AVEC( ), AMAT( , )
```

then   AVEC(+) means the vector is shifted one place left
and   AVEC(−) means the vector is shifted one place right.

Any value shifted off the end of one vector reappears at the other end thus AVEC( ) + AVEC(+) corresponds to the additions

```
AVEC(1) + AVEC(2), AVEC(2) + AVEC(3),... AVEC(64) + AVEC(1)
```

where the shifted value AVEC(1) has reappeared at the opposite end of the vector.

For a matrix there are four possibilities, namely,

```
AMAT(+, )  means the matrix is shifted one place north,
AMAT(−, )  means the matrix is shifted one place south,
```

AMAT(,+)   means the matrix is shifted one place west, and
AMAT(,−)   means the matrix is shifted one place east.

Any values shifted off one edge reappear at the opposite edge of the matrix. For example, on a 4 by 4 DAP when a north shift is applied the following data is produced:

$$
AMAT(,) = \begin{pmatrix} 1 & 2 & 3 & 4 \\ 5 & 6 & 7 & 8 \\ 9 & 10 & 11 & 12 \\ 13 & 14 & 15 & 16 \end{pmatrix} \quad AMAT(+,) = \begin{pmatrix} 5 & 6 & 7 & 8 \\ 9 & 10 & 11 & 12 \\ 13 & 14 & 15 & 16 \\ 1 & 2 & 3 & 4 \end{pmatrix}
$$

while for an east shift and a north-west shift the following data is produced:

$$
AMAT(,−) = \begin{pmatrix} 4 & 1 & 2 & 3 \\ 8 & 5 & 6 & 7 \\ 12 & 9 & 10 & 11 \\ 16 & 13 & 14 & 15 \end{pmatrix} \quad AMAT(+,+) = \begin{pmatrix} 6 & 7 & 8 & 5 \\ 10 & 11 & 12 & 9 \\ 14 & 15 & 16 & 13 \\ 2 & 3 & 4 & 1 \end{pmatrix}
$$

All shifts in these examples are applied to the original values of AMAT.

Hence, for example, a solution of Laplace's equation can be specified as

U(,) = 0.25 * (U(,−) + U(,+) + U(−,) + U(+,))

where U is the matrix on which a solution is to be found. The north, south, east and west values of each point are used in the calculation to produce a new value. All shifts are applied before the expression is evaluated.

Shift operators may be used in conjunction with the indexing techniques considered earlier in which case the appropriate shift is performed before the selection takes place. For example, the expression AMAT(3,+) shifts the matrix AMAT one position to the west and selects the third row of the resulting matrix. On a 4 by 4 DAP with the following values this corresponds to

$$
AMAT(,) = \begin{pmatrix} 1 & 2 & 3 & 4 \\ 5 & 6 & 7 & 8 \\ 9 & 10 & 11 & 12 \\ 13 & 14 & 15 & 16 \end{pmatrix} \quad AMAT(,+) = \begin{pmatrix} 2 & 3 & 4 & 1 \\ 6 & 7 & 8 & 5 \\ 10 & 11 & 12 & 9 \\ 14 & 15 & 16 & 13 \end{pmatrix}
$$

so that AMAT(3,+) is the vector consisting of the values 10, 11, 12, 9.

In the above examples when a vector or matrix shift is performed and a value is shifted off one edge it is shifted in at the opposite edge. It is also possible for values to be shifted off one edge and not reappear at an opposite end. The former type of shift in DAP terminology is referred to as a cyclic shift and the latter as a plane shift. The user specifies how the edge values are to be treated by means of a special GEOMETRY statement.

As shown above a matrix can be shifted in two directions, north-south or east-west, and the user can specify the type of geometry to be used in each of these directions when a shift is applied. The form of the statement to establish the geometry is

GEOMETRY(NS, EW)

where the two parameters determine how the edge values are to be treated in the north-south and east-west directions respectively. They may have either of the values PLANE or CYCLIC.

When a shift is performed in a direction for which PLANE geometry has been specified the values shifted in are zero, .FALSE., or the null character depending on the type of the vector or matrix. When a shift is performed in a direction for which CYCLIC geometry has been specified, values that are shifted off one end are shifted in at the opposite end.

By combining these two geometries in the north-south and east-west directions the DAP can be made to resemble a plane or a cylinder in either of two orientations. For example, on a 4 by 4 DAP with the following matrix of values:

$$AMAT(,) = \begin{pmatrix} 1 & 2 & 3 & 4 \\ 5 & 6 & 7 & 8 \\ 9 & 10 & 11 & 12 \\ 13 & 14 & 15 & 16 \end{pmatrix}$$

and GEOMETRY(PLANE, CYCLIC) then

$$AMAT(+,) = \begin{pmatrix} 5 & 6 & 7 & 8 \\ 9 & 10 & 11 & 12 \\ 13 & 14 & 15 & 16 \\ 0 & 0 & 0 & 0 \end{pmatrix} \quad AMAT(+,+) = \begin{pmatrix} 6 & 7 & 8 & 5 \\ 10 & 11 & 12 & 9 \\ 14 & 15 & 16 & 13 \\ 0 & 0 & 0 & 0 \end{pmatrix}$$

This example illustrates how on the shift north, zero values are shifted in while on the shift west values shifted off an edge reappear at the other edge. In the case of a vector, where shifts are made in one direction only, the NS parameter only is significant.

Matrix shifts which are to be made over a distance greater than 1 position must be performed by using specially provided functions which are formed from the following entities

SHift {North or South or East or West} {Plane or Cyclic}

giving rise to 8 possible combinations. This can occur with the movement of a matrix in one of the 4 cardinal directions with a choice of two geometries, namely, SHNP, SHNC, SHSP, SHSC, SHEP, SHEC, SHWP and SHWC.

SHEP(AMAT,2) means the matrix is shifted 2 positions to the east using plane geometry so that the first two columns of the matrix AMAT become zero, that is,

$$AMAT = \begin{pmatrix} 1 & 2 & 3 & 4 \\ 5 & 6 & 7 & 8 \\ 9 & 10 & 11 & 12 \\ 13 & 14 & 15 & 16 \end{pmatrix} \quad SHEP(AMAT,2) = \begin{pmatrix} 0 & 0 & 1 & 2 \\ 0 & 0 & 5 & 6 \\ 0 & 0 & 9 & 10 \\ 0 & 0 & 13 & 14 \end{pmatrix}$$

while SHEC(AMAT,2) means the first two columns are moved to last two columns of the matrix AMAT as in

$$AMAT = \begin{pmatrix} 1 & 2 & 3 & 4 \\ 5 & 6 & 7 & 8 \\ 9 & 10 & 11 & 12 \\ 13 & 14 & 15 & 16 \end{pmatrix} \quad SHEC(AMAT,2) = \begin{pmatrix} 3 & 4 & 1 & 2 \\ 7 & 8 & 5 & 6 \\ 11 & 12 & 9 & 10 \\ 15 & 16 & 13 & 14 \end{pmatrix}$$

These functions can be combined to perform shifts in more than one direction. For example, the shifts in the following expression

SHNP(SHEP(AMAT,2),2)

are illustrated in the following diagrams:

$$AMAT = \begin{pmatrix} 1 & 2 & 3 & 4 \\ 5 & 6 & 7 & 8 \\ 9 & 10 & 11 & 12 \\ 13 & 14 & 15 & 16 \end{pmatrix} \quad SHEP(AMAT,2) = \begin{pmatrix} 0 & 0 & 1 & 2 \\ 0 & 0 & 5 & 6 \\ 0 & 0 & 9 & 10 \\ 0 & 0 & 13 & 14 \end{pmatrix}$$

$$SHNP(SHEP(AMAT,2),2) = \begin{pmatrix} 0 & 0 & 9 & 10 \\ 0 & 0 & 13 & 14 \\ 0 & 0 & 0 & 0 \\ 0 & 0 & 0 & 0 \end{pmatrix}$$

It is also possible to shift each row or column of a matrix by a different distance. This is achieved by using a vector to specify the different shift distances. For example, the expression

SHEC(AMAT,AVEC)

where

$$AMAT = \begin{pmatrix} 1 & 2 & 3 & 4 \\ 5 & 6 & 7 & 8 \\ 9 & 10 & 11 & 12 \\ 13 & 14 & 15 & 16 \end{pmatrix} \qquad AVEC = (-1\ 0\ 1\ 2)$$

gives

$$SHEC(AMAT,AVEC) = \begin{pmatrix} 2 & 3 & 4 & 1 \\ 5 & 6 & 7 & 8 \\ 12 & 9 & 10 & 11 \\ 15 & 16 & 13 & 14 \end{pmatrix}$$

The functions SHRP, SHRC, SHLP and SHLC can be used to indicate right and left shifts greater than 1 position on vectors and are comprised from the entities

SHift {Right or Left} {Plane or Cyclic}

The function SHLC(AVEC,2) shifts the vector AVEC two places to the left using cyclic geometry.

A more substantial example of the use of a shift function occurs when it is required to sum the elements of a 64×64 matrix, AMAT. This summation can be performed in $\log_2 4096$ iterations by using a shift with increasing shift distances each time round a loop. A DAP FORTRAN segment to do this is

```
        REAL AMAT( , )
        J = 1
        DO 1 I = 1,12
            AMAT = AMAT + SHLP(AMAT,J)
            J = J + J
1       CONTINUE
```

In this solution the matrix is treated as a vector with 4096 elements. On the first iteration neighbouring values are added, on the second iteration values a distance 2 apart are added, etc. Because plane geometry is being used any values shifted off the edge are replaced by zero values at the other edge. Hence after 12 iterations the summation of the values is given in AMAT(1).

Thus there are many very flexible methods for a DAP programmer to specify the shifting and rotation of data for both vectors and matrices.

13.4   Conditional expressions

All the elements of an array are processed on the DAP except where a processing element is excluded by the programmer establishing a mask index either explicitly as above or by means of a logical expression. In both cases this corresponds to the activity registers of some of the processing elements being set, enabling those processing elements to execute the broadcast instruction. A logical expression can be established as follows, given the declaration

REAL AMAT(,)

whose elements are already assigned values then

AMAT.GT.0.0

enables a logical matrix of values to be established with a value true where the corresponding value of AMAT is positive. This matrix of logical values can then be used as a mask in a subsequent assignment statement as in

AA(AMAT.GT.0.0) = 0.0

The result of this statement's execution is that the value 0.0 is assigned to the elements of the matrix AA where the corresponding elements of AMAT are positive.

The use of logical matrices expands the flexibility of the DAP since the above example can also be written as

```
REAL AMAT( , ), AA( , )
LOGICAL NONZER( , )
– – –
NONZER = AMAT.GT.0.0
AA(NONZER) = 0.0
```

More specifically if

$$
\text{AMAT} = \begin{pmatrix} -1.0 & 1.0 & 1.0 & -1.0 \\ 1.0 & -1.0 & -1.0 & 1.0 \\ 1.0 & -1.0 & -1.0 & 1.0 \\ -1.0 & 1.0 & 1.0 & -1.0 \end{pmatrix} \quad \text{then NONZER} = \begin{pmatrix} F & T & T & F \\ T & F & F & T \\ T & F & F & T \\ F & T & T & F \end{pmatrix}
$$

where F represents false and T represents true. Hence after the execution of the second assignment statement we have:

$$
\text{AA(NONZER)} = \begin{pmatrix} -1.0 & 0.0 & 0.0 & -1.0 \\ 0.0 & -1.0 & -1.0 & 0.0 \\ 0.0 & -1.0 & -1.0 & 0.0 \\ -1.0 & 0.0 & 0.0 & -1.0 \end{pmatrix}
$$

The GOTO and DO statements of FORTRAN are also available in DAP FORTRAN and can be used in conjunction with expressions containing vectors and matrices provided that they evaluate to single scalar values.

13.5 Subprograms

DAP FORTRAN provides a set of functions which take vectors and matrices as arguments. For example, the SUM function which returns the scalar sum of all the components of its vector or matrix argument while the functions SUMC and SUMR return vectors obtained by summing all the columns or rows of a single matrix argument respectively.

Two other interesting and useful functions are MATC and MATR which take a vector as an argument. MATC returns a matrix whose columns are equal to the vector argument as in:

$$
V = (1\ 2\ 3\ 4)
$$

$$
\text{MATC(V)} = \begin{pmatrix} 1 & 1 & 1 & 1 \\ 2 & 2 & 2 & 2 \\ 3 & 3 & 3 & 3 \\ 4 & 4 & 4 & 4 \end{pmatrix}
$$

while MATR returns a matrix whose rows are equal to the vector argument as in:

$$V = (1\ 2\ 3\ 4)$$

$$MATR(V) = \begin{pmatrix} 1\ 2\ 3\ 4 \\ 1\ 2\ 3\ 4 \\ 1\ 2\ 3\ 4 \\ 1\ 2\ 3\ 4 \end{pmatrix}$$

By using these functions the problem of multiplying two 64×64 matrices can utilize the full parallelism of the machine. As in the following code segment

```
      INTEGER AA( , ), BB( , ), CC( , )
      CC = 0
      DO 1 K = 1,64
          CC = CC + MATC(AA( ,K)) * MATR(BB(K, ))
1     CONTINUE
```

Each column of AA is used to form a matrix, while each row of BB is used to form a second matrix. The corresponding elements in the two matrices are then multiplied. This process is repeated for each column of AA and row of BB with the results being summed. For example, on a 2×2 DAP with the following initial values:

$$AA = (1\ 2) \quad BB = (5\ 6) \quad CC = (0\ 0)$$
$$(3\ 4) \quad (7\ 8) \quad (0\ 0)$$

on the first iteration we have:

$$CC = CC + (1\ 1) \times (5\ 6) = (\ 5\ \ 6)$$
$$(3\ 3) \quad (5\ 6) \quad (15\ 18)$$

and on the second iteration:

$$CC = (\ 5\ \ 6) + (2\ 2) \times (7\ 8)$$
$$(15\ 18) \quad (4\ 4) \quad (7\ 8)$$

giving the final result for matrix multiplication of:

$$CC = (19\ 22)$$
$$(43\ 50)$$

DAP FORTRAN provides a standard function TRAN which will transpose a matrix. For example, on a 4×4 DAP the effect is as follows:

$$LM = \begin{pmatrix} F\ F\ T\ T \\ T\ T\ F\ F \\ T\ F\ T\ F \\ F\ T\ T\ F \end{pmatrix}$$

$$TRAN(LM) = \begin{pmatrix} F\ T\ T\ F \\ F\ T\ F\ T \\ T\ F\ T\ T \\ T\ F\ F\ F \end{pmatrix}$$

This can be used even for matrices which are greater than the size of the DAP. For example, assuming we have a 4×4 DAP and wish to transpose a 16×16 matrix. This can be achieved by dividing it into four equal submatrices, transposing each submatrix and then exchanging the off diagonal submatrices. This can be programmed as on a 4×4 DAP

```
        REAL A( , ,2,2), T( , )
C       store 16 × 16 matrix as four 4 × 4 submatrices

C       transpose each submatrix

        A( , , 1,1) = TRAN(A( , ,1,1))
        A( , , 2,2) = TRAN(A( , ,2,2))
        A( , , 1,2) = TRAN(A( , ,1,2))
        A( , , 2,1) = TRAN(A( , ,2,1))
C       exchange the off-diagonal submatrices

        T( , ) = A( , , 1,2)
        A( , ,1,2) = A( , ,2,1)
        A( , ,2,1) = T( , )
```

The same principle can be applied to even larger matrices.

There are many other DAP standard functions which are provided to enable users to exploit the parallel processing capability of the machine.

User defined functions and subroutines are also possible. The arguments may be scalars, vectors or matrices. In addition a function can return a scalar, vector or matrix result.

COMMON and EQUIVALENCE statements are also available, however the programmer must be careful because scalars, vectors and matrices are each mapped onto the DAP store in different ways.

DAP FORTRAN has no input/output facilities and all calls from the host computer are parameterless subroutine calls, data is passed between the host and the DAP sections of a program via named COMMON blocks. The DAP FORTRAN COMMON blocks are held in the DAP store, but are accessible to both the DAP and the host.

13.6 Summary

Thus, like CFD for the Illiac IV, DAP FORTRAN is based on the syntax of the underlying machine architecture. This facilitates the generation of code within the compiler. However, if the parallelism required in the application does not match the parallelism of the machine this requires the programmer to modify the data structures. This, in turn, can cause difficulties if the program is required to be modified.

DAP FORTRAN does provide an extra dimension of parallelism in both the declaration and manipulation of data structures and provides extremely flexible methods of shifting and masking data structures. However, all operations are based on the factor of 64.

Hence because of their machine dependency these languages do not form a basis on which languages for this type of parallel programming can evolve.

EXERCISES

13.1 Construct a DAP FORTRAN program to multiply a matrix by a vector.

13.2 On a 4 × 4 DAP with the following declarations

```
INTEGER S
INTEGER V( )
INTEGER AMAT ( , )

S = 4
V = (1,2,3,4)
            /1 5  9 13\
AMAT   =   | 2 6 10 14 |
           | 3 7 11 15 |
            \4 8 12 16/
```

Evaluate the following statements

(a) AMAT = MATR(V)

(b) AMAT = MATC(VEC(S))

(c) AMAT = AMAT − MATR(V + S)

13.3 Construct a DAP FORTRAN program which will calculate the exponential of each component of a real matrix.

13.4 Construct a DAP FORTRAN program which will take a vector of integers and use this to select from a vector of characters the characters corresponding to the vector of integers.

13.5 Given a 64 × 64 matrix **AMAT** generate the numbers 1 to 4096 and assign them to the elements of AMAT such that the element (i,j) contains the value

$$1 + (i − 1) + 64 * (j − 1)$$

Hint A solution can be obtained using the built-in function ALT(N) which returns a vector with alternating groups of N TRUE and FALSE components.

13.6 Determine the solution of the quadratic equation

$$Ax^2 + Bx + C = 0$$

for N^2 sets of values A, B and C on the DAP ($N = 64$).

13.7 Construct a DAP FORTRAN program to sort N^2 numbers ($N = 64$) using the Bubblesort technique.

EXPRESSION OF PROBLEM
PARALLELISM LANGUAGES

Chapter 14 **Actus: a Pascal Based Language**

14.1 Introduction

The synchronous parallel programming language described in this chapter differs from the previous languages which were considered for programming array and vector processors in that this language is not biased towards either existing programs or existing machine architectures. The language considered, Actus (Perrott, 1979), follows the programming philosophy which emerged for sequential machine architectures, namely, that programming features should be independent of any particular hardware.

The approach used in designing the language has been to consider the problem areas in which such computers are used, and to isolate the relevant features of the problems. The next step was to form the syntactic and semantic rules for these abstractions while at the same time trying to ensure that a compiler for these features could be reasonably efficiently implemented. In this way the parallelism of the problem can be expressed directly. Actus is, therefore, an example of an expression of problem parallelism type language.

The language enables the user:

1. to ignore the idiosyncrasies of the hardware;
2. to express the problem parallelism directly;
3. to design a problem solution in terms of a varying rather than a fixed extent of parallel processing;
4. to control parallel processing through explicit control structures and through the data, as applicable.

More specifically, Actus extends the program and data structures of Pascal (with the exception of sets, variant records and pointers) for this type of parallel programming. In effect, the language has adopted those structures which are thought to be appropriate for a scientifically orientated programming language, and it has incorporated extensions to enable the user to take advantage of the parallel nature of array and vector processors.

Since these parallel computers were developed as a means of performing the same operation on independent data in parallel, it is the data which should indicate the extent of parallelism. To realize this principle in a high level language, it is proposed that each declaration of a data item should have associated with it a maximum extent of parallelism.

The extent of parallelism on an array processor is the number of processors that could logically compute upon a particular data structure at the same time (this may be greater than, less than or equal to the number of actual processors available); for a vector processor it is the length of the data structure presented to the processor for computation. The extent of parallelism is, thus, explicitly indicated by the data declarations and manipulated by the language statements.

It should be emphasized that the extent of parallelism is a central concept in the language and enables a joint syntax for programming array and vector processors to be developed.

The main features of the language are

1. user constructed data types and program structuring facilities;
2. a means of expressing the parallel nature of a problem at the data declaration and statement level;
3. static control of the extent of parallelism by means of index sets;
4. dynamic control of parallelism;
5. alignment of operands and independent indexing.

The following sections contain a description of particular features of Actus and demonstrate the philosophy of machine independent programming for array and vector processors.

14.2   Data types

The array data structure is the only structure which can be declared to have an extent of parallelism. It is used as a means of expressing the extent of the parallel actions which are intended to be applied to that data structure. Scalar variables therefore include all the data structures declared in a program except those arrays which have an extent of parallelism.

For example, in the declarations

```
const
  N = 200 ;
var
  PARALLEL : array [1:N] of REAL ;
  SCALAR : array [1..N] of REAL ;
```

the parallel dots : indicate that the maximum extent of parallelism for the array PARALLEL is N. The N elements can be manipulated in identical fashion at the same time. Thus an expression involving PARALLEL[1:200] will cause all 200 elements of the array to be accessed in parallel. In contrast the elements of the array SCALAR can only be manipulated one element at a time.

In general, PARALLEL[I:J] will select the elements from I to J inclusive from the declared extent of parallelism, where I >= lower index and J <= upper index and J >= I, otherwise an error occurs. Thus, I and J can vary dynamically in a loop, for example, provided they adhere to these conditions.

Unlike the previous FORTRAN based languages a parallel array can be declared to have elements of any of the language's available simple or structured types. For example,

```
type
  POSITION = record
                X, Y, Z : REAL
             end ;
  DIRECTION = (NORTH, SOUTH, EAST, WEST) ;
var
  COMPASS1, COMPASS2 : array [−180:180] of DIRECTION ;
  POINT : array [1:2000] of POSITION ;
```

and the expression POINT[1:2000].X will access all the X co-ordinates of the 2000 points in parallel.

Thus, the data declarations are used to indicate the maximum number of elements that can be considered in parallel as well as the type of the elements.

In Actus, as in the previous languages, operations are applied on an element by element basis for expressions which involve more than one parallel variable. In addition, the extent of parallelism must be the same for all the parallel operands, that is, individual elements of the arrays are paired off and the operation applied. For example, the expression

```
A[1:50] * B[1:50]
```

causes each element of array A to be multiplied by the corresponding element of array B, in parallel.

In the case of an expression involving a parallel variable and a constant or scalar variable, these latter two entities can be regarded as assuming the extent or parallelism of the parallel variable for the purposes of expression evaluation.

When declaring a two- or higher-dimensioned array to be operated upon in parallel, the programmer must indicate the index with which the extent of parallelism is to be associated. The declaration

```
const
  M = 200 ; N = 100 ;
var
  GRID : array [1:M, 1..N] of REAL ;
```

indicates a two-dimensional array with dimensions M and N; the M × N elements are of type REAL. The array is to be processed in parallel M elements at a time as indicated by the parallel dots : in the first index. Hence, a maximum of M elements can be accessed in parallel and the second or sequential index is used to select the particular M elements. For example, the declaration

```
var
  BB : array [1:4, 1..5] of INTEGER ;
```

represents the elements

```
BB[1,1] BB[1,2] BB[1,3] BB[1,4] BB[1,5]
BB[2,1] BB[2,2] BB[2,3] BB[2,4] BB[2,5]
BB[3,1] BB[3,2] BB[3,3] BB[3,4] BB[3,5]
BB[4,1] BB[4,2] BB[4,3] BB[4,4] BB[4,5]
```

The declaration indicates that a maximum of four elements can be processed in parallel; selected from different rows with the second index indicating which column. More specifically, BB[1:4,2] is equivalent to referencing BB[1,2] BB[2,2] BB[3,2] BB[4,2] in parallel; BB[2:3,1] is equivalent to referencing BB[2,1] BB[3,1] in parallel and BB[4:4,1] references the single element BB[4,1]. Hence, this array can be efficiently referenced by column but not by row.

A declaration such as

```
const
  P = 60 ; Q = 150 ;
var
  GRID1 : array [1..P, 1:Q] of INTEGER ;
```

indicates that the user wishes to process the array in parallel by rows (or part rows) rather than columns; Q elements can be envisaged as being selected in parallel. Hence, it is possible to select a complete row or part of a row for parallel processing.

For example, the declaration

```
var
  CC : array [1..5, 1:3] of INTEGER ;
```

represents the elements

```
CC[1,1] CC[1,2] CC[1,3]
CC[2,1] CC[2,2] CC[2,3]
CC[3,1] CC[3,2] CC[3,3]
CC[4,1] CC[4,2] CC[4,3]
CC[5,1] CC[5,2] CC[5,3]
```

A maximum of three elements can be selected for parallel processing; the elements are selected from different columns with the first index indicating which row.

Example: linear transformation

To illustrate some of the above features consider the multiplication of a matrix AA of dimensions M * N by a vector W of length N, that is,

U[M] = AA[M , N] * W[N]

The method used is to multiply, in parallel, the elements of a column of AA with a single element of W; this will be repeated for each column of AA and each element of W. After each multiplication, the results are added. (The statements which are used in the solution are treated in more detail in later sections.)

```
const
  M = 200 ; N = 123 ; (*arbitrary values*)
var
  AA : array [1:M, 1..N] of REAL ;
  W : array [1..N] of REAL ;
  U : array [1:M] of REAL ;
  J : 1..N ;
begin
  U[1:M] := 0.0 ;   (* all elements of U assigned zero *)
  for J := 1 to N do   (* repeat N times *)
    U[1:M] := U[1:M] + AA[1:M,J] * W[J]
end.
```

Example: initialization

Another example which illustrates the flexibility which can be applied to the extent of parallelism is to initialize the elements of an array BB to 0 above the main diagonal and 1 elsewhere.

```
const
  N = 100 ;
var
  BB : array [1..N, 1:N] of INTEGER ;
  I : 1..N ;
begin
  for I := 1 to N − 1 do
    begin
      BB[I,1:I] := 1 ;
      BB[I,(I + 1):N] := 0
    end ;
  BB[N,1:N] := 1
end.
```

The extent of parallelism is changed each time round the loop as each row of BB is manipulated. On each iteration the elements of a row of the array BB are assigned either the value zero or one. The last row where each value is the same has been treated separately.

Thus, compared to the earlier languages, Actus offers more flexibility in how data may be structured and how the extent of parallelism may be associated with that structure. However, the evaluation of expressions which contain parallel variables is like earlier languages based on element by element pairing.

14.3 Parallel constants

Constant identifiers can be defined which have more than one value and can subsequently be used in expressions or assignments to parallel variables; the number of values must be the same as the extent of parallelism of the variable or expression. The form of a parallel constant is as follows:

```
parconst
  SEQUENCE = 1:50 ;
```

which causes the 50 sequential values 1, 2, 3 ..., 50 to be recorded and identified by the identifier SEQUENCE.

The following example illustrates the use of a parallel constant to initialize the elements of the array AA such that AA[I,J] := I + J.

```
const
  N = 100 ;
parconst
  SEQUENCE = 1:N ;
var
  AA : array [1:N, 1..N] of INTEGER ;
  I : I..N ;
begin
  for I := 1 to N do
    AA [1:N,I] := SEQUENCE + I
end.
```

The expression SEQUENCE + I causes each individual value of the parallel constant to be increased by I. Such parallel constants can be set up at compile-time and their use throughout the program text makes a program more readable.

Any starting, finishing and increment integer values can be used to define a parallel constant. The constant increment value is enclosed in square brackets; for example,

```
parconst
  PC1 = 100:[− 2]84 ;   (* 9 values *)
  PC2 = − 2:[4]14, 1:[3]22, − 17:[6]91 ;   (* 32 values *)
```

A broken range in a sequence can be indicated by using a comma to represent the missing values as in

```
parconst
  BROKENSEQUENCE = 1:12, 20:58;
```

which represents a parallel construct with 51 integer values.

14.4 Manipulation of parallelism

The extent of parallelism can be changed each time a data structure is referenced by explicitly indicating appropriate lower and upper indices or by means of an **index set** which identifies the data elements that can be altered. The members of an index set are (ordered) integer values, each of which identifies a particular element of a data structure that can be accessed in parallel.

This, in effect, means that statements become more readable since they use the index set identifier, and that the extent of parallelism can be evaluated before the statement is encountered (and thus permit greater efficiency in execution).

An index set is defined after the declaration of the variables and takes the form

```
index
  IS = I:J ;
```

where I, J are constant integer values such that I $<=$ J. For example

```
const
  M = 200 ; N = 100 ; M1 = 199 ;
var
  GRID : array [1:M, 1..N] of REAL ;
index
  INSIDE = 2:M1 ;
```

Only constants can be used in the definition of an index set. Again, the parallel dots : in the index set definition are used to indicate parallelism. The identifier INSIDE is used to identify the elements 2 to M1 in a parallel array which has that extent of parallelism (at least). This means that the elements 1 and M are excluded whenever GRID[INSIDE,J] is used in an expression to reference the Jth column of the parallel array GRID.

Specific values can be excluded from a consecutive parallel index set by using a plus symbol (+) to form the union of the two (or more) index sets as in

```
index
  PARTS = 1:9 + 12:17 ;
```

where elements 10 and 11 and all elements above 17 and below 1 are excluded.

If there is regularity in the required parallel subscript, this can be defined in an index set by inserting the constant increment in square brackets between the two terminal values. For example

```
index
   ODD = 1:[2]99 ;
   EVEN = 2:[2]100 ;
```

would enable the manipulation of various parts of an array with an extent of parallelism 1 to 100 (at least). The expression A[ODD] * 2 would double the values of the odd elements of the array A leaving the values of the even elements unchanged.

Index sets cannot be reassigned during execution of a program, however, they can if required be manipulated by the following operators:

union (+)
intersection (*) and
difference (−).

For example, given the declarations

```
var
   A : array [1:20] of INTEGER ;
index
   SET1 = 2:15 ;
   SET2 = 6:18 ;
```

then

A[SET1 + SET2]   means elements A[2:18], a union operation;
A[SET1 * SET2]   means elements A[6:15], an intersection
                 operation;
A[SET1 − SET2]   means elements A[2:5], a difference operation.

Alternatively a programmer can use explicit variables or values and manipulate them using the above operators. For example, using explicit values then A[2:15 * 6:18] is equivalent to the intersection example given above.

Thus index sets provide a flexible means of manipulating parallel data structures by enabling the programmer to establish appropriate processing patterns.

14.5 Data alignment

Array and vector processors do not have the synchronization problems which can occur with independent processors since all their processors are constrained by the hardware to act in unison. However, they do have problems associated with the movement of data between parallel processing streams.

It is therefore necessary in any language to provide features which specify the movement of data either within the same data structure or between different data structures. It is also necessary to specify whether the data is shifted over the edge of an extent of parallelism or rotated within a given extent of parallelism.

In Actus these two actions are represented by **shift** and **rotate** operators respectively; they are referred to as alignment operators and can only be used as part of a parallel array index. Thus the form of a parallel index is as follows:

extent of parallelism   **alignment operator**   integer expression

Here the extent of parallelism is either explicitly defined or is an index set identifier and the alignment operator is either **shift** or **rotate**. The sign of the integer expression indicates the direction of the alignment: when combined with the extent of parallelism it defines the source operands, that is, the values which are to be moved to the positions indicated by the extent of parallelism. For example, given

```
var
  A : array [1:100] of REAL ;
index
  CONTROL = 4:60 ;
```

then A[CONTROL] accesses elements 4 to 60, and A[CONTROL **shift** 3] accesses elements 7 to 63. The expression

```
A[CONTROL] + A[CONTROL shift 3]
```

will therefore cause these elements to be added in parallel, i.e., A[4] + A[7]; A[5] + A[8]; A[6] + A[9]; – – –; A[60] + A[63]. The distance of the shift, 3, is added to the index set values to find the source operands, the destination indices being the extent of parallelism.

Data alignment can also be used with a broken range of parallel processing as illustrated in the next code fragment:

```
var
  A, B : array [1:100] of REAL ;
index
  CONTROL = 4:25 + 30:40 ;
```

the expression A[CONTROL] + B[CONTROL **shift** − 1] causes the additions

```
A[4] + B[3]; A[5] + B[4]; – – – – – – – – – – – – –
A[22] + B[21]; A[23] + B[22]; A[24] + B[23]; A[25] + B[24];
A[30] + B[29]; A[31] + A[30]; – – – – – – – – – – – –
A[40] + B[39]
```

to be performed in parallel.

Thus the **shift** operator works on the current extent of parallelism of a parallel variable, and any alignment must be within the declared (or maximum) extent of parallelism of that array variable. Otherwise an error occurs.

The elements of a parallel variable can be reordered by means of the other binary alignment operator **rotate**. This operation causes the data to be shifted circularly with respect to the current extent of parallelism, only the elements indicated in the extent of parallelism will be affected. Hence this operator is used to alter the order in which elements are accessed, rather than to introduce new elements, which was the case with the **shift** operator. For example, given

```
var
  A : array [1:100] of INTEGER ;
index
  SET1 = 80:100 ;
```

then the expression A[SET1] + A[SET1 **rotate** 1] will cause the additions (in parallel) of the elements

A[80] + A[81]; A[81] + A[82]; – – –; A[99] + A[100]; A[100] + A[80] ;

The same principle as for the shift operator is applied to calculate the source and destination indices, the main difference being that no new elements of the array are introduced into an expression when using the **rotate** operator.

The rotation of the data can also be applied to a broken parallel index range. For example, given

SET2 = 1:2 + 99:100 ;

then the expression

A[SET2] + A[SET2 **rotate** 1]

will cause

A[1] + A[2]; A[2] + A[99]; A[99] + A[100]; A[100] + A[1];

to be added in parallel.

These two alignment operators thus provide the major method of moving data within a data structure or between data structures in Actus.

14.6 Assignment statements

Each statement in Actus which contains parallel variables must have associated with it a single extent of parallelism. This must be less than or equal to the declaration extent of parallelism for the variables involved. In practice this means the assignment statement is the smallest unit for which the extent of parallelism can be defined.

In those assignment statements which involve data alignment, it is the left side of the assignment operator which determines in which elements of a parallel variable the results are to be stored. For example, given the declarations

```
var
  A : array [1:50] of REAL;
index
  SET = 11:20;
```

the statement

```
A[SET] := A[SET shift −1] + A[SET shift +1]
```

causes the elements 10 to 19 to be added to elements 12 to 21 and the results to be stored in elements 11 and 20 of the array A. While the statement

```
A[SET shift 2] := A[SET shift −1] + A[SET shift +1]
```

causes the results to be stored in elements 13 to 22 of the array A. In either case there is a single or base extent of parallelism, SET, associated with the statement to which data alignment operators can be applied.

To avoid repeatedly indicating the extent of parallelism whenever it will be the same for a series of statements, the **within** construct can be used. It takes the form

within EOP **do** statement part

The specifier EOP is an index expression (either explicit or implicit) indicating the extent of parallelism for the following simple or compound statement; a sharp symbol # is then used to indicate the extent of parallelism implied by the specifier. For example

```
within N:M do
  begin
    A[#] := B[#] + C[#] ;
    B[#] := B[#] − 1
  end
```

the extent of parallelism N:M is applied to both statements.

When using a **within** construct, the extent of parallelism will not be re-evaluated until either the construct is exited or another extent setting construct is encountered. In such a situation, the extents of parallelism are stacked as new constructs are encountered and then unstacked as the constructs are exited (see Section 14.7).

14.7 Conditional statements

When programming array and vector processors it is frequently required to perform conditional and repetitive actions. It has been discovered that the semantics of the Pascal **if**, **case**, **for** and **while** statements can be extended to take account of the extent of parallelism and parallel array variables.

In the case of the **if** statement there are several possibilities which can occur depending on whether the test expression or the statement part contain parallel variables.

If the test expression is scalar the extent of parallelism for any parallel variables of the statement part must be explicitly indicated or inherited from an enclosing extent setting construct. For example

if J > 0 **then** A[1:N] := A[1:N] / 2.0 ;

causes the N elements of A to be halved if J is positive, while the statements

if A[1] > 0.0 **then**
   A[1:N] := A[1:N] / 2.0
else
   B[1:M] := B[1:M] − 1

cause the N elements of A to be halved if the first element of A is positive otherwise the M values of B are changed. In each example the extent of parallelism for the statement part is explicitly defined, whereas in the following statements it is inherited:

within 2:49 **do**
  begin
    A[#] := − B[#] ;
    if J > 0 **then** A[#] := A[#] / 2.0
  end

The extent of parallelism of the **if** statement, represented by the sharp symbol #, is inherited from the surrounding **within** statement. Thus the sharp represents the extent of parallelism 2 to 49 for all the parallel variables.

A more interesting situation occurs when the test expression involves array variables which are acted upon in parallel, in this case the test is evaluated for each element. If the test is true for an element, the statement part is applied to that element, otherwise it is not. For example, given

if A[1:N] > 0.0 **then** A[#] := − A[#]

the sharp abbreviation # is used to represent those elements that found the test true, that is, if A[I] is positive then I is a member of the extent of parallelism represented by #. The test expression therefore determines the extent of parallelism for the statement part and it is not determined until execution time. If the extent of parallelism evaluates to zero the statement part is not executed. When used in this way, the **if** statement is an extent setting construct. After execution of the **if** statement, the extent of parallelism is determined by the next statement, or inherited from a surrounding construct. This is illustrated in the following example:

```
within 1:P do              (* extent of parallelism *)
  begin
    B[#] := 1.0 ;                     (* 1:P *)
    if A[#] > 0.0 then                (* 1:P *)
      A[#] := A[#] − 1.0 ;    (* 1 <= # <= P *)
    X[#] := A[#]                      (* 1:P *)
  end
```

The **if** statement causes the elements 1 to P of the array A to be examined and for those values which are positive 1.0 is subtracted. The sharp # may therefore have a different value in the statement part than in the test expression A[#] > 0.0. After the **if** statement is executed, the old value of # (i.e. 1 to P) is unstacked and used for the remaining statements of the **within** construct.

If an **else** part is given then its extent of parallelism is the complement of the extent of parallelism for the **then** part; it is determined by those values which found the test expression false. For example, in the statement

```
if A[1:N] > 0 then
  A[#] := A[#] + 1
else
  A[#] := A[#] − 1
```

the extent of parallelism (1:N) is split among the two statements in a ratio which is determined by testing the N values of the array A. The sharp # must be used to represent the unknown extent of parallelism in each statement.

Where the test expression involves more than one parallel variable, the extent of parallelism of the variables must be the same. For example, in the statement

```
if A[2:N] < B[2:N] then statement part
```

a pair-wise comparison of the elements of A and B is performed to determine the extent of parallelism for the statement part.

Two special quantifiers **any** and **all** are available for parallel variables only. They can be used to apply a test across an extent of parallelism as in

```
if any (test) then statement part
if all (test) then statement part
```

The statement part is either executed with the extent of parallelism indicated or else skipped. Such quantifiers are used to determine whether at least one or all of the elements of a parallel variable obey the test. For example

```
if all (B[1:N] > A[1:N]) then B[1:N] := 0.0
```

means that if all the elements of B are greater than the corresponding elements of A then all the elements of B will be assigned the value zero.

Example: neighbourhood sort

The following example illustrates how to sort P numbers in parallel using the method known as neighbourhood sort. In this sort the odd numbered elements are compared with their right neighbours and exchanged if the neighbours are smaller. A similar comparison is performed for the even numbered elements. On each pass through the data the most out of place data item is moved two places towards its correct position. Hence if there are P items to be sorted, P / 2 passes through the data guarantees that the data is sorted. A solution can be programmed in Actus as follows:

```
const
  P = 100 ; P1 = 99 ; P2 = 98 ;
var
  TEMP, NUMBERS : array [1:P] of INTEGER ;
  N : INTEGER ;
index
  ODDP = 1:[2]P1 ; EVENP = 2:[2]P2 ; (* assume P is even *)
begin
  for N := 1 to (P div 2) do
    begin
      if NUMBERS[ODDP] > NUMBERS[ODDP shift 1] then
      begin
      (* exchange values *)
        TEMP[#] := NUMBERS[#] ;
        NUMBERS[#] := NUMBERS[# shift 1] ;
        NUMBERS[# shift 1] := TEMP[#]
      end ;
      if NUMBERS[EVENP] > NUMBERS[EVENP shift 1] then
      begin
        TEMP[#] := NUMBERS[#] ;
        NUMBERS[#] := NUMBERS[# shift 1] ;
        NUMBERS[# shift 1] := TEMP[#]
      end
    end   (* Nloop *)
end.
```

The other type of conditional statement which is available in Actus is based on the sequential **case** construct. It is available for those situations in which there are several alternative execution paths which can be selected. The selection is dependent upon the value of a selector variable or expression. The possible values of the selector variable must therefore be associated with a statement of the **case** construct. For example, given

```
var
  I : 1..15 ;
case I of
  1,2,3 : statement1 ;
  4,15  : statement2 ;
  5..14 : statement3   (* all the values from 5 to 14 *)
end
```

the possible values of I are used as labels for the statements of the construct. One of the statements is selected depending on the value of the selector variable I; if necessary each statement can indicate a different extent of parallelism or involve scalar variables only.

In the situation where the selector expression involves parallel variables, more than one statement can be selected depending on the value of the selector expression for each element. Each element evaluates the selector expression and determines which of the statements is applied to that element. For example, given

```
type
  GROUNDCOVER = (OCEAN, ICE, SNOW, DESERT, FROST) ;
var
  SURFACECONDITIONS : array [1:50] of GROUNDCOVER ;

case SURFACECONDITIONS[10:50] of
  OCEAN          : statement1 ;
  SNOW, FROST    : statement2 ;
  DESERT         : statement3 ;
  ICE            : statement4 ;
end
```

when the case construct is encountered the values of SURFACECONDITIONS in the range 10 to 50 are evaluated and the results determine which statement is applied to each element. The selector variable's extent of parallelism is, thus, distributed among the four labelled statements so that each element is associated with one of the statements only. The sharp abbreviation is used to represent the unknown extent of parallelism for each of the labelled statements since they are determined by the current values of the selector variable.

14.8   Repetitive statements

The execution of a group of statements a number of times can be specified using one of three constructs. These constructs correspond to enhancements of the sequential **repeat**, **while** and **for** constructs with the introduction of an extent of parallelism to test expressions and control variables as required.

In the case of the **while** statement,

```
while test do statement part
```

if the test contains scalar variables only, an extent of parallelism must be explicitly defined or inherited for any of the statements in the statement part which involve parallel variables. For example

```
while J > 0 do
  begin
    A[1:N] := B[1:N] + C[1:N] ;
    B[2:M] := C[2:M] + 1 ;
```

```
      J := J − 1
   end
```

If the test contains parallel variables, it is evaluated for each element and if it is found to be true, the statement part is applied to that element. The extent of parallelism for the statement part is therefore determined by the test expression. The re-evaluation of the test expression is applied to the elements which found it true on the previous evaluation. Hence, the number of elements which have the statements applied to them is non-increasing. If the extent of parallelism of the test expression is zero the statement part is not executed. For example, given the statement

```
while A[1:N] > 0 do
   begin
      A[#] := A[#] − 1 ;
      B[#] := B[#] * A[#]
   end
```

every time the test is evaluated, only those elements which are greater than zero have the two statements applied to them. Hence, each element can be operated upon a different number of times and execution stops for the same reason for each element. The N elements of A are, thus, less than or equal to zero after the **while** statement is executed. As usual the sharp # abbreviation must be used to represent the unknown extent of parallelism for each statement.

A less flexible means of specifying repetition is by using the **repeat** statement. It is less flexible because the test expression comes after the statement part and so it is not possible to have a varying extent of parallelism in the statement part. A possible use is

```
var
   A, B : array[1:100] of INTEGER;
   I, J : 1..100;
repeat
   A[1:N] := B[1:N] ; I := I + 1 ; J := J − 1 ;
   within 1:N − I:J do
      if B[#] < 0 then B[#] := B[#] + 1 ;
until all (A[1:N] > 0)
```

In the situation where it is known in advance the number of times a group of statements will be executed, the **for** statement can be used, as in

```
for control := start by increment to finish do
      statement part
```

or

```
for control := start by decrement downto finish do
      statement part
```

The control variable can be a parallel variable with parallel variables or constants used for the start, increment and finish entities. Since this construct is closely related to independent indexing it is examined after consideration of that topic in the next section.

14.9   Independent indexing

The process of selecting a random series of elements from an array is referred to as independent indexing. It is achieved in Actus by using a one-dimensional parallel integer array to pick out the appropriate elements of another array. For example, given the declarations

```
parconst
  DIAGONAL = 1:100 ;
var
  ID : array [1:100] of INTEGER ;
  AA : array [1:100, 1..100] of REAL ;
```

and the assignment ID[1:100] := DIAGONAL ; then AA[1:100,ID[1:100]] accesses the diagonal elements of AA in parallel and the statement

within 1:100 **do** AA[#,ID[#]] := 1.0

causes the diagonal elements to be assigned the value 1.0 in parallel, that is, the elements AA[1,1], AA[2,2], – – – AA[100,100]. The extent of parallelism for the indexing array ID and the indexed array AA must be the same.

The previously defined alignment operators can also be applied to an indexing array to enable different off diagonal elements to be accessed. For example, the first off diagonals can be accessed using the following indexing arrays

ID[1:100] := ID[1:100 **rotate** 1]   (* 2, 3, 4, ..., 100, 1 *)

so that AA[1:99,ID[1:99]] references AA[1,2], AA[2,3], AA[3,4], – – – AA[99,100]; while the lower off diagonal can be accessed using

ID[1:100] := ID[1:100 **rotate** – 1]   (* 100, 1, 2, 3,..., 99 *)

so that AA[2:100,ID[2:100]] references AA[2,1], AA[3,2], – – – AA[99,98], AA[100,99].

Independent indexing can be usefully employed in conjunction with the parallel version of the **for** statement. For example,

```
for ID[1:N] := DIAGONAL to 100 do
  begin
    AA[#,ID[#]] := BB[#,ID[#]] + C[#] ;
    – – –
  end
```

can be imagined as N loops operating in parallel. The first loop has values 1 to 100, the second 2 to 100 etc. The N loops terminate at different times and after a different number of iterations after reaching the terminal value, 100.

Thus the **for** loop when used in this way provides a powerful tool for manipulating parts of a parallel data structure other than a row or column.

Example: matrix transposition

The following example transposes an (N + 1) by (N + 1) matrix OLD by creating one row of the NEW matrix from a column of the OLD matrix each time round a loop. Independent indexing is used to ensure the appropriate indices are being used each time round the loop.

```
const
  N = 200 ;
parconst
  DIAGONAL = 0:N ;
var
  OLD, NEW: array [0:N, 0..N] of REAL ;
  I, J : array [0:N] of INTEGER ;
  K : 0..N ;
begin
  within 0:N do
    begin
      I[#] := DIAGONAL ; J[#] := DIAGONAL ;
      for K := 0 to N do
        begin
          NEW[#,J[#]] := OLD[# rotate – K,I[#]] ;
          I[#] := I[# rotate + 1] ;
          J[#] := J[# rotate – 1]
        end (* K *)
    end (* within *)
end.
```

The elements of the indexing arrays I and J are paired on a one to one basis with the extent of parallelism of the parallel arrays OLD and NEW respectively, therefore, the extent of parallelism for these arrays must be the same.

14.10 Subprograms

In Actus a function can be used to isolate a section of code which returns a result value or values to a data structure depending on whether the structure is scalar or parallel. In either case the parameters may be scalar or parallel and may differ in the extent of parallelism from that of the result.

The following function uses a scalar and parallel variable as input parameters and produces a parallel result of real numbers.

```
type
  VECTORA = array [1:50] of REAL ;
  VECTORB = array [1:100] of INTEGER ;
```

```
var
  A : VECTORA ; B : VECTORB ; Z : REAL ;

function CALCULATE (N:REAL ; Y:VECTORB) : VECTORA ;
  const
    P = 200 ; Q = 50 ; P1 = 199 ;
  var
    ZZ : array [1:P, 1..Q] of REAL ;
  index
    INSIDE = 1:P1 ;
  begin
    statements
    CALCULATE := ZZ[1:50,1]
  end   (* calcuiate *) ;
```

The function heading includes the result type, which in the case of a parallel type is restricted to a one-dimensional array. The statements of the function can use any of the language constructs previously defined and are governed by the same rules, for example, the extent of parallelism must be consistent on both sides of an assignment statement.

A function is invoked by specifying its name plus the actual parameters with their dimensions and the variable in which the result(s) is to be stored. An extent of parallelism for the result must also be included. The above function might be called as in

```
A[I:J] := CALCULATE(Z,B) [I:J]
```

where the values of I and J determine the number of values returned and ensure that the extent of parallelism is the same on both sides of the assignment operator.

There are several standard functions which can be used to calculate a value for each element of a parallel array or yield a single result using several elements of a parallel variable. In addition, there are functions which deal with the extent of parallelism only, such as, FIRST(#) which returns the first member of the extent of parallelism, #.

The following program fragment finds the average of the positive elements of an array X by using the standard function SUM.

```
const
  N = 100 ;
var
  A, X : array [1:N] of REAL ;
  AVERAGE : REAL ;
begin
  A[1:N] := 0.0 ;
  if X[1:N] > 0.0 then
    begin
```

```
        A[#] := 1.0 ;
        AVERAGE := SUM(X[#])/SUM(A[#])
     end
  end
```

Procedures, like functions, can be used as an abstraction mechanism. They enable several scalar or parallel variables or a combination of each type to be returned to the calling subprogram after the execution of the procedure. The parameters must be declared in a formal parameter list with those parameters which can input a value and return a result preceded by the reserved word **var** for each different type. For example,

```
type
  VECTOR = array [1:100] of REAL ;
  MATRIX = array [1:50, 1..10] of INTEGER ;

procedure DAX (S,T : MATRIX ; var P:REAL ; var U,V : VECTOR) ;
(* procedure body *)
```

This procedure requires as parameters two two-dimensional arrays formally identified as S and T with extent of parallelism 50 and depth 10, a scalar variable P and two vectors U and V. As a result of its execution with actual parameters results can be returned in the variables formally identified as U,V and P. These results can then be used in the calling subprogram.

A procedure may be called recursively and corresponds to the execution of that procedure a number of times which is dependent on the data context. Similarly, a function may be activated recursively.

To provide more flexibility with the use of procedures it is possible to pass an array parameter with different bounds on each procedure call. Such a parameter is referred to as a conformant array parameter. It takes the form

```
procedure P (var A : array [EXTENT] of REAL) ;
```

where the identifier EXTENT is used to indicate an extent of parallelism, which can vary each time the procedure is called. Non-parallel indices of an array parameter can also be conformant. Sample procedures calls would be

```
P(B[1:10]) ;
P(B[I:J]) ;
P(B[#]) ;
P(B[ODDS])
```

where ODDS is an appropriately defined index set.

14.11 Summary

The language which has been developed in this chapter has taken a different approach to the programming of array and vector processors than the languages considered in previous chapters. Actus is based on the expression of problem parallelism approach and provides a number of language features which facilitate the expression of the parallelism inherent in problems suited to the type of environment represented by array and vector processors.

It has benefited from the experience which has been gained in the design and implementation of abstract programming languages for sequential machines.

It provides parallel data structures to define the parallel nature of a problem's data and statements to manipulate this parallelism. These features are not dependent on the architecture of a particular machine or influenced by existing programs which is the case with previously defined languages.

The central concept of the language is the extent of parallelism which has enabled a joint syntax to be developed for both array and vector processor type processing. This should enable some measure of program portability to be introduced to this type of parallel programming environment.

Case study: sorting

Consider the problem of sorting N numbers using an extent of parallelism P where N is much larger than P. For example if $N = 16$ and $P = 4$ then the objective is to rearrange the numbers as follows:

P1	P2	P3	P4		P1	P2	P3	P4
16	19	97	41		2	16	27	51
32	6	5	96	→	5	18	31	89
12	51	27	2		6	19	32	96
18	31	89	20		12	20	41	97

before sorting   after sorting

Sorting consists of two phases. First, the numbers associated with an individual member of the extent of parallelism 1:P are sorted using any sequential sorting algorithm, in this case bubblesort, applied in parallel. This will produce P sequences of data which are individually sorted. Using the above data this would produce

P1	P2	P3	P4
12	6	5	2
16	19	27	20
18	31	89	41
32	51	97	96

The second phase is to merge these P sequences using the neighbourhood sort technique applied to sorted sequences; the odd numbered members of

1:*P* are used to merge two neighbouring sequences in parallel, then the even numbered members of 1:*P* are used to merge two neighbouring sequences. Special rules apply at the boundaries. This alternation between the odd and even numbered members is continued for *P* / 2 passes of the algorithm. It can be shown that this will ensure the data is sorted.

For example, using the above data this would produce (the active processors have been underlined in the following diagrams)

P1	*P2*	*P3*	*P4*		*P1*	*P2*	*P3*	*P4*	
6	19	2	41		6	2	27	41	
12	31	5	89	→	12	5	31	89	→
16	32	20	96		16	19	32	96	
18	51	27	97		18	20	51	97	

P1	*P2*	*P3*	*P4*		*P1*	*P2*	*P3*	*P4*
2	16	27	51		2	16	27	51
5	18	31	89	→	5	18	31	89
6	19	32	96		6	19	32	96
12	20	41	97		12	20	41	97

To simplify the discussion assume the number of numbers to be sorted is a factor of the extent of parallelism, (N = 2 × K × P), and that the data is held in the Actus array

NUMBERS : **array** [1:P, 1..K2] **of** INTEGER ;

where K2 = 2 * K.

Bubblesort can be constructed in parallel by extending the sequential version as follows:

```
const
  N = 10000 ; P = 100 ; K = 50 ;   (* N = 2 * P * K *)
  K2 = 100 ;
var
  NUMBERS : array [1:P, 1..K2] of INTEGER ;
  J : 1..K2 ;
  I, TEMP : array [1:P] of INTEGER ;
begin   (* parallel bubblesort *)
  for J := 1 to K2 do
  begin
    I[1:P] := J ;
    while I[1:P] < K2 do
    begin
      if NUMBERS[#,I[#]] > NUMBERS[#,I[#] +1] then
      begin
        TEMP[#] := NUMBERS[#,I[#]] ;
        NUMBERS[#,I[#]] := NUMBERS[#,I[#] +1] ;
        NUMBERS[#,I[#] +1] := TEMP[#]
      end   (* if *) ;
```

```
            I[#] := I[#] + 1
        end   (* while *)
      end   (* for *)
    end   (* parallel bubblesort *)
```

The next phase is based on the extension of the earlier neighbourhood sort algorithm (Section 14.7) to a sequence of values. First a procedure MERGE is defined which takes two array parameters and sorts their values into a third array. This can be defined using conformant array parameters to increase the range of application of the procedure as follows:

```
procedure MERGE (var A,B : array [EOP, 1..K1] of INTEGER ;
                 var C : array [EOP, 1..K2] of INTEGER) ;
```

This procedure merges the values of A and B into a sorted sequence for each member of the extent of parallelism EOP, the result of the merger is to be found in the array C.

```
    var
      I, J : array [1:P] of INTEGER ;
      Q : 1..K2 ;
    begin
      I[EOP] := 1 ; J[EOP] := 1 ;
      A[EOP,K1] := INFINITY ; B[EOP,K1] := INFINITY ;
      (* large sentinel values *)
      for Q := 1 to K2 do
        if A[EOP,I[EOP]] > B[EOP,J[EOP]] then
          begin
            C[#,Q] := B[#,J[#]] ; J[#] := J[#] + 1
          end
        else
          begin
            C[#,Q] := A[#,I[#]] ; I[#] := I[#] + 1
          end
    end ;   (* merge *)
```

The arrays I and J are used to indicate which elements in the arrays A and B are under consideration. These elements of the arrays A and B are then compared in parallel EOP elements at a time. The smaller elements in each of the EOP comparisons are stored in the array C and the indexing arrays I and J incremented appropriately.

This procedure can be used for both the odd and even numbered members of the extent of parallelism since it has been defined using conformant array parameters.

Hence the algorithm can be expressed as follows, where the code given above has not been repeated.

```
    const
      P = 100 ; P1 = 99 ; P2 = 98 ; N = 10000 ;
      (* N = 2 * P * K *) K = 50 ; K1 = 51 ; (* K +1 *)
```

```
  K2 = 100 ; (* K*2 *)
var
  FIRST, SECOND : array [1:P, 1..K] of INTEGER ;
  NUMBERS : array [1:P, 1..K] of INTEGER ;
  M, I, J, K : INTEGER ;
index
  ALLP = 1:P ; ODDP = 1:[2]P1 ; EVENP = 2:[2]P2 ;
  (* declaration of procedure MERGE as before *)
begin
  (* bubblesort is applied *)
  for M := 1 to P div 2 do
    begin
      (* create the sequences to be merged *)
      for J := 1 to K do
      begin
        FIRST[EVENP, J] := NUMBERS[EVENP, J] ;
        SECOND[EVENP, J] := NUMBERS[EVENP shift 1, J]
      end ;
      MERGE(FIRST[EVENP, 1..K + 1],SECOND[EVENP, 1..K + 1],
            NUMBERS[EVENP, 1..2*K1]) ;
      (* similarly for the odd numbered elements *)
    end   (* M loop *)
end.
```

EXERCISES

14.1 Construct an Actus program which will multiply two matrices AA and BB to produce a third matrix CC.

14.2 Construct an Actus program which represents the main loop in a Gauss-Jacobi solution of Poisson's equation.

14.3 Given an $N \times N$ matrix write an Actus program to generate the numbers 1 to $N \times N$ and assign them to the elements of the matrix such that element (i,j) contains the value $1 + (i - 1) + 64 \times (j - 1)$.

14.4 Write an Actus program to find the inverse of an $N \times N$ triangular matrix.

14.5 Devise an Actus program which will sum the N values of an array in parallel.

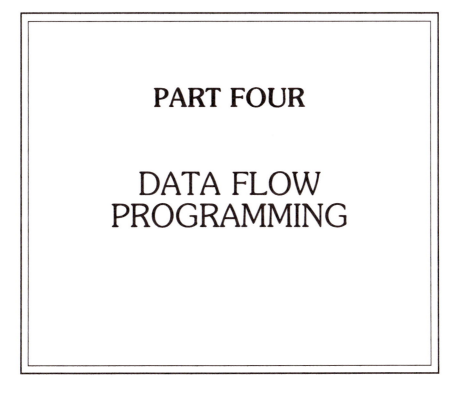

PART FOUR

DATA FLOW PROGRAMMING

Chapter 15 Data Flow Programming

15.1 Introduction

The von Neumann model of computer organization can be summarized as one in which there is single control of the computation flow. In this model a program is stored in memory and a single control unit is used to interpret the instructions sequentially; a sequence control register determines the next instruction to be executed. Data is passed between instructions by means of references to shared memory locations. Since its introduction in the late forties this model has been used for the majority of general purpose computers which have been designed and built. As a consequence the languages which have been developed for this model can be described as control flow languages. Many of these earlier control flow languages reflected the properties of this model rather than the way in which a programmer thinks about a solution to a problem. This, in turn, has given rise to two main criticisms of the von Neumann model and control flow languages, namely:

1. the model is unsuitable to represent and utilize parallelism;
2. programs designed to execute on this model lack useful mathematical properties which aid program verification.

Array and vector processors represent one departure from the von Neumann type of architecture which have introduced parallelism to the design; data flow machines represent another.

Control flow languages display a common characteristic in that the execution sequence of the program's statements is dictated by the order in which the statements are textually composed by the programmer, in other words, the instructions drive the program's execution. Normally if statement A is encountered before statement B then this is the order in which the statements are executed; explicit transfers of control can be caused by goto statements etc. An alternate method of selecting statements for execution is to regard a statement as being ready for execution if the data that it requires is available. Hence the sequence in which the statements are textually composed is unlikely to be the order in which they are executed. In addition, if the data is available for more than one statement then these statements can be executed in parallel. This is referred to as data flow programming since it is the availability of the data which drives the program's execution. The data flows from one instruction to another and the order of execution of the instructions does not depend on the location of the instructions in memory.

Hence the parallelism which is associated with data flow programming is within a statement or among a group of statements. Because the parallelism is at such a low level it is not feasible to establish a process or task for each part of the program which can be executed in parallel; the overheads would be too large. Thus the approach used in languages like Ada which provide the task feature, is at too high a level for a data flow programming language.

To facilitate data flow programming, language features are required which enable the user to write a program which lends itself to the easy detection of any parts which can be executed in parallel when the required data is available. As a result most data flow languages provide a syntax which enables a programmer to describe a problem solution while at the same time enabling the easy detection of which statements can be executed in parallel. Essentially this amounts to being able to isolate data dependencies among statements and for a compiler being able to determine these dependencies.

To illustrate what is involved in determining the execution sequence for a data flow computer consider the following Pascal statements:

```
A := B + C ;        (1)
D := A * C ;        (2)
E := B / A ;        (3)
F := D * A ;        (4)
G := D - E ;        (5)
H := D + E ;        (6)
I := F + G + H ;    (7)
```

If this program fragment is submitted to a Pascal compiler then code will be generated to perform the calculations in the order indicated reflecting the control flow model of computation. If each statement unrealistically takes 1 time unit then the time to execute the statements is 7 time units. A closer examination of the statements indicates that statement (2) cannot be executed until statement (1) has executed because of the data dependency on A, similarly for statement (3). However statements (2) and (3) could be executed at the same time. Also statements (4), (5) and (6) can be executed at the same time provided statements (2) and (3) have been executed.

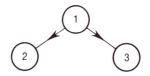

Figure 15.1

Data dependencies can be represented and detected by constructing a graph, for example, in the form shown in Figure 15.1 where each node, indicated by its number, is a statement and a path or arc into the node means that the statement at the other end of the path must be executed before the current node can be executed.

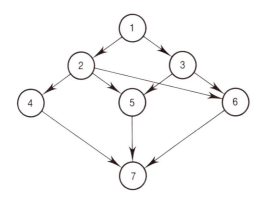

Figure 15.2

All seven statements of the above example can be represented as in Figure 15.2 which indicates the constraints placed on the order of statement execution. In fact, there are several possible execution orders ranging from purely sequential to 1, [2,3], [4,5,6], 7 where the numbers in brackets indicate possible parallel execution of the statements concerned. Hence the time to perform the required calculations on a data flow machine could be 4 time units, a substantial improvement over the sequential or control flow model execution.

While the above example considered the data dependencies among a group of statements, the same principle can be applied to individual statements or expressions. In this case the nodes contain operators and the arcs contain data values. For example, given the statement

$Z := X + Y$

this would be represented on the graph as illustrated in Figure 15.3.

The values represented by X and Y flow along the arcs and are consumed by the node operator to produce the value Z.

The statement

$Z := (X + Y) \times (X - Y)$

would be represented as in Figure 15.4 where the values X and Y are input to more than one node operator to produce new values which are then

Figure 15.3

multiplied. The operators + and − can be applied in parallel since their operands, X and Y, are both available. The final value produced could, if required, be broadcast to several other nodes.

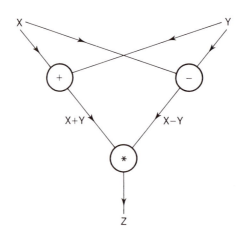

Figure 15.4

To further illustrate what is required in a data flow computer consider the multiplication of two complex numbers X and Y, that is,

(A + iB) * (C + iD).

A graph can be constructed to represent this expression as shown in Figure 15.5 where the required operators have been placed at the nodes of the graph and the required data has been duplicated and broadcast appropriately.

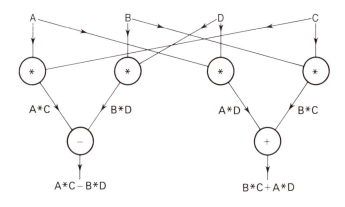

Figure 15.5

Thus a graph must be constructed for each program that is to be executed on a data flow machine. On the graph each operation is assigned to a node. Each node is enabled for execution (usually called firing), when data (usually called tokens), arrive on the set of input paths of the node. The number of input paths is the number of tokens required to arrive before the node can execute. The firing of the node thus consumes the input values and produces tokens on its output paths. There may be more than one output path, indicating that the single data value produced as a result of firing that node is required by several other nodes. In this case separate copies of the data values are created and dispatched. This should be compared with a control flow model where a data value is placed in a memory location and shared between instructions as a result of the instructions accessing the memory location. The graph has been executed when all nodes that have received the required data have been fired.

A more substantial example is the solution of the quadratic equation

$$AX^2 + BX + C = 0$$

with real solutions

X1 = (− B + SQRT(B × B − 4 × A × C)) / (2 × A)
X2 = (− B + SQRT(B × B − 4 × A × C)) / (2 × A)

Figure 15.6 illustrates a solution in graphical form where operators on the same line can be executed in parallel if the data on their input arcs is available.

As can be seen by these examples a data flow model does not equate a variable with a storage location and a programmer deals only with values. As a result a data flow language can be described as a value orientated language. A value cannot be changed and once it is produced at a node it must be transmitted unchanged to all the other nodes which require it as an

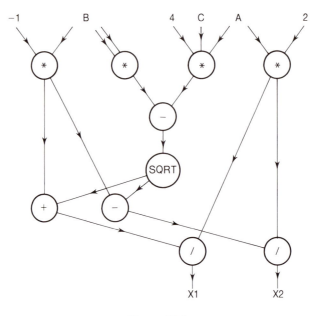

Figure 15.6

input value. In contrast, a control flow language can be described as a variable or object orientated language since it deals with variables rather than values.

Hence when using a data flow programming language it is necessary to be able to generate a graph such that the data dependencies are easily identified. The techniques used to translate a source program into a data flow graph are similar to the methods used in a conventional optimizing compiler to analyse the paths of data dependency in a source program. Once the graph has been constructed it is then possible to determine which statements can be executed in parallel. As the above examples illustrate, the level of parallelism is at such a low level that it is unreasonable to expect a programmer to detail the data dependencies in the syntax of a programming language itself, rather it is only reasonable to expect a programmer to stay within certain guidelines which facilitate the detection of data dependencies. This is the approach adopted by most languages designed for data flow programming.

15.2 Hardware considerations

There have been several experiments to implement a hardware system based on the data flow model of computation. To give some idea of the structure of a data flow machine and how it differs from earlier machines one is chosen for further examination: the Manchester Data Flow machine (Gurd *et al.*, 1985); an outline of its structure is given in Figure 15.7.

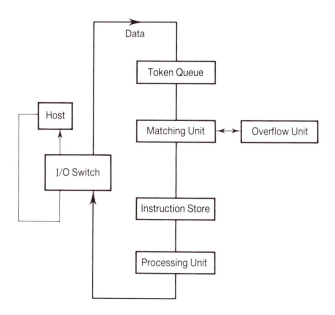

Figure 15.7   The Manchester Data Flow computer.

An important component of this machine is the ring around which the data flows. The basic structure of the ring contains four modules connected to a host system. The modules operate independently and in a pipelined fashion. Any items of data which are required for a particular instruction must first be brought together; this task is performed in what is known as a Matching Unit. An auxiliary store, called the Overflow Unit, is used in the situations where there are large sets of data. Once the data has been matched the required instruction is selected from the Instruction Store. At this stage the instruction is ready for execution which is performed in the Processing Unit. If as a result of the execution of the instruction, data is produced, this data is then transmitted back around the ring to be matched with other data and then to activate other instructions.

The execution parallelism of the machine is contained in the Processing Unit. Here there are up to 20 units which perform the execution of the instructions and pass any output data onto the ring. These units can operate in parallel. The Token Queue is a first in first out buffer which is used to smooth out any uneven rates of generation and consumption of data in the ring. The I/O Switch allows programs and data to be loaded from a host processor, and permits results to be output for inspection. Such a machine has been operational at the University of Manchester since 1981. The performance of the system for reasonably large user programs has been measured at maximum rates of between 1 and 2 million instructions per second.

15.3   Data flow language criteria

In this section we consider what features make traditional languages, like Pascal, unsuitable for the detection of data flow dependencies and what properties are required of a data flow programming language.

15.3.1   Locality of effect

In Pascal it is possible to use the same variable name in different parts of a program and as a consequence the value of this variable can be changed several times. It may be that the use of the same variable in different parts of the program is for different computational purposes. However, the problems of detecting this type of data dependency and determining that the dependency is such that statements involving the same variable can be executed in parallel are very demanding. It would require a very clever compiler to detect that any dependency was not real between computations involving the same variable. This problem can be made even more difficult if there is an undisciplined use of control structures such as the goto statement.

Hence data flow programming, like structured programming, advocates the disciplined use of programming constructs in order to limit their effect. Also because data flow computing is influenced by the dependency between variables it is necessary to restrict the scope in which a variable is active. This is usually referred to as the locality of effect, and ensures that instructions do not have unnecessary far reaching data dependencies.

15.3.2   Side effects

Another feature of languages like Pascal which make them unsuitable as data flow programming languages is that side effects are possible. A side effect can occur when a procedure or function changes the value of a variable in an enclosing subprogram, for example, if a procedure P which is called by another procedure Q, changes some of the values of the variables of procedure Q. This is a side effect and gives rise to a data dependency which is difficult to detect. The effect is even more damaging when structured data values are involved. If these structured values are manipulated by several statements then it is virtually impossible to determine when, and what effect that change will have in another part of the program. An example of this type of situation is when elements of the same array are manipulated by several statements.

Thus one of the main properties of a data flow programming language is that any subprograms which are used in a program must be free from side effects.

15.3.3 Aliasing

In Pascal the parameters of a procedure or function can give rise to side effects and also to a more serious problem known as aliasing. Aliasing occurs when different formal parameters refer to the same actual parameter whenever the function is activated. For example, given

```
type
  VECTOR = array [1..100] of REAL ;
var
  A : VECTOR ;
  procedure MULT(var P,Q : VECTOR) ;
```

then a procedure call such as

```
MULT(A, A)
```

is an example of aliasing. The definition of the procedure MULT specifies two formal parameters P and Q implying that perhaps some of the statements of procedure MULT could be executed in parallel using the variables P and Q. However, if the actual parameter for both P and Q is A, then some of the statements could be simultaneously changing the same variable leading to inconsistencies.

Many of these effects can be limited by using the call-by-value rather than the call-by-reference parameter passing mechanism. With the call-by-value mechanism a copy of the parameter is taken and used during execution while with call-by-reference a pointer is used to indicate where the value is stored. However it is not a sufficient solution for a data flow programming language.

Even if aliasing does not occur, two activations of the same procedure can give rise to problems on a data flow computer. For example, given the procedure VSUM, where I and J are index values for the vector P,

```
procedure VSUM(var P : VECTOR ; I,J : INTEGER) ;
```

then if

```
VSUM(A, K, L) ;
VSUM(A, M, N) ;
```

appear in a program, a data flow computer will attempt to execute the two procedure calls in parallel. Since the values of K, L, M and N are not known at compile-time it is possible that there will be an overlap in the parts of the array that are to be manipulated. The values may only be assigned at run-time, so it must be assumed that they will conflict and therefore they can only be executed in the order listed without any overlap in execution.

15.3.4 Single assignment rule

The single assignment rule simply stated means that a variable is assigned a value by one statement only. The assignment statement therefore has the effect of providing a value and binding that value to the name appearing on the left side. The statement $Z := X + Y$ is interpreted as a definition rather than an assignment. As a consequence a new name must be chosen for any redefined variable. For example

```
Z := X + Y ;
Z := Z * A
```

should be written as

```
Z1:= X + Y ;
Z := Z1 * A
```

to adhere to the single assignment rule. Hence statements such as $J := J + 1$ are forbidden.

Each time a function is entered a new binding is made which remains in force until that scope of access is completed. This is somewhat similar to a constant in Pascal except that a different value on each activation of the procedure or function is used.

Structured data types such as the array and record are most affected by such a rule since they must be considered as single values. Thus they cannot be modified, the only possibility is to build a new array or record with some of the values changed.

The main advantage of the single assignment rule is that the corresponding data flow graph can be obtained directly. In practice it is not essential that a data flow language conform to the single assignment rule; multiple assignments can be handled provided the scope of a variable extends only from its definition to the next definition of the same variable name. This means that once an identifier is bound to a value the binding remains in force for the entire scope of access to that identifier.

There have been languages developed under these criteria before the proposals for data flow computers emerged, these are the functional or applicative languages where program transformations are simply the result of applying functions to their arguments. One of the oldest of these languages is LISP, but recently other languages have emerged such as FP (Backus, 1978), LUCID (Ashcroft et al., 1977), ID (Arvind et al., 1978) and VAL (Ackerman and Dennis, 1979; McGraw, 1982). It is this last language which has been chosen as the subject matter of the next section to illustrate the properties of an existing data flow language.

15.4   VAL: a Data Flow Programming Language

VAL is a data flow programming language which was developed at the Massachusetts Institute of Technology by Jack Dennis and his colleagues (Ackerman and Dennis, 1979). Their objective was to provide a notation to describe an algorithm which can be executed in parallel on a machine with multiple processors. The language is not intended to reflect a particular application area or target machine and it is hoped that VAL will evolve into a general purpose language for use on general purpose data flow computers.

VAL does not contain features which explicitly indicate which parts of a program can be executed in parallel, rather the parallel features are implicit. Only when the graph representation of a program is constructed is the order in which statements are to be executed determined. From the graph it is also possible to determine which statements can be executed in parallel.

The language provides features which cannot give rise to side effects and introduces new features to guide the user in the construction of programs in which data dependencies can be easily determined. The detection of these dependencies is easily determined and performed automatically. To facilitate such a task the user should be aware of how the parallelism in a program is detected and, where possible, provide as many clues as possible.

A programmer must write expressions and functions which take input values and produce a result or results without side effects, that is, without altering the program environment. This means that whenever all the input values are available an expression or function can be executed and it cannot affect the execution of any other expression or function. All expressions or functions which are ready to execute may do so in parallel. Subexpressions may be evaluated in any order without effect on computed results. New values are defined and then used in many places but no value may ever be modified.

Thus the major feature of VAL which makes it different from the other languages considered in earlier chapters is the restriction of allowing only expressions and functions.

VAL handles run-time errors differently from conventional languages like Pascal. In Pascal a run-time error stops program execution while in VAL a run-time error is well defined. For example, if an array reference exceeds the bounds of the array then VAL specifies what results are produced. This is achieved by associating special error elements with each data type (see Section 15.4.4).

15.4.1 Data types

VAL provides the usual standard types of Boolean, integer, real and character. These are introduced when required by using a declaration of the form

```
I : INTEGER := 1 ;
R : REAL := 0 ;
B : BOOLEAN := FALSE ;
```

where each variable has also been given an initial value. Each of these types has an appropriate set of operators and predicates. For example, the values which a Boolean type can have are TRUE and FALSE, known as the proper elements, and **undef**[BOOLEAN] and **miss_elt**[BOOLEAN], known as the error elements. The error elements correspond to the situation where the Boolean variable is undefined and the element value is missing respectively (see Section 15.4.4). The Boolean operations include **and**, **or**, **not**, **equal** and **not equal** with tests for **undef** and **miss_elt**. Each data type has its own set of possible values and operators.

Data structured values are either record values or array values and are treated as mathematical sets of values just like the standard types. The operations for arrays and records are chosen to support identification of concurrency for execution on a parallel processor.

There are three ways in which new or compound types can be constructed in VAL, namely, by using **array**, **record** and **oneof** definitions; **oneof** corresponds to a discriminated union definition. The specification consists of a type constructor giving the name of the compound type followed by the necessary additional information within brackets.

An *array* type definition takes the form

```
type ATYPE = array [INTEGER] ;
type BTYPE = array [REAL] ;
```

where the type of the components but not the bounds of the array are given. Thus a type definition describes all finite length ordered sequences of its components. The actual bounds of an array are associated with each individual array when it is used in the program. Since there is no bound information associated with the type, it means that arrays of different sizes can be passed to a single procedure for manipulation.

As can be seen the only type information associated with an array is its component type which may be any type including an array, enabling arrays with more than one dimension to be described. For example

```
type CTYPE = array [array [REAL]] ;
```

defines a two-dimensional array type.

Access to individual elements of an array is achieved by using an integer index, if the index is not within the range the result is undefined.

Some or all of the elements of an array can be specified and evaluated simultaneously. The syntax for such a specification is a list of ordered pairs enclosed in square brackets. The first of the pair is the index position in the array and the second is an expression representing the value to be held in that position. For example

    [1 : EXPRESSION1 ; 2 : EXPRESSION2]

is an expression that creates an array of two elements. The values bound to the two identifiers, EXPRESSION1 and EXPRESSION2, become the values for the corresponding array elements. Both expressions can be computed simultaneously. Hence it is possible to provide an arbitrarily long list of ordered pairs which can be executed in parallel.

The expression

    A[I : V]

creates a new array with only one value changed where I is the index position of the changed position and V its new value. More specifically, if A has the values 1,2,3,4 the expression

    A[3 : 0]

leaves A with the values 1,2,0,4. The range of A is expanded as needed to include index I and any intervening elements in the expanded range are given the value **miss_elt**. For example, if A has the bounds 1 and 4 with values 1,2,3,4 then A[6:0] will give element 5 the value **miss_elt** and element 6 the value 0.

Thus an array is not considered as an object but rather as a group of values, and if one value is changed the whole array is regarded as having been changed. Thus treating structured data types as values instead of objects is one of the most profound differences in data flow programming. As a result it is possible to deduce the data dependencies for arrays using the same techniques as in the case of simple values.

The method of constructing a *record* is similar to the way in which an array is constructed. For example, a record type is defined as

    type ARECORD = **record** [FIELDS] ;

where FIELDS represents the identifier and type associated with each component as in

    record [I, J : INTEGER ; TEMP : REAL] ;

The fields may also contain record or array types as in the following example

    record [A : **record** [X : **array** [REAL] ; Y : CHARACTER] ;
             B : REAL] ;

The method of assigning values to the fields of a record is to list the field identifiers with expressions of the appropriate type in square brackets as in

```
[FIELD1 : EXPRESSION1 ;
 FIELD2 : EXPRESSION2 ;
 FIELD3 : EXPRESSION3]
```

In this example each of the three field identifiers is followed by an expression representing the value to be entered in the record. All the expressions may be computed at the same time. For example, given

record [X, Y : INTEGER ; Z : BOOLEAN] ;

then

record [X : 100 ; Y : I * 2 ; Z : FALSE] ;

establishes values for the three fields X, Y and Z; the values can be computed and assigned simultaneously. Individual fields of a record may be accessed using the usual dot notation.

The type of a record is based on its constituent field identifiers and their associated types. This means that neither the order of the definitions nor any type name bound to the structure influences the type matching process.

A *discriminated union* is a grouping of several types only one of which will be required at any time in the program. Such a data type can be represented in VAL by means of the **oneof** constructor. The definition of such a type takes the following form:

type RESULT = **oneof** [A : ATYPE ; B : ARECORD] ;

Each field consists of a tag and the type associated with that tag. The tag identifiers must be distinct. In this example an instance of the type RESULT can represent either an array (ATYPE) or a record (ARECORD). The details of these two types having been defined previously. The two tags A and B are used to identify the constituent types and to indicate which value is intended.

Recursive type definitions can be used to construct types composed of array or record structures of unlimited depth. For example, a stack of real numbers can be defined as

```
type STACK = oneof [EMPTY : null ;
                    ELEMENT : record [VALUE : REAL ;
                    REST : STACK]] ;
```

where the type **null** can be used to represent an alternative where no data value is required.

VAL imposes strong structural type checking so that if two types have identical structures they are equivalent; the identifiers associated with the types do not influence the equivalencing. Automatic type conversions are never made by the language although a number of functions are provided to aid with conversion when necessary.

There is associated with each data type a number of special error values such as overflow, for example. They provide a mechanism for handling run-time errors without violating any type correctness properties; this is considered later.

15.4.2 Expressions and functions

In VAL there are no statements in the conventional sense, rather the main vehicle for calculations are expressions and functional operators. They are constructed so that there is no possibility of side effects occurring and such that any implicit concurrency is easily identified. For example

```
function F(B : BOOLEAN returns REAL) ;
  EXPRESSION
endfun
```

defines a function F which returns a real result, it has a single parameter B of type Boolean. The scope of the formal parameter B is the entire function definition, less any inner scopes that reintroduce the same value identifier.

The body of a function is an expression which produces the result. In the statements of the body only the formal parameters and locally defined identifiers may be accessed; no access to global identifiers is permitted. This is to ensure that there are no side effects. All the parameters are passed by value and their evaluations can proceed concurrently.

Thus a VAL function receives its input through its parameters and defines an execution environment after which it computes a result. The environment defined by a function is only available during the execution of the function and it disappears when the function returns a result.

In addition, an expression can provide an execution environment by giving a list of identifier value bindings in a header to the actual expression. This is achieved by means of the **let-in** structure. Its purpose is to introduce one or more value identifiers; define their values, and evaluate an expression within their scope. In the first part of the structure temporary bindings can be specified before the result is generated in the **in** clause. All the bindings are made at the beginning of the expression and disappear as soon as the result value has been computed. In this way the environment of an expression can be expanded, and possible concurrency in the data constructions or the evaluation of the expression introduced. For example

```
let A : REAL ; B : REAL ;
  A := X ;
  B := A + 3.14 ;
in
  A * B
endlet
```

where X is imported from the outer context. The other identifiers are declared exactly once and defined exactly once in that block. If X had been defined in the **let** clause the outer value of X would not be available. Also a value identifier may not be used until after it is defined and must be defined only once in a block.

In languages like Pascal a function can only return a single value as a result of its execution. If more than one value is required it is returned through the parameter list or global data; this can give rise to side effects. A VAL function can return more than one value as a result of its execution, the most common way of specifying multiple results is by writing a comma delimited list of expressions. Multiple results can then be used in a program anywhere that a list of the particular type is expected. This is illustrated in the following function which finds the real roots of a quadratic equation:

```
function REALROOTS (A,B,C : REAL returns REAL REAL)
  let
    X : REAL := SQRT(B * B – 4 * A * C) ;
    Y : REAL := 2 * A ;
  in
    (– B + X) / Y , (– B – X) / Y
  endlet
endfun
```

15.4.3 Parallel expressions

Parallel expressions in VAL have three basic parts, a range specification, an environment expansion and a result accumulation. The range specification is indicated by means of a **forall** which is a contiguous integer interval or a cross product of a contiguous integer interval that defines the scope of the parallelism. For example,

```
forall X in [1,4]
forall Y in [I,J], Z in [K,L]
```

where X, Y and Z range over the values specified in the square brackets known as the index values. The types of the index are integer. When more than one index is given it is the Cartesian product of the ranges that is applied.

The body of the **forall** expression contains an environment expansion section which is executed once for each element in the **forall** range. If the range size is N then N parallel paths can be in execution, after which, the results must be accumulated into one object either as an array or as the result of some operation on them. The former case is indicated by the word **construct** the latter by the word **eval** followed by the name of the operator. The values may not depend on each other.

In a **construct** part, the expression is evaluated for each index value which generates a value and becomes an array element, its index position corresponding to the range index associated with that path. For example,

```
forall X in [1,4]
   construct X * X
endall
```

creates an array of 4 values, namely, 1,4,9,16.

If an **eval** part is used in a **forall** construct the values generated from each path are merged into one result. The merging takes the form of a binary tree evaluation. Only six operators can be used in the merge operation, namely, **plus**, **times**, **max**, **min**, **and**, **or**. For example,

```
forall X in [1,4]
   eval plus X * X
endall
```

returns the value $1 + 4 + 9 + 16 = 30$.

A **forall** may produce multiple result values using either **construct** or **eval** any number of times in an expression. For example,

```
forall X in [1,4]
   eval plus X * X
   construct X, X * X
endall
```

is an expression which yields the value 30 and two arrays of 4 values each. Expressions can be sequenced to ensure logical correctness by using:

1. **if** test **then-else** enables selection of expression results according to the test value. The **if** construct introduces no value identifiers, all values are passed into the construct.

2. **tagcase** can be used to interrogate values of a discriminated union type. The entire construct is an expression whose values are those of the expression whose tag identifier matches the value of the test expression. If no match is found an **otherwise** part is chosen. It takes the form

```
tagcase P := X ;
   tag A : P + 4
   tag B : P[6]
   otherwise 5
endtag
```

   where P is a value identifier and X an expression. If X has tag A and P the value 3 then the above expression yields the value 7.

3. **for-iter** is used with loops which cannot execute in parallel because values produced in one iteration must be used in the next. The initialization part appears between the reserved words **for** and **do** and all loop parameters must be declared and given initial values here. The loop body is an expression that is repeatedly evaluated until a final

result can be computed; this is usually determined by some form of conditional expression. For example, the following code computes the factorial of N:

```
for I : INTEGER := 1 ; P : INTEGER := N ; do
  if P > 1 then iter I := I * P ; P := P - 1 ; enditer
  else I
  endif
endfor
```

The loop names I and P are initialized, only once, to the values indicated in the definitions appearing after the word **for**, and the first iteration cycle begins. During each iteration cycle these identifiers have fixed values. The body consists of an **if-then-else** construct whose first arm is a redefinition and whose second arm is the expression I. At the start of each cycle P is tested, if it is greater than 1, I and P are given new values and another cycle begins. If P is 1 the iteration terminates with the value I. It should be noted that within such a construct it is legal to redefine a value as in the statement I := I * P where the old value of I is multiplied by P.

As an example of the use of some of these constructs consider the calculation of the square root of a real number X using Newton's Method,

```
for T : REAL := X ; do
  let D : REAL := (X/T - T)/2.0 ;
  in if D < EPS then T
    else iter T := T + D ; enditer
    endif
  endlet
endfor
```

The iteration body uses a **let** block to introduce the temporary identifier D and initializes it with an estimated value for D. The value of EPS, which determines the accuracy of the result, is imported. The iterations are continued until the desired accuracy is achieved.

15.4.4 Error handling

A VAL function can never abort in the middle of a calculation, it must either correctly terminate or run forever. This is possible since every data type contains error values in addition to the values commonly associated with the type, known as the proper values. When an operator cannot carry out its assigned task it returns an appropriate error value. A programmer can test for the presence of error values so that alternate results can be provided when an anticipated error arises. Two error values are members of every data type:

1. the element **undef** [type] which results when operand values are not in the domain of an operator, for example, if an array access operation is outside the range of the array;

2. the element **miss_elt** [type] which results if the index of an array accesses within the range of the array but no data value exists at that index. For example, if array A has bounds 1 and 3 then A[6:0] will append element 6 to the array and the intervening elements, 4 and 5, will have the value **miss_elt**.

There are specific error values belonging to each of the appropriate basic language types; the full name of an error type consists of an error name followed by the type specification enclosed in brackets, as follows:

- **pos_neg** [T], **neg_over** [T] which represents numbers known to pass the magnitude capability of the machine;

- **pos_under** [T], **neg_under** [T] which represents numbers known to require greater precision than the machine can supply;

- **zero_divide** [REAL] which is the result of a zero division for real numbers while **zero_divide** [INTEGER] is the result of a zero division involving integers;

- **unknown** [T], which represents any number whose value cannot be accurately determined due to previous magnitude or precision errors.

All error test operations return true or false, never an error value.

Example: Matrix multiplication

In earlier chapters we considered the multiplication of two matrices to demonstrate the different techniques required with the different types of parallelism. Here we consider the same example using data flow parallelism. The arrays to be multiplied are declared as parameters to a function MATRIXMULT as follows:

```
function   MATRIXMULT (A : array [array [REAL]] ,
                       B : array [array [REAL]] ,
                       N : INTEGER
                       returns array [array [REAL]])
```

where N is the size of the arrays. The result of executing this function will be to produce an array, also of size N, which is a product of the two input arrays A and B.

This solution works by forming the inner product of a row of A and column of B and then summing the values. This can be expressed by using the **forall** statement with the **eval** construct as follows:

```
forall I in [1,N]
  eval
    plus X[I] * Y[I]
endall
```

and incorporating this into a function we have

```
function INNERP (X : array [REAL], Y : array [REAL],
                 N : INTEGER
                 returns INTEGER )
    forall I in [1,N]
      eval
        plus X[I] * Y[I]
    endall
  endfun
```

Using this function a solution can be expressed as

```
function MATRIXMULT (A : array [array [REAL]],
                     B : array [array [REAL]],
                     N : INTEGER
                     returns array [array [REAL]])
    forall I in [1,N]
      construct
        forall J in [1,N]
          construct
            INNERP (A[I], B[J], N)
        endall
    endall
  endfun
```

15.5 Summary

In recent years data flow machines have been proposed as an alternative to conventional machines as a means of obtaining greater execution speeds. Such machines are based on the principle that an instruction is ready for execution when its data is available. A language suitable for a data flow computer consists of values, expressions and functions instead of variables, statements and procedures. Such expression based features prohibit all forms of side effects and simplify the task of identifying concurrency.

The use of implicit concurrency and implicit synchronization means that data flow languages have no features for forcing any kind of concurrent activity such as the process and the monitor; the programmer does not have to add sequencing constraints beyond those imposed by the algorithm.

An example of such a language is VAL which is not dependent on any machine structure and is suitable for a data flow architecture. It provides functions without side effects which enables a formal definition of the language to be specified. The syntactic and semantic rules can then be checked at compile-time so that any program that starts execution has a well defined result. No aspect of the language is left undefined and hence open to different interpretations by compiler writers.

One weakness of VAL is its input/output because no input/output can be done within a function itself, it is the responsibility of the system environment. This means a user cannot interact with a program while it is running. Also, since there can be no output prior to program termination database applications are excluded. Input/output implies side effects which conflicts with the language's philosophy.

EXERCISES

15.1 Write a VAL program to perform the operations of addition, subtraction, multiplication and division on a pair of complex numbers.

15.2 Write a VAL program to calculate the Nth power of a real number X.

15.3 Devise a data flow program which reverses a list of characters by using a recursive data structure.

15.4 Construct the graph representation of a function for computing the mean and standard deviation of 3 given input values.

15.5 Write a VAL program which will sort N numbers using the method of Quicksort.

15.6 Write a VAL program to generate primes according to the Sieve of Eratosthenes algorithm.

References

Ackerman, W. B. (1979). 'Data Flow Languages' *Proc. Nat. Comp. Conf.*, **48**, 1087–1095

Ackerman, W. B. and Dennis, J. B. (1979). 'VAL – a Value Orientated Algorithmic Language' *Technical Report MIT/LCS/TR-218*, Laboratory of Computer Science, MIT

'American National Standard Programming Language FORTRAN' *ANSI X3.9-1978* American National Standards Institute Inc., New York

Arvind, Gostelow, K. P. and Plouffe, W. (1978). 'The ID Report. An Asynchronous Programming Language and Computing Machine' *Technical Report 114a*, Department of Information and Computing Science, University of California

Ashcroft, A. and Wadge, W. W. (1977). 'LUCID, a Nonprocedural Language with Iteration' *Comm. ACM, 20*, 519–526

Backus, J. W. (1978). 'Can Programming be Liberated from the von Neumann Style? A Functional Style and its Algebra of Programs' *Comm. ACM*, **21**, 613–641

Backus, J. W. (1981). 'The History of FORTRAN I, II and III' *The History of Programming Languages*. (Ed. R. W. Wexelblat), London and New York: Academic Press

Barnes, G. H., Brown, N. M., Kato, M., Kuck, D., Slotnick, D. and Stokes, N. A. (1968). 'The Illiac IV Computer' *IEEE, Trans. on Computers*, **17**, 746–757

Barnes, J. G. P. (1984). *Programming in Ada*. Second Edition. London: Addison-Wesley

Batcher, K. E. (1968). 'Sorting Networks and Their Applications' *Spring Joint Computer Conf.*, **32**, 307–314

Batcher, K. E. (1979). 'MPP – a Massively Parallel Processor' *Proc. Int. Conf. on Parallel Processing 1979*, **249**. (Ed. O. N. Garcia), New York: IEEE Inc.

Bell, C. G., and Newell, A. (1971). *Computer Structures: Readings and Examples*. New York: McGraw-Hill

Brinch Hansen, P. (1972a). 'A Comparison of Two Synchronising Concepts' *Acta Informatica*, **1**, 190–199.

Brinch Hansen, P. (1972b). 'Structured Multiprogramming' *Comm. ACM*, **15**, 574–578

Brinch Hansen, P. (1973). *Operating Systems Principles*. Englewood Cliffs, New Jersey: Prentice-Hall

Brinch Hansen, P. (1975). 'The Programming Language Concurrent Pascal' *IEEE, Trans. on Soft. Eng.*, **1**, 199–207

Brinch Hansen, P. (1978). 'Distributed Processes: a Concurrent Programming Concept' *Comm. ACM*, **21**, 934–940

Control Data Corporation. (1982). 'CDC Fortran 200 Reference Manual Version 1' *Control Data Corporation Publication 60480200*

Conway, M. E. (1963). 'Design of a Separate Transition-Diagram Compiler' *Comm. ACM*, **6**, 396–408

CRAY-1 Computer Systems. (1981). 'Fortran (CFT) Reference Manual' *Publication No. SR-0009*, Rev H

Dahl, O. and Nygaard, K. (1966). 'SIMULA – an ALGOL-based Simulation Language' *Comm. ACM*, **9**, 671–678

Dennis, J. B. (1979). 'The Varieties of Data Flow Computers' *Proc. Int. Conf. Distr. Comput. Syst.*, 430–439

Dijkstra, E. W. (1965). 'Solution of a Problem in Concurrent Programming Control' *Comm. ACM*, **8**, 569–570

Dijkstra, E. W. (1968). 'Co-operating Sequential Processes' in *Programming Languages*. (Ed. F. Genuys), 43–112. London and New York: Academic Press

Dijkstra, E. W. (1972). 'Hierarchical Ordering of Sequential Processes' *Operating Systems Techniques*. (Eds. C. A. R. Hoare and R. H. Perrott), 72–79. London and New York: Academic Press

Dijkstra, E. W. (1975). 'Guarded Commands, Non-determinacy, and Formal Derivation of Programs' *Comm. ACM*, **18**, 453–457

Foster, M. J. and Kung, H. T. (1980). 'The Design of Special Purpose VLSI Chips' *Computer*, **13**, 26–40

Gostelow, K. P. and Thomas, R. E. (1980). 'Performance of a Simulated Dataflow Computer' *IEEE Trans. Computers*, **29**, 905–919

Gurd, J. R., Kirkham, C. C. and Watson, I. (1985). 'The Manchester Prototype Dataflow Computer' *Comm. ACM*, **28**, 34–51

Hoare, C. A. R. (1972). 'Towards a Theory of Parallel Programming' *Operating Systems Techniques*. (Eds. C. A. R. Hoare and R. H. Perrott), 61–67. London and New York: Academic Press

Hoare, C. A. R. (1974). 'Monitors: an Operating System Structuring Concept' *Comm. ACM*, **10**, 549–557

Hoare, C. A. R. (1978). 'Communicating Sequential Processes' *Comm. ACM*, **21**, 666–677

Hockney, R. W. and Jesshope, C. R. (1983). *Parallel Computers*. Bristol: Adam Hilger

Holland, D. A. and Purcell, C. J. (1971). 'The CDC Star-100: a Large Scale Network Oriented Computer System' *Proc. IEEE Conference*, 55–56

Hord, R. M. (1984). *The Illiac IV – the First Supercomputer*. Maryland: Computer Science Press

Hwang, K. and Briggs, F. A. (1985). *Computer Architecture and Parallel Processing*. New York: McGraw-Hill

Inmos Ltd. (1984). *Occam Programming Manual*. Englewood Cliffs, New Jersey: Prentice-Hall

International Computers Ltd. (1980). 'DAP Fortran Language' *ICL Technical Publication 6755*

International Standardisation Organisation. (1982). 'Computer Programming Language Pascal' *ISO International Standard (DIS) 7185*

Kung, H. T. and Leiserson, C. E. (1979). 'Systolic Arrays (for VLSI)' *Sparse Matrix Proc. 1978*, 256–282. Society for Industrial and Applied Mathematics

Lincoln, N. R. (1982). 'Technology and Design Tradeoffs in the Creation of a Modern Supercomputer' *IEEE Trans. on Computers*, **31**, 349–362

May, D. (1983). 'Occam' *ACM SIGPLAN Notices*, **18**, 69–79

McGraw, J. R. (1982). 'The VAL Language: Description and Analysis' *ACM Trans. on Programming Languages*, **4**, 44–82

Millstein, R. E. (1973). 'Control Structures in Illiac IV Fortran' *Comm. ACM*, **16**, 622–627

Naur, P. (1963). 'Revised Report on the Algorithmic Language Algol 60' *Comm. ACM*, **1**, 1–17

Parkinson, D. (1983). 'The Distributed Array Processor' *Computer Physics Comm. ACM*, **28**, 325–336

Perrott, R. H. (1979a). 'Languages for parallel computers'. In *On the Construction of Programs*. (Eds. R. M. McKeag and A. M. Macnaghten), Cambridge University Press

Perrott, R. H. (1979b). 'A Language for Array and Vector Processors' *ACM Trans. on Prog. Lang. Syst.*, **2**, 177–195

Perrott, R. H. and Stevenson, D. K. (1981). 'Considerations for the Design of Array Processing Languages' *Software – Practice and Experience*, **11**, 683–688

Randell, B. (Ed.) (1975). *The Origins of Digital Computers – Selected Papers*. Berlin: Springer-Verlag

Rosen, S. (1969). 'Electronic Computers: a Historical Survey' *Comput. Surv.*, **1**, 7–36

Russell, R. M. (1978). 'The Cray-1 Computer System' *Comm. ACM*, **21**, 63–78

Smith, B. J. (1981). 'Architecture and Application of the HEP Multiprocessor Computer System' *Real Time Signal Processing IV*, 298

Stevens, K. (1975). 'CFD – a FORTRAN-like Language for the ILLIAC IV'. *Sigplan Notices*, **10**, 72–80

Stevens, K. (1979). 'Numerical Aerodynamics Simulation Facility Project' *Infotech Supercomputers*, **2**, (Eds. D. Hockney and C. R. Jesshope), 331–341. Maidenhead: Pergamon Infotech Ltd

Swan, R. J., Fuller, S. H. and Siewiorek, D. P. (1977). 'Cm* – a Modular, Multi-Microprocessor' *AFIPS Conf. Proc.*, **46**, 637–644

Treleaven, P. C. (1979). 'Exploiting Program Concurrency in Computing Systems' *IEEE Computer*, **12**, (1) 42–50

USA Standards Institute. (1966). 'Standard Fortran' *USAS X3.9 – 1966*. New York

U.S. Department of Defense (1983). 'Reference Manual for the Ada Programming Language' Washington D.C. (ANSI/MIL-STD 1815). Government Printing Office Order 1008-000-00354-8

Welsh, J. and Bustard, D. W. (1979). 'Pascal Plus – Another Language for Modular Multiprogramming' *Software – Practice and Experience*, **9**, 947–957

Welsh, J., Lister, A. and Salzman, E. (1980). 'A Comparison of Two Notations for Process Communication' in *Language Design and Programming Methodology* (Ed. J. Tobias). Lecture Series in Computer Science, **79**. Berlin: Springer-Verlag

Wilkes, M. V. and Renwick, W. (1949). 'The EDSAC, an Electronic Calculating Machine' *J. Sci. Instrum.*, **26**, 385–391

Wirth, N. (1971). 'The Programming Language Pascal' *Acta Informatica*, **1**, 35–63

Wirth, N. (1977). 'Modula: a Language for Modular Multiprogramming' *Software – Practice and Experience*, **7**, 3–35

Wirth, N. (1983). *Programming in Modula-2*. New York: Springer-Verlag

Wulf, W., Russell, D. B. and Habermann, A. N. (1971). 'BLISS: a Language for Systems Programming' *Comm. ACM*, **14**, 780–790

Index